Persuaded
↳by the evidence

Persuaded
by the evidence

True Stories of Faith, Science, & the Power of a Creator

Compilation Editors

DOUG SHARP & DR. JERRY BERGMAN

First printing: August 2008

ISBN-13: 978-0-89051-545-7
ISBN-10: 0-89051-545-X
Library of Congress Number: 2008929654

Scripture taken from the HOLY BIBLE, NEW INTERNATIONAL VERSION.® Copyright © 1973, 1978, 1984 International Bible Society. Used by permission of Zondervan. All rights reserved.

Scripture taken from the New King James Version. Copyright © 1982 by Thomas Nelson, Inc. Used by permission. All rights reserved.

Cover design by Diana Bogardus.

Printed in the United States of America

Please visit our website for other great titles:
www.masterbooks.net

For information regarding author interviews,
please contact the publicity department at (870) 438-5288.

Master Books
A Division of New Leaf Publishing Group

Acknowledgments

We wish to thank Steve Edwards for his excellent contribution in editing each of these testimonies. We are also grateful for each of the contributors who were willing to share a part of their personal lives as part of this book. Finally, we acknowledge the influence of the Creation Research Society and the CRS network of researchers, where discussion of the topic of creation and evolution spurred interest in creating a book containing individual testimonies as to the power of God showing himself through His creation.

Contents

what he was taught in Sunday school as a child and atheistic arguments against the Bible.

Chapter 25: John Sanford: The Making and Unmaking

As a godless youth in college, John had no foundation for life, and was very empty. He marvels at God's grace that led him through all that darkness without being destroyed. John was chosen *Progressive Farmer*'s Man of the Year in January 2001.

Chapter 26: Donald D. Ensign: Dinosaurs Capture

As a child, Don discovered the world of dinosaurs and fossils through the popular media. He was raised in a Bible-believing home and eventually realized that his Christian experience and beliefs were not reconcilable to evolutionary deep-time thinking. Thus began a search that allowed him to gain insights into the correct relationship between Scripture and nature.

Chapter 27: Victor Marshall: From New Age to

Victor was a truth seeker who studied philosophy, Hinduism, Buddhism, Islam, theosophy, spiritualism, animism, pantheism, New-Age beliefs, and the occult. He tells the story of his conversion to Christianity and how creationism played an important part. He is now a corrections chaplain with the State of Ohio.

Dr. John Doughty talks about his training as a mechanical engineer and tells how the laws of thermodynamics were primary pieces of evidence that persuaded him of the truth of the creation model.

Dr. Walter T. Brown is the founder and director of the Center for Scientific Creation based in Phoenix, Arizona. His story is included in the book *Christian Men of Science: Eleven Men Who Changed the World* by George Mulfinger and Julia Mulfinger Orozco, along with those of Kepler,

Faraday, Maxwell, Henry Morris, and other Bible-believing scientists.

Dr. Raymond Damadian, the inventor of the MRI machine, tells his story. To see inside a living body in fine detail, without the harm of x-rays, was a doctor's impossible dream then; today it is a reality, thanks to Magnetic Resonance Imaging.

Frank Sherwin tells about the steps that led him to become convinced of the truth of creation. The fact of God, historical evidence, the reliability of Scripture, the foolishness of the religion of naturalism, and the failure of neo-Darwinism all caused him to conclude that all science is creation science!

Dr. Richard D. Lumsden was fully grounded in Darwinian philosophy, and had no reason or desire to consider Christianity. Science was his faith: the facts, and only the facts. But at the apex of his professional career, he had enough integrity to check out the facts, and made a difficult choice to go where the facts led. His life took a dramatic turnaround, from Darwinist to creationist, and from atheist to Christian.

A persuasive instructor in college caused Nick to become unsure of his Christian faith and for a time compromised his beliefs and caused him to doubt. It took the birth of his son and a serious accident to jar him into reexamining his beliefs about God.

SPECIAL FEATURE: FOUNDING FATHERS OF THE CREATION MOVEMENT

Dr. Henry M. Morris is often regarded as the founding father of the modern creationist movement. His book *The*

Genesis Flood, co-authored by Dr. John C. Whitcomb, was the foundation that started several creationist organizations, including the Institute for Creation Research, Answers in Genesis, and the Creation Research Society. Dr. Morris recounts the events in his scientific career and Bible study that led him to devise the modern young-earth creationist model.

Having made a decision to follow Christ at ten years old, Dr. Duane Gish recounts how information about creation science added to the foundation of his faith, to the point that he has become one of the most sought-after creation debaters in the modern creation era.

As a teacher, Dr. Gary Parker not only taught evolution, but he also preached it. He believed that it was his duty to steer young people away from what he regarded as silly myths. But he was challenged by several Christian professors to reexamine the science upon which his beliefs in evolution were founded, and after about three years of study, he also became a believer.

Dr. Andrew Snelling tells of his journey as a geologist whose Christian faith was challenged by evolution, and how he searched for answers and finally was persuaded that the rock layers showed evidence of catastrophe.

Long before the intelligent design movement was making news, Dr. A.E. Wilder-Smith was already making the same arguments. His analysis of genetic information influenced Dean Kenyon, the evolutionary origin of life researcher turned creationist, to call Dr. Wilder-Smith one of the two or three most important scientists in his life. Much of the literature coming out of the modern intelligent design movement contains echoes of powerful arguments made by A.E. Wilder-Smith decades ago.

SPECIAL BIOGRAPHY

Dr. Mortimer Adler (December 28, 1902–June 28, 2001) was considered one of the greatest thinkers of all time, and according to a 1987 *Time* magazine article was the "last great Aristotelian." Adler wrote (or co-authored) more than 45 books (all of them very successful) and more than 200 articles. He was also chairman of the board of editors of *Encyclopedia Britannica* for many years. His 54-volume *Great Books of the Western World* has sold more than a quarter of a million copies since 1952.

Introduction

It has been my pleasure to review and edit the personal testimonies of individuals whose lives have been changed by the knowledge of and a personal experience with our Creator. I have had the privilege of interviewing many of these people, and I interact with some of them often. Many have advanced degrees. And a few have not yet had that privilege or opportunity, yet each one has had his faith in God strengthened by scientific evidence for creation.

Persuaded by that evidence, they have integrated biblical principles in their lives, and each one tells a story of how that has satisfied his hunger for God. One of the facets of the Christian faith is that a person's experience with Christ is subjective and personal, and often it isn't easy to share this with someone who hasn't had that experience. That only comes through faith, and a person who has a logical mind will want more proof. These testimonies share both aspects — a personal experience as well as the scientific evidence that convinced the individual to take the steps needed to establish a relationship with the risen Christ.

What is amazing about each of these stories is that they are all different, and yet God individually tailored the evidence for each person's personality, causing a defining moment that persuaded him to consider his spiritual life. Some received Christ first and sorted out their belief in Him as Creator much later. Others grew up in a Christian home but were never taught that science and Scripture could be reconciled, and eventually went through a crisis motivating them to research the issue. Still others had no Christian influence at all in their early years, but were confronted with the evidence only later in life. There were also a few who wanted to submit their stories, but they felt that if they did so, it might jeopardize their employment. Discrimination against creationists is a real problem discussed by several of the contributors. It is also interesting to note that evidence that causes some to make a pivotal decision in their spiritual life might not be as convincing to others. Although I do not think that these individuals are in complete agreement on every aspect of Christian doctrine, I do know that the hand of the Master has touched each of their lives.

As you read these testimonies, ask yourself, "What is it that motivates me in my Christian faith?" Do you have unshakable reasons for your faith that stand the test of careful scrutiny? Or if you are not yet persuaded or are an unbeliever, ask yourself if you should be skeptical of your skepticism. Are the reasons given in this book enough motivation for you to take the challenge of following Christ? Or is your skepticism rooted in tradition, fear, or comfort?

Evolution is a stumbling block for many people that will prevent them from accepting simple faith in Jesus Christ. This collection of personal experiences will give you some idea of what helps many people overcome this common stumbling block.

— Douglas B. Sharp

Information Tends Toward Chaos

Chapter 1
Eric Blievernicht

Because I grew up in the public school system where censorship of creation is rampant, I was not exposed to a creationist viewpoint until I was in college. *I believed in the Darwinian story for the origin of the earth, living things, and mankind by default.* As a rationalistic teen, I had deduced that the concept of God was a "philosophically necessary" concept to make sense of the world, but I had no concept of a personal, loving, involved Creator.

As a bookworm, I was always reading everything I could get my hands on. In the public schools, this meant a heavy indoctrination in secular humanism, whether from school textbooks (which I usually read cover to cover early in each semester) or from the library. Most sci-fi authors, such as H.G. Wells, Arthur Clarke, and Isaac Asimov, for example, were hardcore Darwinists whose beliefs are strongly reflected in their writing.

I was fascinated by the principle of natural selection in my early teens and spent a great deal of time pondering it. I quickly realized that in the absence of natural selection — that is, if most mutations persisted whether good or bad — the result would be a degeneration of the genetic pool, because most mutations that cause phenotypic changes are, in fact, harmful. This early thinking about *degenerative* evolutionary trends would later play a significant role in my development as a creationist.

Another early conclusion I reached was that Darwinism had no competent explanation for the origin and development of dynamically stable ecosystems. Darwinism is only concerned with the origin and persistence of mutations that benefit individual organisms. It did not explain why the ecosystem recycles numerous biological waste products so that life does not become buried in its own wastes and die out.

For example, suppose an organism arose that utilized photosynthesis, producing oxygen as it broke down carbon dioxide in the photosynthetic cycle. Why should it in turn give rise to life that did the exact opposite, inhaling oxygen and replenishing carbon dioxide in the atmosphere? There was no valid reason for blind Darwinian evolution, which cares only whether a mutation brings immediate benefit to its host, to create such cyclical systems. Yet this is only the simplest of many examples necessary for life to persist indefinitely on earth. And so I became a skeptic of totally atheistic Darwinism, unaware that I was not alone in my dissent.

Further movement away from Darwinism came during my sophomore year in college when I attended a church youth rally and heard a speaker *criticize evolutionism*. After his presentation, I picked up *Blind Faith: Evolution Exposed*[1] by Howard Peth. The book had limited effect. Since I read books by the dozens, it was unusual for any one book to have a major effect on my thinking. It did continue my movement away from Darwinism, since I could see now that rejection of Darwinism was not unthinkable. This rejection was based upon sound theoretical objections, absence of mechanisms to explain it, scientific laws hostile to it, and an unhelpful fossil record. After my sophomore year in college, I was a theistic evolutionist, or even an anti-evolutionist, though not yet a creationist in any positive sense. *I knew what I didn't believe, but I didn't know what to believe.*

Peth's appeal for faith in Genesis was simply a foreign concept to me. I had attended church while growing up, but "Bible history" was a fantasy history in my mind, completely divorced from the "real history" I learned in school and in textbooks. The idea that the Jesus of the Bible was an inhabitant of the same historical Roman Empire I studied with such interest in school, for example, was practically unthinkable to me. Genesis as real history, supplanting the textbook orthodoxy of Darwinism, was not even an option in my mind.

Nevertheless, God was guiding me home. By my senior year in college, I was visiting Internet newsgroups such as talk.origins (this was

---

1. Howard Peth, *Blind Faith: Evolution Exposed* (Roseville, CA: Amazing Facts, Inc., 1990).

before the web), sometimes speaking against naturalistic Darwinism. I soon discovered the fanaticism and fury of many committed Darwinian fundamentalists. This did nothing to persuade me of the accuracy of their beliefs, but actually helped prime me for a final break with the Darwinian worldview.

The break came in the winter of my senior year at Michigan State University when I discovered a cache of creationist literature in the back of a church I was attending. Almost simultaneously, the Christian apologist Dr. Josh McDowell came to speak on campus. Suddenly I was being confronted with an array of evidence supporting the historical *accuracy* of the entire Bible. Even more importantly, Dr. McDowell emphasized God was a personal, loving, caring being — not a cold philosophical concept.

Between McDowell's *A Ready Defense*,[2] Henry Morris and Gary Parker's *What Is Creation Science?*[3] and other books, I soon realized that I was in no position to stand in judgment over the Bible. It stood in judgment over me. I found that I could trust Genesis. Now, once a skeptic finds that he can believe in Genesis, the rest of the Bible is easy. Indeed, God loomed so large before me in those days that to put Him off would have been impossible. I was no longer a "churchian"; I had become a young-earth creationist, and so I could hardly avoid becoming a Christian.

My acceptance of faith has since been confirmed both by reading creationist and Christian works on the one hand, and anti-creationist works on the other. The latter (such as Niles Eldredge's *Monkey Business*,[4] Hugh Ross's *Creation and Time*[5] and Karl Giberson's *Worlds Apart*[6]) uniformly fail to cope with most creationist arguments, either caricaturing or ignoring them in favor of minor criticisms. Although they do point out occasional errors in creationist thinking, they do not hold a candle to works like Leonard Brand's *Faith, Reason and Earth*

2. Josh McDowell, *The Best of Josh McDowell: A Ready Defense*, compiled by Bill Wilson (Nashville, TN: Thomas Nelson Publ., 1993).

3. Henry M. Morris and Gary E. Parker, *What Is Creation Science?* (Green Forest, AR: Master Books, 1982).

4. Niles Eldredge, *Monkey Business: A Scientist Looks at Creationism* (New York: Washington Square Press, 1982).

5. Hugh Ross, *Creation and Time* (Colorado Springs, CO: NavPress, 1994).

6. Karl Giberson, *Worlds Apart* (Kansas City, MO: Beacon Hill Press, 1993).

History,[7] Lee Spetner's *Not by Chance!*[8] or *The New Answers Book*[9] from Answers in Genesis.

The biblical record of Genesis was exciting to me because it helped fulfill a major intellectual goal of my life — a demand for intellectual consistency across all disciplines and realms of thought. For example, I had long heard that God was perfectly loving and good. Why did I not accept this belief until my senior year?

Like most people, I could not make sense of that claim in terms of what we see in the world around us. Around us we see suffering. We see death. We see people in pain and agony. If God is (1) all-powerful and (2) perfectly good, then how can this be? Logic seemingly demanded that either (1) or (2) had to be false. Since the concept of an all-powerful First Cause is something that *can* be deduced from sheer logic, I rejected (2).

But this raises further questions — as the former atheist intellectual C.S. Lewis pointed out in *Mere Christianity*,[10] good and evil are concepts that only make sense if they originate in the will of an Almighty God. Otherwise, they are mere personal opinions. I do not like anchovies on my pizza, but I do not call such a thing evil *in the same way the Holocaust was evil*. If the universe is "unjust" only in my personal opinion, then how can that be an argument against a perfectly just God? In order for it to be a valid argument, the universe really must be unjust whether I think so or not, but that requires an absolute standard of justice that can only come from God himself.

Genesis untangles this paradox. It teaches that there is a perfect, loving, good God, but that He created a world in which humans had freedom to choose obedience or disobedience, and that Adam did, in fact, choose the latter. It teaches that the universe was originally perfect, but that our disobedience led to the introduction of death, pain, and decay. In response, God set in motion a path of redemption that would save those who turned back to Him in repentance and sorrow, without any cost. His perfect love was reflected on the Cross and in Christ's payment for our crimes against God.

---

7. Leonard Brand, *Faith, Reason and Earth History* (Berrien Springs, MI: Andrews University Press, 1997).

8. Lee M. Spetner, *Not by Chance! Shattering the Modern Theory of Evolution* (New York: Judaica Press, 1999).

9. Ken Ham, ed., *The New Answers Book* (Green Forest, AR: Master Books, 2006).

10. C.S. Lewis, *Mere Christianity* (London: G. Bless, 1952).

I now had an explanation for the co-existence of suffering and evil in a universe with a perfect, all-powerful, good Creator. By contrast, consider the theistic evolutionary view. In this model, pain and suffering and death, such as are reflected in the fossil record, pre-date the fall of man. They are instituted by God not in response to mankind's sin, but are a reflection of His own will and character. The result is a sadistic, malicious god who prefers pain and suffering in his creation. This is not the God of the Bible.

This intellectual reality was reflected in my personal outlook in life. Earlier in my sophomore year in college, I had attempted suicide over a failed romantic expectation, leaving a scar along one side of my neck. Fruitless time wasted with psychologists grounded in Darwinian beliefs did nothing to help me, for my depression was grounded in a false worldview. Belief in Genesis *and* the resulting Christian faith was the *perfect* antidote.

Genesis also brings consistency to science. For example, the law of entropy in thermodynamics demands that, in a closed system, entropy (that is, disorder) always increases. Since the whole natural universe can be thought of as such a system, it follows that the universe was maximally ordered in the very beginning and has become more disordered since then. This is not very consistent with popular naturalistic models such as the big-bang theory (where disorder gives rise to order on a *universal* scale) but it is completely consistent with Genesis.

Finally, consider evolutionary biology itself. I am not speaking here of Darwinism (the belief that life evolves from primitive to complex, with all life stemming from one or a very few ancestors), but rather of the scientific study of changes that are occurring in life today. Biological change itself does not prove Darwinism, as is commonly claimed. Darwinism requires millions of *innovative* mutations. That is, for Darwinism to be true, most beneficial mutations must add information to an organism, generating new systems and integrating greater and greater complexity into organisms as they evolve from single cells to the present vast array of life.

Genesis teaches the opposite: not stasis, but rather a perfect creation that was marred by a Fall that has resulted in decay throughout the universe. Biological changes (such as the appearance of carnivorous animals and thorns) are *known to have resulted from the Fall*. From a perfect beginning, there is only one direction that change can take: downward. The difference between Darwinism and Genesis is not change versus stasis but rather innovative evolution versus degenerative evolution.

Darwinists frequently proclaim that there is a vast amount of evidence for "change" in biology. There is, but they do not admit to the nature of the change. The result is the curious fact that modern Darwinian fundamentalists vaguely proclaim evolutionary biology to be the great proof of their belief system, yet it is 180 degrees the opposite of what they claim. Ironically, Darwinian fundamentalism is in an all-out war *against* evolutionary biology.

There are no exceptions: all known cases of beneficial mutations are either neutral or result in loss of information and are therefore degenerative in nature. There are no examples of beneficial mutations that create new functions or biological systems in an organism. Genesis explains and predicts this pattern, which is completely incompatible with Darwinism.

Consider, for example, vestigial organs. Darwinists relying on their caricature of "Genesis = stasis" long proclaimed them to be proofs against creation, because they claim a God would not create useless structures in living things. It is true a perfect Creator would not create structures with no function, but vestigial organs by definition are structures that were once useful. The argument is refuted by the recognition that degenerative change is vital to the creationist paradigm.

Most claims of "vestigial organs," such as the human appendix, coccyx, and tonsils, were based on ignorance of their true functions. The advance of science has thus debunked most claims of "vestigial organs." Nonetheless, examples such as loss of eyesight and pigmentation in cave-dwelling creatures remain. Flightless birds and wingless beetles are other good examples. These fit more naturally with the degenerative paradigm of Genesis than the innovative paradigm of Darwinism. Darwinism needs to explain how sight *and wings and pigmentation* arose, not how they disappear!

What about the hundreds of examples of antibiotic, herbicide, and pesticide resistance arising by mutation? These are frequently held up as proofs of Darwinism, but are they?

Antibiotic resistance occurs by several mechanisms, none of which involve innovation. For example, penicillin resistance in *Staphylococcus* bacteria is observed due to damage to a control gene that leads to unregulated production of penicillinase, which breaks down penicillin. Under normal circumstances, these bacteria are just wasting resources overproducing penicillinase, but in the presence of penicillin, only they survive. *Mycobacterium tuberculosis* bacteria have an enzyme that, in addition to useful functions, alters the antibiotic isoniazid into a lethal form that destroys the bacteria. A mutation that eliminates the enzyme cripples the bacteria but prevents the antibiotic from killing it.

Some toxins work by binding to certain sites on target cells. A point mutation can alter the geometry of the binding site and protect the organism while degrading or destroying the useful function for which the site exists in the first place. For example, 4-quinolone is an antibiotic that attacks the gyrase enzyme in bacteria. A neutral mutation in one amino acid alters the binding site on the enzyme and as a result, prevents the interaction.

Streptomycin kills bacteria by binding to their ribosomes and interfering with vital protein production. Mutant bacteria have been observed with *damaged* binding sites. As a result, the antibiotic can no longer bind, but the speed and efficiency of protein production is reduced due to the *altered* binding site. Some cases of pesticide resistance occur because of damage to the cell membrane that slows the uptake of the pesticide into cells, preventing cells from accumulating toxic concentrations of the pesticide.

Warfarin is a rat poison that works by inhibiting an enzyme that metabolizes vitamin K, which is vital for life. Resistant rats have a damaged enzyme so that 13 times as much vitamin K is needed for them to stay alive. However, warfarin does not recognize the damaged enzyme, so when warfarin is used on rats, only the crippled mutants survive.

Examples could be multiplied, from seedless fruits that proliferate because of human preference for them, to farm animals and crops with increased yields due to damage to protein regulator functions. This damage leads to uncontrolled protein production, wasteful in most circumstances but preferred by farmers trying to maximize food production.

As this new degenerative paradigm takes over evolutionary biology, further insights will be gained. For example, parasites *now appear to be* degenerate forms of once-helpful symbionts or independent, free-living organisms that lost the ability to survive on their own. Bacteria and viruses that now cause disease show evidence of degeneration from their original altruistic roles in supporting the ecosystem of life. Far from stifling scientific research, insights from Genesis are opening new frontiers for research and understanding of God's fallen, yet still wondrous, creation.

A Reluctant Convert from Evolutionism

Chapter 2
David A. Bradbury

In 1949, I graduated from the University of Michigan with a science degree and a firm belief that biological evolution was the proper scientific explanation for life as observed on earth today. From this background, augmented by the flow of authoritative-sounding materials in technical journals and the popular media, I abandoned the worldview earlier instilled in me by my Christian parents. This classic "dualistic" worldview is that both physical and nonphysical influences exist, each playing an important role in one's life. Instead I adopted the "monistic," or mechanistic-evolutionary, worldview where only physical matter/ energy existed . . . and which my textbooks presented as scientifically explaining the formation of simple first life and its evolution upward to complex mammalian life forms by chance natural mechanisms.

I was a firm believer in and outspoken defender of chance evolution for the next three decades. Even today I still well recall (now with some embarrassment) the warm glow of intellectual superiority I felt as I confidently assured less well-educated others about how "molecules to man" evolution (the title of the most widely used introductory biology text of all time) was well and scientifically established. This same attitude of superiority is still alive and well amongst those selectively (partially) educated and unconsciously indoctrinated into "believing" the fascinating concept of evolution indeed has proper "scientific" credentials.

It wasn't until some 20 years out of school that I had first occasion to question and personally seek out and examine the evidence supporting the evolutionary explanation. Like most students, I unquestioningly accepted that the necessary evidence indeed *did* exist. Surely, all the impressive, factual-sounding claims presented in our textbooks were confirmed by the repeatable research experiments required in science, weren't they?

Interestingly, the circumstance prompting my first, admittedly belated, effort to examine this evidence came only upon a surprise encounter with what I perceived to be a totally reckless and unfounded challenge made before the Texas State Board of Education in November 1969. This was in the form of a $1,000 (more than $10,000 in today's value) offer by a Mr. John Grebe to anyone (board member, scientist, college professor, or other) able to provide any *first* example of physically verifiable evidence (or even a basic mathematical model) sufficient to elevate the then hypothesis of macroevolution up to the status of scientific theory as then being proposed for inclusion in new textbooks under consideration.

Once I discovered that this challenge was still open, I seriously set out to collect this easy money. Sure, the dollars involved provided immediate incentive, but my greater desire at the time was to publicly embarrass this Mr. Grebe and put an end, once and for all, to such irresponsible attacks by so-called "creationists" on what I then accepted as well-established scientific determinations.

I started by leafing through multiple textbooks to select representative claims. Then it was off to the science archives in local and university libraries (these were pre-Internet days) to locate and copy the original source data from the supporting experiments that would compel Mr. Grebe to part with his money and eat humble pie. At the time, I expected to quickly select from any number of verifiable confirmations that the progressive steps involved in macroevolution had indeed been checked and double-checked by responsible scientific experiments. However, to my disappointment and near disbelief, I could find *no* such objective confirming evidence anywhere then — nor after following years of continuing search is there any to be found, even today.

Indeed, this continuing absence only further confirmed that none of the claims purporting to qualify macroevolution as scientific are supported by the physical verification criteria required in the universally taught empirical (or Baconian) scientific method. Though it took some time before I was ready to accept it, I finally began to question, and even accept, that all evolutionary explanations presented to students and the public as science must necessarily have been qualified as science based on some new, different, and at the time unshared, non-Baconian scientific method. I recognized that this was as confusing as it was disturbing. Nowhere were we informed that the criteria of empirical science taught and applied in other science courses (chemistry, physics, etc.) were *not* being applied to qualify the Darwinian, or neo-Darwinian, evolutionary explanations as science in our biology textbooks. This was as difficult and troubling for me to understand then — as it undoubtedly is for others who may only be becoming aware of this little appreciated, much less understood shift today.

Finding that *no* empirical (objective, physical, inductive, or hard) evidence confirming evolution was available, while still difficult to believe, did make me want to know more about what the nonempirical criteria was that was now being substituted. At the time, details on the alternate steps applied and accepted by evolutionary textbook authors as sufficient to qualify their physically unverifiable explanations as science was difficult to pin down. All I could find in general-use texts then, and still in most texts today, were unsupported claims, statements, and assertions reflecting the consensus acceptance ("beliefs") of the prevailing evolutionary community.

Even with this troubling realization, my school-instilled trust in science as the best, if not only, method to compellingly establish physical truths was so deeply embedded, I continued to wrestle with this problem for a number of additional years before finally conceding that perhaps Dr. Grebe's $1,000 challenge was not in as much danger as I had initially presumed. This change was also further influenced by my learning that the man issuing this challenge was actually Dr. John J. Grebe, the excellently credentialed director of basic research for the Dow Chemical Company, and not the irresponsible know-nothing I initially presumed. Also, that his offer was directed toward the leading evolutionists of the day (Simpson, Dobzhansky, Ayala, Grant, etc.) then championing the elevation of evolution from its long-accepted status of hypothesis to far higher status of theory in the next generation of undergraduate science textbooks. In a way, this new understanding provided a welcome relief ... after all, if evolutionary leaders such as these could *not* provide even a single example of the requested empirical evidence, and even appeared reluctant to share, much less defend, the alternate criteria necessarily applied ... who was I to continue to insist that Dr. Grebe's position was the one in error?

Gradually, over the course of these years, my independent study led me into related fields previously ignored, or actually purposefully avoided. Three early texts then available were *Evolution: Possible or Impossible?* by Dr. James Coppedge[1]; *The Logic of Scientific Discovery* by Dr. Karl Popper[2]; and *The Genesis Flood* by Drs. Whitcomb and Morris.[3] The first addressed mathematics and probability; the second addressed philosophy of science; and the third provided pertinent evidence from hydrology and geology. Each acquainted me with previously unfamiliar scientific evidence and introduced me to thought-provoking alternate hypotheses (explanations) and views not mentioned (i.e., omitted, censored) in earlier classroom materials. As informative as these were at the time, folks today are fortunate to have a great many more books and materials by evolutionists, nonevolutionists, and creationists, all openly providing new, more balanced information helpful in clarifying this long-standing controversy. It was while trying to stay abreast by reading a cross-section of material from both evolutionists and creationists alike that it became clear that researchers from *both* camps all work from the very same physical evidence ... and about which there is little, if any, controversy. If there is *no* controversy about the observable facts themselves, then controversy, where it is encountered, must result from the way these facts (the language) are presented or interpreted. When this alternative registered in my thinking, it was a eureka moment. Possibly the problem responsible for so much controversy was more semantic (how evidence is presented or mentally interpreted) rather than scientific (physically confirmable) as the problem was being addressed up until now.

At this point, dictionaries, encyclopedias, and related English texts were added to my reading list. These were added in the effort to locate the precise, universally accepted definitions and usage for terms most frequently involved in these controversies. Starting with the basic term science, I found the default definition invariably to be empirical

---

1. James Coppedge, *Evolution: Possible or Impossible?* (Grand Rapids, MI: Zondervan, 1973).

2. Karl Popper, *The Logic of Scientific Discovery* (New York: Basic Books, 1959).

3. John C. Whitcomb and Henry M. Morris, *The Genesis Flood* (Philadelphia, PA: Presbyterian and Reformed Publ. Co., 1966).

science, where conclusions earned the envied designation of scientific only after successful physical verification under the Baconian scientific method. Should any other nondefault definition be intended, it is every author's primary responsibility to share this variation with his readers by inclusion of an appropriate adjective modifier — as theoretical-science, mathematical-science, pseudo-science, and more recently as Hypothetico-Deductive (HD) science (which will be discussed further shortly).

In one of the language books, *The Practical Stylist* by Sheridan Baker, I was surprised to read: "For the word *science* is at present used in at least two meanings, and the whole question of scientific education is obscured by the current tendency to dodge from one meaning to the other."[4] I had to read this twice. For a scientifically impartial semanticist to select the word *science* to illustrate the problems caused by ambiguity (imprecise definitions) in science education really appeared to hit the nail on the head.

A second helpful clarification appeared in *The Language of Argument* by Daniel McDonald, where he states: "It is foolish to try to disprove a conclusion which was never proven in the first place."[5] This quickly paraphrased itself in my mind as, "It would be foolish to try to disprove 'evolution' as science by empirical standards (which is Dr. Grebe's approach) if it has been 'established' as science by some different 'second' criteria of science." Wow, are we finally making progress after all this time or what?

It was during continuing correspondence with the very patient and helpful evolutionist Dr. Ralph Lewis at nearby Michigan State University that I first became aware of the unfamiliar terminology "hypothetico-deductive" as a form of science. This was in a copy of an article he wrote titled "Biology: A Hypothetico-Deductive Science," as published in a specialized, smaller circulation journal. It opens with this paragraph:

> During the 50 year life of *The American Biology Teacher* there has been a change in the general view of method in

---

4. Sheridan Baker, *The Practical Stylist*, 5th edition (New York: Harper & Row, 1982), p. 49.
5. Daniel McDonald, *The Language of Argument*, 2nd edition (New York: Crowell Publishing Co, 1975), p. 137.

biological science. A brief look at this change and its possible consequences for biological education may interest those who are searching for ways to improve education at the high school and college levels. The change was from descriptive biology to hypothetico-deductive (HD) biology, that is, to theoretical biology.[6]

This five-page article should be mandatory reading for those interested in science education today. He provides practical (but sometimes overlapping) definitions for terms such as hypothesis, theory, postulates, premises, etc., along with admonitions as to how this shift away from empirical science in biology should be taught to the students saying, "Starting in high school, the HD nature of biology should be prominent" (p. 366). Unfortunately, authors (and probably uninformed teachers) during my school years did *not* share this change with us — and it appears in only a few, if any, public school biology books today. Going further, I searched this new phrase on the then-infant worldwide web and found a wide-ranging, and often heated, debate between various groups of scientists concerning its pros and cons and whether it was sufficiently rigorous to qualify untested evolutionary conclusions as scientific. Even now, with a Google search returning far more than 100,000 hits (most by evolutionists defensively justifying its usage), instruction in the strengths and weaknesses of HD science is still conspicuously absent from public school textbooks today. Little wonder that those currently involved in this controversy cannot resolve this troubling issue. They just don't know what the issue is and continue to believe the (untaught, mental, HD) claims for evolution reflect the same level of physically verifiable scientific certainty as that universally taught in chemistry and physics texts.

Indeed, ask them about the differences between HD and empirical science, or which one was used to qualify evolution as science in biology texts, and most would have no clue. In fact, this is a good question to ask those reading this today. But all is not lost. As you and the public become more aware of this situation, the stronger background in English and language skills possessed by teachers, judges, and

---

6. Ralph Lewis, "Biology: A Hypothetico-Deductive Science," *The American Biology Teacher*, vol. 50, no. 6, 1988: p. 362.

lawyers (wordsmiths) will allow them, after some bit of further study, to properly identify and inexpensively resolve this ongoing (semantic, not scientific) dichotomy.

This won't be easy. I know it took several years of digging before I was ready to accept that this switch in the meaning of "science" had surreptitiously been introduced in our classrooms — and probably nearly as long to realize that this alone is responsible for more than 90 percent of *all* controversy over evolution in our schools today. Hopefully, the following brief summary might make such realization a little easier for others. Basically, Hypothetico-Deductive science simply drops the "Physically test the *hypothesis* to be proven" step in the Baconian scientific-method and substitutes a series of individually less compelling steps roughly as follows:

1. From the physically untestable *hypothesis*, mentally draw secondary *deductions* that can be physically tested.

2. Test the *deductions* (not the *hypothesis* itself).

3. Do this for as many *deductions* as possible. No single deduction, whether confirmed or falsified, is sufficient to validate, or invalidate, the *hypothesis*.

4. As more *deductions* are successfully tested, validity of the *hypothesis* is progressively corroborated.

5. After some subjectively determined number of validated *deductions*, the *hypothesis* can then be accepted as scientific (by HD standards).

While such progressive steps may initially appear reasonable to a casual reader, particularly when presented in authoritative science texts, discussion of the major unavoidable uncertainties in the deduction-drafting step are seldom mentioned. *Deductions*, by definition, are "logically deduced" (mentally) from "observed facts" (evidence) and a "select set of premises."[7] Possible premises (called postulates or hypotheses by Dr. Lewis) are numerous. The researcher selects from these, typically about five, from which to draw his *deduction*. But this step produces

---

7. Premise: A statement that is assumed to be true and from which a conclusion can be drawn; WordNet 2.0, Princeton University, 2003.

unavoidable uncertainty. Presuming the observations are correct and the logic sound, a wide range of different and often conflicting deductions can be drawn, each reflecting the different premise sets selected. And here lies the root cause of almost all controversy. Which set of unverifiable *premises* should be accepted as providing scientifically useful (certain) *deductions*? The sets of premises that indicate evolutionary explanations are true, or the sets of premises indicating them to be invalid? Unfortunately, in only rare cases do those defending their particular *deduction* include a list of the premises available, or those selected to reach their preferred conclusion. And when they are listed, it quickly becomes recognizable that the controversy is not over science but rather over which set of philosophically preferred (assumed, untestable) premises is to be accepted.

Similar philosophical (quasi-scientific) disagreement has long been comfortably accommodated in other investigative fields where physical duplication of events or claims cannot be provided. Here this limitation is recognized, and prolonged debate is both expected and accepted as useful in leading to possible ultimate resolution in the future as new information may be developed. Some examples would be: How were the pyramids built? By crude tools only, or by use of some yet-to-be-discovered more advanced technology? By slave labor or by indigenous citizens when their fields were flooded? Many different answers can be proposed, discussed, and considered, all without animosity and none with scientific certainty.

So what is it about evolution, then, that makes it so bitterly controversial? It becomes controversial where evolution is involved only because its proponents insist it be universally presented at the taxpayers' expense to our children as scientific (near fact), but indemonstrable, with explanations compatible with some, but not all, religions. In particular, where the key aspect of the demonstrations are fully compatible with the *science* where evolution and its religious implications, both pro and con, are involved.

Gradually, throughout the course of this now 50-year, sometimes wavering, and often sputtering venture, many unexpected good things have come my way. I started out as a happy, trusting, but scientifically misinformed atheist thinking I knew a lot more about evolution than I really did, whereas today, thanks to a loving Christian wife, much fascinating research (all within the range of those seeking to separate wheat from chaff), thoughtful advice from patient evolutionists and nonevolutionist advisors, and a resultant deeper understanding of the intricate processes involved in macroevolution, I've come full circle. Once the artificial "intellectual" (scientific) barrier against religion posed by evolution was exposed, and serious consideration again given to spiritual matters, my return to Christianity has been personally most rewarding. For a while I was led to accept Richard Dawkins's view that "Darwin made it possible to be an intellectually fulfilled atheist,"[8] but having once been blind, it makes the truth and light available to all mankind in Scripture all the more appreciated.

---

8. Richard Dawkins, *The Blind Watchmaker* (England: Longman, 1986), p. 6.

"The Words of the Lord Are Flawless"

Chapter 3
Dr. David A. Dewitt

I grew up attending church and went to a Roman Catholic school. Although I believed in God, I also believed evolution was true. I considered myself to be a creationist because I thought that God created us — He just used evolution to do the job. I didn't sense any conflict between my religious beliefs and the evidence for evolution.

I went to Michigan State University and majored in biochemistry. When evolution came up in my biology class, the professor had an exercise at the beginning of the section. He placed an object on the front desk and asked students to draw the object from different points in the room. Of course, the students — although looking at the same thing — drew very different pictures because of their perspective. The professor made the point that evolution was similar — depending on how you looked at the evidence, you would come to different conclusions. Even though he never mentioned the Bible or God, the conclusion was obvious: if you believed in God, then you would interpret the evidence in line with that belief. This simply reinforced my belief at the time that there was no conflict between the Bible and evolution.

During my sophomore year, I attended a Bible study in the dorm with Matt Shantz and Mike Sochay. Matt had given me a Bible, and Mike gave me a book about creation called *The Revolution Against Evolution* by Doug Sharp.[1] He said, "David, I know that you are majoring in science. I thought that you should take a look at this book." I read the back cover and placed it on my bookshelf, where the book sat for about a year.

---

1. Doug Sharp, *Revolution Against Evolution* (Lansing, MI: Decapolis Books, 1986, 1993).

Over the summer, I came to understand the gospel and that salvation was a free gift by grace through faith rather than by works. My faith became real, but I still held to the false belief that God had used evolution to create. In fact, I would share this view with my friends when I would tell them about my faith in Christ. I even said that I didn't think you could take the Bible literally because it had been translated and retranslated so many times!

A little later, I read a passage from an old book that talked about how important the Word of God was. It emphasized that Jesus had submitted himself to the Scriptures, quoted from them repeatedly, and fulfilled every word of prophecy in them. This stuck with me as I later read in Psalm 12:6: "And the words of the Lord are flawless, like silver refined in a furnace of clay, purified seven times" (NIV). This passage was reinforced when in the book, minutes later, I read Psalm 18:30: "As for God, his way is perfect; the word of the Lord is flawless. He is a shield for all who take refuge in him" (NIV).

These words pierced my heart as I realized that I had been taking a distorted view of God's Word. I claimed to believe the Bible — that God could change water into wine; heal the blind, lame, deaf, and mute; and even raise the dead. Yet I was hesitant to believe that God created everything in six days. This conflict hit me like a ton of bricks. I realized that if I was going to accept the Bible, I had to accept all of it. Moreover, if God said He had made everything out of nothing in six days, who was I to say otherwise?

Another concept later cemented my creationist views. I realized that there was a major conflict between the Bible and the theory of evolution. Evolution requires death — millions of years of death, bloodshed, and survival of the fittest. In fact, natural selection with the death of the less fit is the explanation for the evolution of man. This runs contrary to the clear teaching of Scripture: "Therefore, just as sin entered the world through one man, and death through sin, and in this way death came to all men, because all sinned" (Rom. 5:12; NIV). It became obvious to me that the Bible taught that death was not the means that God used to create. It is the last enemy that Christ came to destroy. I saw that millions of years of struggle for survival, bloodshed, and death was incompatible with a loving God — whose eye is on the sparrow — who saw all that He had made and called it "very good."

Thus, I became convinced from Scripture that young-earth creationism was true and believed it with all my heart.

I later remembered the *Revolution Against Evolution* book that my friend had given me. I pulled it out and began to study it very carefully. It was amazing how much evidence there was that refuted evolution and supported the biblical account of creation. I felt that I had been lied to about the subject for my whole life. I read this book over and over many times because it was the only creation book that I had then, and I started making notes from my textbooks and classes of things that supported the creation account.

I continued with my studies in biochemistry and pursued a PhD in Neurosciences at Case Western Reserve University. While I was at CWRU, some of my fellow students (and a few professors) came to know of my creationist beliefs. Although they would often criticize me or make fun of me for these beliefs, for the most part, they respected my work. One friend who had collaborated with me on three papers told me that I "could never be a good scientist." I said, "How can you say this? We have published papers together." He said that a good scientist would not begin with a conclusion and hold on to it in spite of the evidence against it. He seemed oblivious to the fact that the same could be said about those who believed in evolution! In the end, in spite of the occasional ridicule, I was able to complete my PhD.

As I was considering what to do after I graduated, my advisor suggested that I think about a teaching position at a religious school where I would fit in with the other "fanatics." He was serious and thought that I would be a good fit in a Christian college. So I began to pursue a teaching position at a Christian college. This was an eye-opening experience for me.

I spoke to one chair of biology from a Christian college in Kentucky who told me, "You won't find much difference between what we teach and what is taught at a state university . . . we teach evolution here." When I interviewed at a Christian college in Ohio, I got the impression that they were theistic evolutionists. The chairman asked me what my views were about creation and evolution. I was completely honest and told him where I was coming from, although I expected him to disagree. Instead, he told me, "I agree with you 100 percent, David. But I am probably the only one on campus who would."

This was a shock to me. Even at Christian colleges there were few people who believed the Genesis account of creation. I began to wonder if I would find a college where young-earth creation was accepted.

Then, Liberty University published an ad for a biology professor who "must be compatible with a young-earth creationist perspective." I was absolutely delighted and found out that all of the graduates were required to take a course in apologetics that covered the creation/evolution controversy from a young-earth perspective. The department chair told me that if I were interested, I could probably teach that course. In 1996, I started teaching at Liberty University and began teaching the History of Life course in the second semester (and every semester since). Through teaching this course, I have learned more about evolution than I did throughout my entire college and graduate studies.

Since joining the faculty at Liberty, I have been very active in the creation community. I taught cell biology at the Institute for Creation Research and have also worked with Answers in Genesis. I have given presentations on creation at colleges and churches across the country and have now taught thousands of Liberty University students about the evidence for biblical creation.

On one speaking trip, I went back to Michigan. While there, I thanked Doug Sharp for writing his book on creation. It was a privilege to tell him how God had used his book. Doug invited me to give a presentation at his church and did an interview with me on his cable TV show. I also met with Matt Shantz, who was serving as a pastor for a campus ministry group. I showed him the Bible that he had given me more than a decade before. When I spoke to his group on campus, I told the students about the Bible and the creation book. "I have heard that you give out Bibles on campus and hope and pray that God will use them to change a life. I want to show you one Bible, given at a campus Bible study, that has changed a life. Let me encourage you in your efforts." Had I not been given that first creation book, my life would be completely different.

Now, when I give out creation books and materials on campuses, it is my prayer that the Lord might use them in someone's life and that they will have an even greater impact than they had in my life.

Cultlike Characteristics of Atheism

Chapter 4
Dr. Jerry Bergman

Ever since I can remember, I have been interested in science — especially biology, astronomy, and chemistry. No doubt, this interest stemmed in part from my father's lifelong involvement in science. In the 1950s, when I was a young child, I remember how my dad designed and drew by hand (no computer-assisted design technology existed then), using only ink and drafting tools, an 8' x 10' wall chart of the elements known today as the periodic table. He then silk-screened the charts and sold them to colleges and universities throughout the United States.

Like the stereotypical nerd, when growing up, I never attended sporting events as did most people my age. Rather, my father took me to the Astronomical Society of Detroit, the Engineering Society of Detroit, and other science organizations to attend the many science events that they sponsored. One of our first projects was to make a six-inch reflector telescope for which we ground the mirror by hand. The astronomical society met on the Wayne State University campus in Detroit (the alma mater of my father, my brother, and myself). The campus later became a familiar place where I would study for my bachelor's, master's, and doctorate degrees. After nine years on that campus, you get to know the place pretty well!

My religious upbringing was pulled primarily in two contradictory directions. My mother became an active Jehovah's Witness (usually called "Witnesses") in the early 1950s, as did also many members of her side of the family. I remember as a child going to hear hour-long talks given by my cousins, and "Witness talk" was common in our household for years.

On the other side of the family, my father was an agnostic and was very involved in various humanist movements and activities during his whole life. Even though most of my relatives (and all of my many first cousins who lived in the Detroit area) were Witnesses, my father had a critical influence on my life. He was more affectionate than my mother, who tended to be somewhat rigid and legalistic. It was my father whom I could go to when I was troubled or needed comfort or attention. Unfortunately, this ended to a large extent after my parents divorced when I was in seventh grade.

Their divorce was by far one of the most traumatic experiences of my life and was to have effects on me that last to this day. A few years later, my father married a younger woman, Dorothy Hart, at the Unitarian Church in Birmingham, Michigan, a church in which they were both involved. Lester Mondale, the brother of former Vice President Walter Mondale, married them.

My father and I had many long discussions about religion and what he saw as the many shortcomings of all theistic beliefs in general. Although his influence was great, even then I tended to see atheism as more of a rebellion against theism than as a logical conclusion based on the empirical evidence. Although he was to become less radical in later life, while I was growing up he championed all of the causes that liberals typically supported then (and often now) including banning guns, abortion rights, strict separation of church and state (which in education amounted to prohibiting favorable mention of religion in the schools while highlighting the events in religious history that are often interpreted today as negative), high taxes for the rich, and generous government benefits for everyone who needed them (mostly the poor).

As a youngster, I was involved in the Witnesses with my family (except my dad, who was always very opposed to them, to an extent that led to the divorce), and as a young adult I decided I would throw my lot in with them. When I look back now, this was partly because the Watchtower was the only faith that I knew then. At that time the Watchtower strongly discouraged attending university, so when I graduated from high school, I soon began working without pay as a full-time Witness in a position they called a Pioneer. We spent around eight hours a day or more in what we called missionary work, which essentially consisted of knocking on doors endeavoring to place (actually sell) Watchtower literature and convince the householder to agree to what we called a Bible study (actually, our goal was to indoctrinate the householder into

Watchtower theology). Frankly, I found this work very depressing, at least partly because I was already beginning to question Watchtower theology and teachings.

Soon I elected to leave the full-time Witness work. In a few weeks, I landed a position as a cabinetmaker. I had always loved working with wood and felt that this was a career that I could enjoy. Unfortunately, though, the cabinetmaking industry was becoming more automated, oriented toward an assembly line. The company I worked for built kitchen cabinets, primarily, and I was not able to indulge in the creative furniture-building activities that I had assumed cabinetmaking involved. My concerns didn't matter much, though, because I was soon laid off, along with several others, and had to seek employment elsewhere. I then moved through a succession of jobs that bored me very quickly, including photography.

About this time, a new state college was opening in my community, Oakland Community College in Bloomfield Hills, and I decided that I would sign up for classes with the goal of improving my knowledge in the areas that would help me to become a better photographer. I knew the Witnesses would give me problems, but I had a perfect excuse. The Watchtower taught that if your father wanted you to go to college, you should try to talk him out of it and pioneer instead, but if he was adamant, you could then (with the Watchtower Society's blessing) attend university. My father clearly *did* want me to go to college and *was* very unhappy with my alternative plans, so I signed up for classes.

The college was experimenting with a new type of learning that relied more heavily upon workbooks, tapes, videos, and other audio-visual equipment than traditional programs. I thrived on this approach and did quite well, transferring to Wayne State University to finish my bachelor's degree. By then I was certain that I wanted to be a teacher. The idea had appealed to me since sixth grade when I was elected president of the astronomy club and was privileged to go around to different classes giving lectures on the space program, astronomy, and science.

Feeling guilty about attending college and being a Witness, I endeavored to become an even better Witness (psychologists call this *compensation*). As a result, I studied Watchtower publications more diligently and endeavored to deal with my previous doubts. I felt that in order to be a more effective Witness, I should be able to deal with the problems I saw in Watchtower theology, and so endeavored to focus on studying these areas in depth. To do this, I began a large collection of thousands of Watchtower publications. I eventually collected an almost complete set of everything the Watchtower published since 1879, save a couple of very rare items for which I obtained photocopies or reprints instead. I read this material voraciously, and, at first, my reading supported the Watchtower, but the more I read (especially in older Watchtower publications), the more problems I encountered. Much of my doubt about theism was due to the steady diet of anti-theistic, anti-religion that I was exposed to in college (I was then starting to work on my second doctorate).

In time, I became totally disillusioned with not only the Watchtower, but also all religion. Soon I was forced, as was René Descartes, to start from square one, assuming only that I and a world out there existed, and felt the place to begin building a new worldview was to try to answer the question, "Does God exist?"

I became involved in the atheism movement and soon knew (and counted as friends) many of the leading atheists of the day, including Gordon Stein, PhD; Garry DeYoung, PhD; and of course, Madalyn Murray O'Hair. I have also published scores of articles in their various magazines. I read atheistic literature religiously for years (and still do). It soon became apparent while I was devouring atheistic literature that the arguments atheists used to prove their worldview boiled down to only two basic concerns — the existence of evil in the world and the assumption that evolution (meaning evolutionary naturalism or Darwinism) could totally explain the existence of the living and nonliving world. Consequently, scientists had "no need of that hypothesis" (the hypothesis that a God exists) because they believed that everything, including life, could be adequately explained by naturalism.

Some persons have concluded that God may exist, but He has had nothing to do in the universe, or, as Phillip Johnson likes to state, He has been *historically permanently unemployed.* The Witnesses are long-age creationists, and thus I had some familiarity with this worldview. I had also studied biology in college (I would later become a high school biology teacher and subsequently taught biology at the college level, which I have done now for more than 20 years), so I was very familiar with the arguments in favor of evolutionism.

To answer the most basic question (*Does God exist?*), I focused on the two most common proofs that atheists use—the existence of evil and whether there is good evidence that the creation in fact created itself by natural law or requires an outside intelligence as postulated by the intelligent design movement. The *existence of evil* problem did not seem difficult to answer because, as a licensed therapist, I knew that people cause most problems today, often the person with the problems (usually due to relationship problems with spouse, family, children, and others). I also knew, as taught by all theistic religions, that free will allows humans to choose, and in choosing some choose to do good, others choose bad. Forcing humans to do only good takes away free will, and we then become robots.

My interest in this area was partly what motivated my study of psychology. As a result of this interest, I eventually became a psychology professor. I also worked for a number of years at various psychiatric clinics, such as Arlington Psychological Associates in Toledo, Ohio, under a licensed psychologist until I was licensed myself. Licensure requires not only graduate degrees in psychology but also several years of supervised experience under a licensed therapist.

The existence of pathogens, such as viruses and bacteria, was also not problematic. I knew that the vast majority of bacteria, viruses, and even insects and plants were not pathogenic — it is relatively unusual for an organism to be pathogenic, and it seemed quite clear from my class work in science that this was usually due to mutations, or an organism infecting an inappropriate host. My college microbiology professor, Dr. Harold W. Rossmore, in an excellent book titled *The Microbes, Our Unseen Friends*,[1] showed eloquently that the common assumption that bacteria are harmful is a distortion. These ideas were also reflected in his lectures.

These answers may not sound very comforting when one is in the midst of suffering. Nonetheless, I concluded after much study and writing many papers on this topic that the historic orthodox Christian answer was the most viable solution to the omnipresent problem of suffering in our world. Furthermore, it was clear to me that atheists did not have a solution except to condemn the Church for not eliminating the

---

1. Harold W. Rossmore, *The Microbes, Our Unseen Friends* (Detroit, MI: Wayne State University Press, 1976).

problem. I am not aware of a single hospital, charity, or school that an atheistic organization started, and few atheists that I knew did much charity work (and I knew many). Most of them lived a life in harmony with their beliefs — there is no God, no heaven, no hell, no Creator, and humans are a cosmic accident. Live and let live, for tomorrow we will die.

Evolutionism was another matter. Since I had become disillusioned with the Watchtower, and found them to be anything but honest, I distrusted all religious literature (even on the topic of creation/ evolution). I had read some of this material before, but most all of my reading and studying for college had been material written by evolutionists. I wanted to name my son after Ashley Montague, the famous anthropologist whom I had read extensively. (My wife did not like that name, so we went with her choice, the biblical Aaron, which we spelled Aeron.) I reviewed many books on Darwinism and from them outlined the chief evidence for evolution, which included vestigial organs, homology, ontogeny recapitulates phylogeny, beneficial mutations, evidence of poor design, the fossil record, atavisms, nascent organs, the argument from imperfection, natural selection, microevolution versus macroevolution, shared genetic errors, the backward retina, junk DNA, and other topics.

I selected the topic I felt was the easiest to answer, specifically the topic of vestigial organs, and delved into the scientific literature. After collecting a list of vestigial organs, I researched each one in turn, using only *secular* academic literature, which I had concluded (wrongly, as it turned out) to be unbiased. After several years of research, I found that I had eliminated all the items on my list (at least for humans) and so began working on animals. I found the same thing there. There were no truly vestigial organs.

I selected the next topic and again delved into the *secular* literature, producing several articles, monographs, or book chapters on my findings. I didn't trust religious literature. This is why the reviewers noted in my early papers on creationism that I did not cite any creationist sources (and often had to add them after the paper was accepted "to acknowledge creationist research in this area"). Slowly, but surely, I was able to eliminate *all* of the main arguments used to support evolutionism by researching secular literature only. At some point I crossed the line, realizing the case against evolutionism was overwhelming and conversely, so was the case in favor of the alternative, creationism.

If this is the case, why are there so many evolutionists? Largely, it is my conclusion, because many are true believers just as the Witnesses are.[2] I had vivid experience of this mindset in the Watchtower: when I presented a concern to the brothers, they would rationalize that the concern didn't exist or was of no importance. When I would show them documentation in the literature (such as the many changes in Watchtower teaching), they would rationalize it as the light getting "brighter and brighter" as the end comes closer. When I showed them that the changes were often back and forth, they would dismiss this concern by such rationalizations as "Jehovah's organization is teaching lies in order to test the loyalty of His people!" Although many Witnesses became disillusioned and left (most all of my friends and all of my family eventually left), there is a core set of true believers for whom no amount of information will be enough to dissuade them from their beliefs. Despite the devastating case against the Watchtower, they still have around ten million adherents.

Likewise, many evolutionists are "true believers" in the full sense of the expression. Most have heard only one side in college, and very few are aware of the weight of evidence on the other side. Unfortunately, proportionately few people have the time or inclination to investigate the case against Darwinism carefully. Nonetheless, many people have. I have in my library more than 5,000 books and monographs written by people critical of Darwinism. Many were written by PhD-level scientists who are not creationists (or even Christians). Unfortunately, the mainline churches tend to uncritically accept social convention, which today is evolutionism (a conformity that gets them in much trouble when fads change). In Nazi Germany, very few churches (and very few "Christians") openly spoke out against Nazism and the Holocaust, as has now been well documented.[3] Likewise, today most mainline churches have openly supported the naturalistic worldview preached

2. Eric Hoffer, *The True Believer: Thoughts on the Nature of Mass Movements* (New York: Harper and Row, 1951).
3. Gordon Zahn, *German Catholics and Hitler's Wars; A Study in Social Control* (New York: Sheed and Ward, 1962); Gordon Zahn, *In Solitary Witness: The Life and Death of Franz Jalgerstaltter* (Boston, MA: Beacon Press, 1968), paperback edition.

by Darwinists and opposed the overwhelming scientific case for an active Creator theism.[4]

Another factor that moved me to the creationist side was the underhanded, often totally unethical techniques that evolutionists typically used to suppress dissonant ideas, primarily creationism.[5] Rarely did they carefully and objectively examine the facts, but usually focused on suppression of creationists, denial of their degrees, denial of their tenure, *ad hominem* attacks, and in general, irrational attacks on their person. In short, their response in general was totally unscientific and one that reeks of intolerance, even hatred.

When I became convinced that evolutionism was simply wrong, just as I had become convinced that the Watchtower was wrong, I was led inevitably to the conclusion that, if life cannot be explained by naturalistic means, it can be explained only by an intelligent Creator, requiring theism. If a Creator existed, this meant that humans might have some obligation to Him. This led me to the conclusion that one of the theistic religions had to be valid. I started exploring the major world religions, and since I was convinced that life required a Creator, I focused on the three main theistic religions, Judaism, Christianity, and Islam, that teach about a Creator God. My study of these three theistic religions has led me to the conclusion that Christianity, specifically historic Christianity, is true.

In short, I took a similar path to that taken by Dr. Mortimer Adler and many others and came to accept Christianity as valid through science, though I recognize that I have much more learning and study to do in this area. Many critics of the creation worldview conclude that creationists accept this worldview *because* they accepted Christianity first (and in many cases this is correct). Many people, though, accepted Christianity *because* they rejected evolutionism and accepted creationism first. Only then were they able to accept Christianity (and many of those who have rejected Darwinism have not yet accepted Christianity). Rejection of evolutionism may be the first step, and then accepting a creation worldview is the *second* step. Then Christianity becomes a third

---

4. Phillip E. Johnson, *Reason in the Balance; The Case Against Naturalism in Science, Law & Education* (Downers Grove, IL: InterVarsity Press, 1995).

5. Jerry Bergman, *Slaughter of the Dissidents: The Shocking Truth about Killing the Careers of Darwin Doubters* (Port Orchard, WA: Leafcutter Press, 2008).

step. The Scriptures teach, "Come now, and let us reason together" (Isa. 1:18; NKJV), stressing the importance of rational discourse.

The many "Christian" religions that I explored included the Christian Science religion founded by Mary Baker Eddy. Soon, I found the same problems I had with the Witnesses. Christian Scientists teach that God is good and God is everywhere, therefore evil could not exist anywhere in fact, and if a person believes that evil (such as sickness) exists, this is an illusion that must be dealt with by the "truth of Christian Science." When the illusion of evil is banished from the mind, evil is eliminated.[6] How they could hold to this belief when, as has been scientifically documented, their children who become Type I diabetics die if not treated by medicine, or when their children who develop normal childhood illnesses die when antibiotics could have saved them, is hard to understand.

The Christian Science church consists of many well-educated individuals, and many are professionals who have done well in the business or professional world (especially law). These people deal with the fact that their behavior results in the loss of many of their children with such rationalizations as "medicine has its failures too." They argue that more than 50,000 children die every year from medical failures and that their few failures should be viewed against that fact. The only way to make comparisons, though, is to use a random sample research design to compare, for instance, diabetic persons treated with Christian Science therapy (which is, in fact, no therapy; it is, rather, doing nothing but often merely trying to convince the person who is sick that he or she is indeed *not* sick) with diabetics treated with insulin.[7] Of course, this experiment will never take place because we all know what the effects would be (and if it did, there would likely be many wrongful death lawsuits). Yet millions of people once adhered to Christian Science, fully believing that it offered a valid view of reality and that medicine was not only an illusion, but perpetuated a wrong belief and, as a result, caused death. I would later find that the specious line of arguments against intelligent design were similar to those used by Christian Scientists.

6. Jerry Bergman, "Religion and Medicine: The Christian Science Holocaust," *Humanist in Canada*, 140 (Spring 2002): 12–17.

7. Dr. Linda S. Kramer, *Religion That Kills: Christian Science: Abuse, Neglect, and Control* (Lafayette, LA: Huntington House Publishers, 2000); Caroline Fraser, *God's Perfect Child: Living and Dying in the Christian Science Church* (New York: Henry Holt, 2000).

At the time I was going through this transition from skeptic to believer, I was a professor at Bowling Green State University in Ohio. My colleagues were very unhappy about the direction my research was taking me, and they made it very clear that they disagreed with my conclusions. I had many long discussions with them and again experienced the same response that I experienced from the Witnesses — many were "true believers" in the full sense of the word and were simply unwilling to look at the evidence. In truth, most knew *little* about either creationism or evolutionism except that evolutionism was "true" and creationism "only religion."

Furthermore, they were not interested in learning much about the evidence. Why should they? They already knew evolutionism was true, so why read about it? My critics invariably questioned my intelligence. The fact that I am a member of MENSA, as are a number of creationists, had a 4.0 GPA for both my PhDs, have close to a 4.0 GPA for all five of my masters degrees, and scored in the 98 percentile for the GRE in my area did not impress them much. They stated that I was like Isaac Newton, a genius, but the last of the magicians.

My research, needless to say, alienated me from my colleagues, and as a result they voted to deny me tenure — and the reasons they gave (in writing) were blatantly clear. The National Education Association evaluated the case and concluded that the university had violated its own procedures and further, that the reason I was denied tenure was quite openly because of my religion. During the ensuing collection of information, letters, depositions, and other information, discussions of my religion clearly dominated — many pages of discussions about their disapproval of the religious path I was taking and my conclusions in this area openly dominated their concerns. I had more than a dozen signed affidavits from colleagues stating that the reason for my problems was openly my religious conclusions. I found the exact same antagonism among my colleagues as I had found among Watchtower adherents! They were simply different forms of "true believers," even though their rationalization was in many ways the same.

I then became an associate professor of psychology at Spring Arbor University. This was basically a good experience but again, even at a "Christian" college, I experienced a lot of the same antagonism from the evolutionists there. Many took a position similar to that which I had adopted while I was in college; namely, that the two belief structures (evolutionism and Christianity) were separate but equal, a rationalization that I now believe is irrational. In fact, the two different belief structures were 180 degrees opposite. Either the universe has a Creator or it does not have a Creator. There is no middle ground. Theism concludes that the universe and life has a Creator, and orthodox evolutionism will not let "a divine foot in the door" (another area I've researched extensively) or tries to get out of conflict by claiming that religion and science are two separate fields, and mixing the two is somehow wrong. I also taught in the math area at the University of Toledo for six years. They treated me exceptionally well, and I never ran into the problem of origins there.

All told, my intellectual journey has resulted in close to 700 publications to date (including 12 books and monographs) that have been translated into 14 different languages. My understanding of the issues has matured considerably since my first publications on this topic in the 1970s. My early works represent my thinking at that time, and since then I have continued to grow and mature in my thinking. Part of my growth has been facilitated by my academic pursuits (I have now completed my ninth college degree, this one from the Medical University of Ohio in Toledo).

There is no question in my mind that evolutionism and its branches of Darwinism will eventually fall, just as Marxism and Freudianism did. The belief structure is wrong and has caused an enormous amount of harm in history. When I mention this, my colleagues (and the atheistic community) typically point to what they believe is the harm caused by Christianity. This putative harm by Christianity, though, often results from *not* following Christianity, not from following it. Those who knew, understood, and lived the teachings of Christ would not have perpetuated the sins attributed to "religion." While still at Wayne State University, I heard a lecture by a well-known philosopher who claimed, "We've given Christianity two thousand years, and it has failed. Now is the time to give atheism a chance." (I heard much in favor of atheism and against Christianity at university.)

In fact, we have *not* yet given Christianity a chance. In Europe and most of the world, even in those portions that claim to be Christian, most of the people are nominal Christians — Christian in name only, at best. They do not have Christianity (or Christ) in their hearts and minds, and do not manifest the fruits of the Spirit (and this, unfortunately, is largely true of many of the major denominations today). I find it appallingly ironic that in the creation/evolution controversy, the mainline denominations invariably line up with evolutionism. As Eugenie Scott has said, in convincing the public of evolutionism, one man in a collar is worth ten scientists any day.

Yes, there are "true-believer" creationists just as there are "true-believer" evolutionists, but many creationists were once on the other side of the fence and converted as a *result* of their openness to the facts, as I did. We have been there and done that and hold to the creation worldview *not* because we were taught it as children. I learned both sides (the theistic side at my mother's knee, and the atheistic side at my father's) as a child and have now been on both sides as an adult. I came down on one side due to my three-decade-long study of the scientific evidence in the lab and in both academic and library settings.

I have also learned that one must become conversant with the science literature in order to make an informed decision on creationism. Only by being a voracious reader can one learn and understand what scientists have found out about reality. One must also let reality speak, and Darwinists today refuse to do this. They insist that the universe and life, although it appears to be designed, really is not, and they hang on to this belief regardless of the evidence. They are "true believers" in the full sense of the word, just like the followers of Jehovah's Witnesses and Christian Science.

ADDITIONAL REFERENCE MATERIAL USED

Jerry Bergman, *The Criterion: Religious Discrimination in America* (Richfield, MN: Onesimus Publishing, 1984).

Edmund C. Gruss, *Jehovah's Witnesses: Their Claims, Doctrinal Changes and Prophetic Speculation. What Does the Record Show?* (Fairfax, VA: Xulon Press, 2002).

Brown, Sticky Goo in a Test Tube

Chapter 5
Douglas Sharp

Since I was a youngster, I have been interested in science. My parents were dedicated Christians and brought me to church. I even remember making a commitment to follow Christ when I was about nine years old and reading Bible storybooks with my mother. However, up through high school, science was number one, and church was somewhere down on my list of priorities.

I was about 13 when I attended a church youth rally where one of the leaders pretended he was an atheist and challenged us to persuade him that there was a God. One of the teenagers piped up and said that the chances of life coming about by chance was much the same as dumping all of the pieces of a jigsaw puzzle onto a table and having them accidentally arrange themselves together. I thought that was a pretty good argument, and I still use it, but this was the very first time that I had heard anyone defend his or her faith that way.

The next time I had a similar encounter with creation and evolution was when I took a high school honors class at Lansing Community College. A high school student won a science fair award by duplicating the Miller-Urey experiment. This intrigued me, and I thought that since amino acids could be created by lightning sparks in a primeval atmosphere, surely all we had to do was to zonk them a little bit more and we could create some proteins. I set up an experiment to try this, and the results were interesting. The electric spark did nothing at all to the simpler amino acids, but the aromatic ringed amino acids tryptophan and tyrosine turned brown. I thought I had something, but I found a piece of research that showed that the same thing happens when they are exposed to ultraviolet light. The resulting compounds are essentially burnt amino acids. No peptide bonds formed at all. I found this puzzling and continued searching for answers about this throughout my college career.

About the same time, I was listening to a radio preacher, Garner Ted Armstrong. He talked about the impossibility of the chemical evolution of life, and much of what he said made sense based upon what I had done experimentally. Since my church never talked about this subject, I was challenged to find out more. I would say that Armstrong's message was a defining moment that put me in the creationist camp. It also caught me up into a maelstrom of Armstrong's strange doctrine, which took me a few years to untangle and finally extricate myself from.

While I was majoring in chemistry in college, I was still trying to sort out all of my questions. I wanted to make sense of what I was being taught (evolution) versus what I knew chemically to be true. I eventually met two key people: Dr. John N. Moore (past managing editor of *Creation Research Society Quarterly*) and Barry Moeckel, a zoology student whose Christian testimony was readily apparent.

Barry was the kind of person who you knew was special even without speaking to him. Dr. Moore helped me sort out the science from a biblical perspective; Barry straightened me out spiritually and got me involved in Bible studies. I think that the thing that impressed me the most about Barry was that he was consistent with his faith. In my youth group at home, I couldn't find very many who really took their faith seriously and made it an important part of their lives. Finding Barry and his group of Christians, who were serious about making Christ number one in their lives, was a defining moment in my life. (Barry's campus group was called Campus Action, now known as Chi Alpha.) Barry was also instrumental in helping me extricate myself from Armstrong's teachings. The lessons I learned there were (a) don't reject the truth because of the error that is mixed in, and (b) don't accept the error along with the truth.

One thing I realized when I became acquainted with Barry was that if I was going to serve God with all my heart, I had to set aside my personal pride and sense of achievement and give all glory and honor to God. This was particularly hard for me to do, since I had built all of my self-worth on the hope that people would honor me for my intelligence and scientific achievement. Once I made the decision to trust God and lay all of that before His feet, I found the assurance and love that He gives is far greater and more permanent than any personal recognition I might get from anyone else I could impress. I think that it is this false sense of pride that is the greatest stumbling block for an evolutionist scientist.

My association with Dr. John N. Moore was another defining moment. I had the opportunity to take a few independent studies with him at Michigan State University where he was a professor of natural science, and he introduced me to the Creation Research Society. I have been a member ever since. These independent studies were challenging. They were arranged with several professors, some evolutionists. One was on the chemical evolution of life; the second was on radiometric dating. The third resulted in a *Creation Research Society Quarterly* article (June 1977).

The Lord brought two more fascinating people into my life. Vivian, a beautiful Chinese foreign student whose family lived in Sao Paulo, Brazil, joined us on a canoe trip with Campus Action. I discovered that she and I had applied to work at the same place that summer, and during that time, we fell in love. The other person was my next-door neighbor, Rich Geer. He had just returned from two years at the University of Wyoming and was full of questions about the Bible, after just finishing a biblical archaeology class. Within a few weeks, God poured out His mercy on Rich, and his life was radically transformed. Rich's transformed life was a great encouragement to me as it provided first-hand evidence that Jesus Christ can renew a person's life. A few years later, Rich married my sister.

The Vietnam War was still dragging on, and the selective service issued me a low draft number. I had no interest in joining the military, but I ended up having to join the navy out of college, right after I married Vivian. While I was in boot camp, she prayed that I would never be away from her for more than two weeks. At the end of the navy training, they gave me the only shore duty assignment: San Diego. I didn't know it at the time, but San Diego was the home of the then-fledgling Institute for Creation Research. Back then, the Creation Science Research Center was almost within walking distance of where I was living, so I got to know Kelly Seagraves and Robert Kofahl. (It is wonderful the way the Lord arranges things, and my wife's prayer was answered.) After my two-year shore duty was up, I was assigned to a ship that was coming into the yards to be refurbished. I never did go to sea, and courtesy of the navy, I got a chance to be further involved with the creation science movement.

After I got out of the navy, we returned to Lansing and eventually joined Mount Hope Church. Our pastor there, Dave Williams, encouraged me to write a book about my experience with the creation-evolution issue as a foundation for a Bible Training Institute course. Since 1993, Rich Geer and I have produced a public access TV show called *Revolution Against Evolution*, where we interview many prominent creation scientists and discuss a wide range of topics relating to the creation-evolution question.

All of these work together to make me a convinced creationist: a Christian foundation, arguments from probability, experimentally verifying that chemical evolution couldn't happen, personal experience with God's direct intervention in my life, a consistent witness from an on-fire Christian, and a professor who stood up for his Christian faith and made an open creationist stand (but paid dearly for it). Through it all, the gentle prodding of the Holy Spirit arranged circumstances in adverse situations to further my interest and education in the creation/evolution issue.

I Could Not Say, "Jesus Is Lord"

Chapter 6
Richard Geer

I grew up in a Roman Catholic family with five brothers and three sisters. My grandmother lived with us, so we had a dozen people living together. Our home was full of wonderful, noisy chaos. I was the oldest of the nine children, and I was raised on peanut butter and Ritalin. My childhood could have been patterned after Calvin of Bill Watterson's *Calvin and Hobbes* cartoon. I was constantly getting into trouble, and after experimenting with jumping out of buildings trying to fly, lighting cherry bombs, chicken bike races, and exploring construction sites, it is a wonder that I am still alive.

I loved dinosaurs, and I could name all of the eras, epochs, and time periods of the evolutionary scale when I was in second grade. There, a nun was teaching evolution and the dinosaur era, when I pointed out an error in her chronology. She had a Jurassic herbivore being confronted by a Cretaceous carnivore. When I tried to correct her (presumptuous brat that I was) she verbally silenced me, but to her credit, she checked my claims out and came back the next day and corrected herself in front of the entire class. Of course, now I don't believe in any of these so-called "facts," and it seems much ado about nothing, but it did help to shape my belief in the evolutionary paradigm of the world.

Practically every kid is interested in the dinosaur era, but I went much further. I always aspired to be a paleontologist in those early days, but later, as my artistic ability grew, I wanted to be a dinosaur illustrator like my hero Charles R. Knight, who painted those wonderful murals for the Chicago Institute of Art (and appeared in every book about dinosaurs I could remember). I remember taking up an entire classroom in the sixth grade with an illustration that covered the entire evolutionary time scale, and it was here that I first heard that there might be conflict between evolution and theism. Of course, I had never really considered that there was any real conflict, but at the time I had no saving knowledge of Christ, and the whole death before Adam argument was not even a glimmer on the horizon. So this was a little confusing to me then. I quickly put it out of my mind, and it remained on the shelf until college.

When I was 15, we moved to Lansing, next door to Doug Sharp. His first impression of our family was looking up at my brother James, who had climbed 60 feet up a huge oak tree. Doug and I became fast friends. He was the mad scientist; I loved to draw and paint.

I had a family friend who took me on trips out west with him. These experiences gave me a love for the geology of America and the national parks. I decided to attend college at the University of Wyoming as an art major.

My art creations reflected the state of my soul at the time. One of my paintings was of a pair of hands trying to crawl out of a hole, but getting cut on sharp objects in the way. I also painted dragons and fanciful creatures. My creativity feasted upon rebellion against rules and standards. One time my art teacher told me that you never should frame a painting on an angle. I asked, "Why?" and did it anyway. I created a sculpture that was a two-dimensional visual in three dimensions but could only be seen if you lined up two points on the sculpture with your eyes. I also created a sculpture that depicted the entire evolutionary process from roots to lizards to humans all in one creature.

My approach to life at college was simply to have a good time: get high and enjoy myself. But I was miserable. I knew I was missing something. Out of curiosity, I took a biblical archaeology class, and I was in for a shock. I never knew that the Bible matched the archaeological facts so well. This started me investigating my beliefs. If the Bible really was true, maybe I needed to do something about it.

I ended my second year by deciding to drive to Florida, sprawl on the beaches, and get high. But my plans didn't work out. I decided to drive back home to Lansing instead. My friend Doug had been attending Michigan State University at the time and had gotten involved in some Bible classes there. I told him about the biblical archaeology class I had, and we had a lot of interesting discussions. I knew Doug was a

Christian, but he hadn't talked much about that part of his life until then.

Doug had been attending a coffeehouse in downtown Lansing called the Master's House, where they conducted street ministry to the addicts and bikers who would hang out on the "gut." He invited me to come with him and see what was happening. There, he opened up the Scriptures to me, and I started talking about what I had learned in biblical archaeology. He explained that he had come to believe that the Bible was true. I knew that Doug majored in chemistry, but he explained how he had learned from his research that the origin of life from nonlife was a chemical impossibility. That night, he showed me 1 Corinthians 12:3, which said that no man speaking by the Spirit of God can call Jesus accursed, and no man can say that Jesus is Lord except by the Holy Ghost. He then asked me if I was a Christian, and I responded, "Well, I'm a Catholic."

That Scripture started bugging me, because I knew that I had used the name of Jesus in vain, and also I could not say, "Jesus is Lord." That night when I went home, it was like Satan had me by my throat, saying, "You're mine, you're mine!" I felt such darkness.

The next day, I had to find Doug. We talked until midnight, and he led me in a prayer to receive Christ. It was like a light was turned on, and the room suddenly got brighter. We went to the Master's House the next evening, and there was a group of people holding hands in a circle, praying. We joined in, and one of Doug's friends, Bill Murphy, laid his hands on me. I cried, "Jesus, come into me, Jesus, come into me!" It was like electricity going through me, and I received wave upon wave of God's love, as He started to clean me up. The change in my life was dramatic. That evening, I stayed up all night reading the Bible and talking to people about the Lord. What was amazing was that I began to say things as God was revealing them to me, and those around me were astonished. They then showed me the Scriptures that I had just paraphrased in my own words.

Over the next few months, many things changed dramatically. I immediately lost my desire for drugs, and I had so much joy, my bad habit of swearing vanished. I made many new friends at the Master's House and on the Michigan State University campus, where I decided to finish my college education. From that dramatic day when God revealed himself to me, I realized that evolution could not possibly be true. I believe that there is an inner revelation that God places in us when we decide to follow Him, and He revealed many things to me in the next year, through the Bible and through my experiences with others.

Doug and I began talking about making a creation movie. There was a tract published by Inter-Varsity Press called *The Western Book of the Dead* that brought out the logical consequences that occur when evolution is assumed as a foundation for one's life. We began filming pieces of this, but shortly afterward Doug graduated from college, got married, and joined the navy. We didn't know it at that time, but this failed film project was the beginning of something the Lord was going to do with us much later.

A few years later, I fell in love with Doug's sister, and I ended up marrying Carol just before Doug returned from the navy. Carol and I started a Christian singing group called Charis, and we played at churches and coffeehouses. A new Master's House was constructed out of an old women's clubhouse in downtown Lansing, and the Lord allowed us to be part of the foundation of that ministry.

Doug was encouraged to write a book about the information he had discovered concerning creation and evolution, and that led to the *Revolution Against Evolution*. I accompanied Doug when he gave seminars, and I would give my testimony.

Eventually, God gave me my dream job as a staff artist for a major Michigan museum. Shortly afterward, Doug and I were asked to be on a public access TV program in East Lansing. This led to several people encouraging us to produce our own show. This was 1993, and since then we have produced more than 400 episodes of *Revolution Against Evolution*. There are indeed that many different topics that can be explored in this major issue. I am thankful to God that we have been allowed this avenue to tell our testimony and give our praise to our Creator God.

We Are More Than Smart Animals!

→ Chapter 7
Wayne R. Spencer

When I was a teenager, one of my nephews — a preschooler at the time — asked me a question that made me realize how much I did not know. I was holding him one evening, and we were looking up at the moon. He asked what the moon was and then asked, "How did it get there?" I thought for a second and I realized that I knew in general terms what science said about the question, but I felt I could not honestly say that I knew for sure, so I felt that I had to tell him that I did not know.

During high school I did well in math and science and had a strong drive to learn all I could about science. During that time, I realized that, though I had gone to church, I did not believe Christianity. In my early years of college, I concluded it was impossible to know if there was a God.

My point of view changed dramatically at age 20. A crisis caused by personal problems and the influence of two Christian roommates led me to accept Jesus Christ as Lord and Savior. At the time, I still assumed that science was correct about issues such as evolution, the big bang, and the age of the earth. Yet I did not claim to know a lot about such things.

Later in college, a fellow student who was a good friend exposed me to creationism. I also had the opportunity to hear presentations at Kansas State University by Drs. Henry Morris, Duane Gish, and Harold Slusher of the Institute for Creation Research. I was excited to learn that the Bible had something to say about science. Then, after reading more creationist books, including some from the Institute for Creation Research, I realized that evolution was in conflict with what the Bible said.

The books of Dr. Henry Morris as well as the writings of Dr. Francis Schaeffer were both very influential in those early years. Their works pointed out clear conflicts between the implications of evolution and Christianity.

Even after I became very interested in creationism and had given up on the idea of evolution, I still thought of it mainly as a science issue. Then, after reading Romans 1 in the New Testament, I realized that evolution had blinded my thinking. Romans 1:18–20 teaches that the basic attributes of God are plain to all people from the way things are made. Evolution was not just a science issue, because the Bible teaches we are the only creatures made in the image of God. Evolution implies we are essentially only smart animals, and the way people behave is a result of our descent from animals. Arguing that humans are evolved animals makes morality vague or nonexistent, depending on which view of evolution you take. This is very convenient because it allows people who do not want to accept the God of the Bible to justify whatever lifestyle they choose. But, if an infinite, personal Creator God created us for a purpose, then we do not have the "right" to live or think however we wish, and we must answer to the Creator God. The Bible is the unique record of the Creator's revelation to mankind. There are many clear indications that it is a uniquely reliable and authoritative source of truth. It gives us answers to all the largest questions people ask, such as about our origins, our purpose for living, and our future.

I asked myself, "Why was it not plain to me?" I realized it was because science and much of my education had taught me to think as if God were irrelevant or nonexistent. As I learned more, I wanted to study the creation issue even more, not just to understand what was wrong with evolution, but also so that I could understand what God was like and so I could learn to think biblically about not just evolution but everything. Eventually, I also became convinced I should do something to pass on the truth about creation to others.

Even today I continue to be amazed at the wonderful things that God created. The order, complexity, beauty, and sophistication engineered into life and the universe teaches us much about the attributes of this Creator. The wonders of nature should motivate us to want to worship and know the Creator personally. For that we must go to the Bible for specifics on how to have a relationship with our Creator.

After the semester in college when I first learned about creationism, I never lost interest and began teaching others what I had learned. I also found that my knowledge of creation had many positive effects on my own personal life. It gave me a greater confidence in the Bible, a sense of the greatness of God, and it helped me to fill in the missing pieces in developing an intelligent faith as a Christian. I began teaching about creation as I had opportunity, first in youth meetings and Sunday school classes. Later I became involved in a more formal sense as vice chairman of the Mid-Kansas Branch chapter of the Bible-Science Association in Wichita, Kansas. I became very active speaking on creationism and organizing conferences in the Wichita area. During this period, I also worked as a science and mathematics teacher in a Christian school, where I taught from a creation perspective. It was also during my ministry with the Bible-Science Association that I began to do some writing for publication.

I also have produced a multimedia slide presentation and video, "Wonders of the Solar System," a creationist program emphasizing worship. I've appeared on television on the *Origins* TV program for Cornerstone Television in Pennsylvania and on the *Science, Scripture, and Salvation* radio program of the Institute for Creation Research. I have preached in churches, youth conferences, home school groups, Sunday school classes, and secular settings as well. In 1994 and 1998, I presented technical papers at the International Conference on Creationism (ICC) in Pittsburgh, Pennsylvania. These papers for the ICC were on the solar system, craters, and earth impact craters. I have published articles in the *Bible Science News*, *Creation Ex Nihilo* magazine, and the *TJ* (*Technical Journal*) from Answers in Genesis. I also provided some graphics for technical illustrations in the book *Voyage to the Planets* published by the Institute for Creation Research, and authored by Dr. Richard Bliss. I now maintain a website (http://creationanswers.net) and produce a free e-mail newsletter called *Creation Answers*.

I hope that my creation ministry will help Christians develop a confidence in the truth of the Bible and help them come to develop an intelligent, consistent, and biblical way of thinking. In my technical-level papers, I want to help creationists to rethink the science of origins to bring it in line with what the Word of God teaches and to avoid the various errors of evolutionary and naturalistic thinking. I try to maintain a high standard of integrity in my ministry and publications. I have on occasion stopped the sale of an item that was out of date, or published corrections to earlier published mistakes. It is important also for creationists to do adequate research before presenting information to others.

I continue to be awestruck at the greatness of God as Creator. Though creation ministry can often be a thankless task, God does bring forth fruit from the effort. Many have turned from being knowledgeable evolutionists and active promoters of evolution to being active promoters of creation because of the evidence. Very few knowledgeable creationists have done the reverse.

Putting on Biblical Glasses

Chapter 8
Carl Kerby

My background is quite different from many of those involved with the creation/evolution issue. I was raised in a very liberal church that did not teach the Word of God. Instead, the focus was on ritual and tradition.

I have two memories of my early days in church. The first was my experience with catechism class. My mother would drop me off at the front door and I would walk in. Instead of going straight to the classroom, though, I would take a left and head out the side door to play. When it was time to leave, I'd walk in the side door, walk out the front door to my waiting mother as if I had been in class. I made a decision to skip these classes and as a result, I had to deal with the consequences for many years.

Years later, after becoming a Christian, I found the book that I had to use in catechism and was angry: the only page I had opened in the book was the front cover — I had written my name on the inside and had never gone beyond that. Nevertheless, I passed the catechism class and served as an acolyte. No one ever cared enough to confront me about not learning what was supposed to be so important. This is one reason why, today, I take very seriously the opportunities that I'm given to teach.

The second memory is of seeing my father, who was 6' 8" tall and 350 pounds, snoring in the pew during service. Mom would elbow him to wake him up. Because my father was a professional wrestler, I had a unique childhood. I now joke with people that growing up around people with one name like, "Crusher," "Bruiser," "Mauler," or "Assassin" had an effect on me. My role models were people like "Dory Funk

Jr." and "Mil Mascaras." Unfortunately, these are not the role models that I should have had: with a background like this, my faith was not something that I took very seriously.

My parents divorced when I was 13, and I lived with my mother and stepfather, who later adopted me. During my senior year in high school, I moved in with a Christian family because my parents moved away and did not want to disrupt my schooling. It was during this time that I first saw *real* Christians. This experience helped me greatly later in life.

During high school, drugs and alcohol were very much a part of my life. I'm not proud of it; I was a very lost young man. The decisions that I made during high school affected me for many years. I did not get my high school diploma in 1979 when I was supposed to; instead I had to finish the requirements while in the military. There, I was stationed in Japan as an air traffic controller. I learned the job that I am doing today and more importantly, I met my wife, Masami, in Japan. We were transferred to Lajes Field in the Azores shortly after being married.

While stationed in the Azores, my wife and I began to have difficulties. Having grown up around the church and thinking that I was a Christian because I had been baptized, I took my wife to church because I thought *she* needed help. The Lord had prepared her heart and mind, and she was born again the first Sunday. I'd never seen anything like that.

We were transferred to Salt Lake City after two years and two months. During this time, my younger brother was also having difficulties: he was making the same mistakes that I had made while in high school with drugs and alcohol. We invited him to come and live with us, and he accepted. I made him go to church with us, even though I still wasn't a Christian. On May 15, 1987, Lowell Lundstrom came to Salt Lake City for an evangelistic outreach. I talked my brother into going to hear him that night because the center for the Utah Jazz, Mark Eaton, was speaking. I felt that *he* needed to hear what these men had to say. In the Huntsman Center, with a few thousand people around us, the Holy Spirit opened my eyes to the fact that I was a sinner and needed Christ as my Savior. That night I was born again.

I still had a lot of difficulties, though, because I really didn't trust the Bible. My Sunday school teacher at that time taught me (and I even wrote it in my Bible) that evolution wasn't a problem. All that you had to do was take it and add it to the Bible, and there weren't any contradictions. I really didn't know how to reconcile this problem.

Because of my job as an air traffic controller, I could fly in the cockpit of commercial aircraft for training. Around March of 1988, I was in the cockpit on a flight to Portland, Oregon, to see my father. To my surprise, the pilot and copilot both turned out to be Christians. During a conversation with the pilots, the creation/evolution issue came up. I indicated that you could accept evolution and add it to the Bible without problems. The copilot sat up straight and looked over at the pilot, and then looked back at me, and said, "I'm sorry, Carl, but that's incorrect!"

The pilot wasn't trying to shove his opinion down my throat. He did exactly what the Scripture calls us to do. He had an answer for the reason for the hope within him, and he shared it with meekness and fear. The way that he went about it was very important, and I'm eternally thankful for this kind gentleman. He went to the Word and explained the world instead of the other way around. In all of my life, I had never met a person who built his or her thinking from the Bible. All I had ever experienced was someone giving his or her opinion and then going to the Bible to find a couple of verses that he or she thought supported his or her view. This pilot showed me from the Bible that evolution was a completely different worldview that could not be found in Scripture. He taught me how to look at the world through biblical glasses.

Needless to say, I was intrigued. I asked him where he had learned this, and he introduced me to Ken Ham's book, *The Lie: Evolution*. After reading it, my faith was totally changed. I then believed that God's Word was true from the very beginning (Ps. 119:160).

A lot has transpired since that day. God has seen fit to move me to O'Hare International Airport as an air traffic controller. I now work part-time, though, so that I can do ministry on the weekends. Answers in Genesis (AiG) has allowed me to start speaking on behalf of the ministry. There is no greater honor than to represent AiG and encourage Christians to trust God's Word completely. The decision to do that will have eternal consequences.

Mutations Do Not Produce DDT-Resistant Bacteria

Chapter 9
John Woodmorappe

I was born in the United States to Polish immigrant parents who had lost everything in World War II. Materially, my life did not get off to a good start. Then things got worse. All my life, I have been afflicted with Tourette's syndrome. This neurological disorder causes me to have spells of torso rocking, finger wiggling, and other unpleasant mannerisms. Although I have had some serious difficulties in life, the grace of God has given me an extraordinary ability in the area of scientific research.

My parents always had a love of learning, and passed it on to me. While all toddlers are naturally curious about the world around them, according to my mother, I was doubly so. I went through phases when I was fascinated with the function of some machine or device. During each obsession, little else mattered. No sooner had I learned to read than my mother began a habit of taking me to the public library to read books related to my then-current interests. I recall a special enjoyment of the "What Is It?" series of books (e.g., *What Is an Insect? What Is a Simple Machine?*). My mother and I also did experiments together. One funny incident comes to mind. My mother planted an avocado seed, and I checked the pot impatiently each day for the first growth to show. When nothing happened, I reasoned that we had planted the seed upside down. Not yet exposed to the fact of geotropism at the tender age of about six, I secretly dug up the seed and put it back in the opposite orientation. Eventually I told my mother what I had done, and she corrected my misunderstanding.

At around the age of ten, I could identify many trees in the neighborhood, and even knew the Latin names of most of them. My friends said I sounded like a priest. It is always good for a gifted child to have a mentor, and I had mine. He was an 80-year-old retired botanist who would visit me. We would go on walks together to talk about and examine different trees. Science was always my favorite subject and by junior high, I was exhibiting my science projects at state fairs.

I was not raised in a church that believed in the fundamentals of the Christian faith. Rather, I was a member of a religion that accommodated what it thought was science. I do recall from childhood a vague feeling that "cavemen" and the story of Adam and Eve didn't mix, but I never pursued it. Of the many science books I read, these inevitably indoctrinated me further into the "fact" of evolution. My childhood training was centered on obedience and conformity. Consequently, any incipient doubts I may have entertained about evolution were squelched by a "Who am I to question the experts?" pattern of thinking. During my religion classes, the topic of evolution and religious faith was ignored, so I assumed that it was not an important part of my religion.

The first whiff of doubt toward standard evolutionary views, as far as I can recall, took place just before I entered the eighth grade. During our family vacation, we visited Dinosaur National Monument at the Colorado-Utah border. I still have the vacation album. Upon noticing the jumble of dinosaur bones, I asked the guide if a flood had been responsible for the death and burial of these dinosaur remains. (I was not asking the question with the biblical flood specifically in mind, only as a result of being amazed by the large number of chaotically distributed bones.) "No! The bones were washed in slowly!" was his indignant reply. I could not understand at the time why he was so angry at what seemed to me to be a reasonable question. However, undoubtedly his anger is what caused me to remember this incident.

I went to one of the most academically demanding high schools in the nation. It was a college preparatory Jesuit school and was liberal theologically as well as politically. I was openly taught that Genesis was a myth and that organic evolution was a proven fact of science. I can still hear Father C saying, "I don't think that there ever was a Noah's ark. It was just a story." Not knowing any better, I accepted it, if only because I was not exposed to any alternative and did not even know that there were any scientists who believed differently.

Unexpectedly, it was my high school experience that finally forced me to confront the implications of organic evolution. In my sophomore year, I took a biology course that approached college level. Not only were we taught evolution as fact, but we were also subjected to Pierre Teilhard de Chardin's ideas as *the* definitive reconciliation between evolution and religion. After organic evolution, we studied ecology, and the left-leaning teacher taught us all the scare-stories of radical environmentalists as proven fact. Parenthetically, *I wonder why we are still here.* At that time (1970) we were told that we would all be dead from pollution, exhaustion of natural resources, and other certain horrors well before 2000 if nothing drastic was done and soon.

Having learned that DDT and organic chlorocarbons accumulate in the biosphere because they do not break down, I wrote my teacher a paper describing an idea I had thought of: scientists should breed bacteria, after subjecting them to radiogenic mutations generation after generation, in progressively greater concentrations of DDT. Finally, we would have a strain of bacteria that not only could break down DDT but also *lived* on DDT. Once released into the biosphere, these bacteria would consume all the accumulated DDT. The teacher replied that this would probably not work, unless perhaps millions of years were available. This planted the first serious seed of doubt about organic evolution in my mind because it showed me that what is often called "molecules-to-man" evolution is theoretical rather than factual.

While a freshman in college, a member of Campus Crusade for Christ won me to Christ. For the first time in my life, I realized that salvation is a free gift of God based on Christ's atoning death, not something to be earned by my good works added to Christ's death on the cross. Eagerly, I went for the follow-up instruction. During one of these sessions, I happened to ask some offhand questions about organic evolution, the global flood, and so on. The Crusade staff lent me a copy of *The Genesis Flood.*[1] I studied this, and other books, and soon became fascinated with this newfound perspective. But when exposed to creationist research, I first went into something that is now called "creation shock." This leads to such thoughts as: *Why did no one ever show me this before? I never realized that evolution was so full of holes!* I was genuinely

---

1. John C. Whitcomb and Henry M. Morris, *The Genesis Flood* (Philadelphia, PA: Presbyterian and Reformed Publ. Co., 1961).

astonished to learn that there are many qualified scientists who question or reject organic evolution.

Just as I had been earlier in life, I was intensely curious and wanted to go deeper. I read everything I could on origins. Being still largely authority-centered in my thinking, I thought of myself as being "free" to question evolution on the basis of the fact that some scientific authorities also questioned it. However, my previous indoctrination had been so solid that at first I found it difficult to contemplate a young earth. For this reason, I was an old-earth creationist (that is, a semi-creationist) for about a year and a half after my conversion. Only after studying geology in more depth did I fully appreciate the flawed reasoning behind the old-earth ideas, and only then was I in a position to accept creationism fully, as well as the complete and literal authority of the Bible in all areas that it addresses.

Forgoing a philosophy major, I decided instead to major in both geology and biology because of the pivotal role of these two disciplines in the study of origins, and because I had been especially interested in the earth sciences all my life. Furthermore, I had geology in my blood, as my grandfather had been a geologist who had owned an oil well (in Boryslaw, now in western Ukraine, following post–World War II border changes). I ended up with a BA in biology, an MA in geology, and an MA in biology.

At that time, I did not consider writing anything for creationist publications. However, the more science I learned, the more fallacies I found in the standard evolutionary-uniformitarian paradigm. Moreover, my eyes became open to many new lines of evidence relevant to creationist science. As a result, I began publishing articles in the *Creation Research Society Quarterly*. In time, all my geology articles were reprinted in a book, *Studies in Flood Geology.*[2] More recently, decades of research on the fallacies inherent in radiometric (actually, isotopic) dating methods culminated in another book, *The Mythology of Modern Dating Methods.*[3] The creationist community has favorably endorsed both.

---

2. John Woodmorappe, *Studies in Flood Geology* (El Cajon, CA: Institute for Creation Research, 1999).

3. John Woodmorappe, *The Mythology of Modern Dating Methods* (El Cajon, CA: Institute for Creation Research, 1999).

I have long been interested in the function of Noah's ark. Having noted that little had been done to relate animal care methods to the actual logistics of the ark, I began studying these methods. I was shocked to discover how many little-known techniques there are for the care of wild animals *en masse*, and how baseless are most of the common criticisms of the ark account, whether they come from infidels or from compromising evangelicals. In no time at all, I had collected hundreds of studies relevant to this topic, and my seven years of work on this project culminated in my book *Noah's Ark: A Feasibility Study*.[4] Judging by the reaction it has received from many supporters (as well as hatred from anti-creationists), it seems to serve a real need.

I have delivered papers at each of the International Conferences on Creationism, and have, in recent years, been a regular contributor of research papers to the *Creation Ex Nihilo Technical Journal*. Periodically, I have also spoken and debated on some topic related to origins. Most summers in recent years have been spent doing geologic or biologic fieldwork. During the year, I am a science teacher in Chicago public schools.

This is truly an exciting time to be a creationist scientist. It is a thrill and joy to help free science from its humanist slave masters and the rationalistic shackles that are holding it in naturalistic thrall. There are so many fascinating questions to investigate, and I can easily conceive of potential research projects that could fill several lifetimes. Looking back on 25 years of creation research, I have only one regret — that I cannot do 100 times the work I do now to speed creationist research forward.

---

4. John Woodmorappe, *Noah's Ark: A Feasibility Study* (Santee, CA: Institute for Creation Research, 1996).

Evidence for the Flood

Chapter 10
Daniel Schobert

My journey toward the creationist position is possibly a little different from that of others. Although I was born into a family where my parents were involved in ministry, I had given little thought about the whole matter of origins until entering college. My father was an American Baptist minister. During the many years I sat under sermons and lived in our home, I don't recall ever hearing him say much about the evolution/creation problem. He was a graduate of Dallas Seminary and had attended Wheaton College in the 1920s. In retrospect, I believe he might have been comfortable as a theistic evolutionist, though this is hard to say.

In a strange turn of events, I began to consider the origins issue shortly after my father died in 1971. It was during the time that we were taking care of his things that I happened to come across the book *The Flood* by Alfred Rehwinkel.[1] I have since lost the book, but it opened my mind to issues I had never before considered. I had had an early run-in with a college professor at Hillsdale College (in Michigan) in my freshman year — an ardent evolutionist I could not see eye-to-eye with. I ended up taking the course again, but at a different institution. At the time, I was simply going on what I knew, or thought I knew, from the Bible that man did *not* come from apes. I had had little ammunition with which to argue.

Even later when I attended the predecessor of Judson College in Chicago, I cannot remember ever hearing much about the relationship between evolution and the Bible and creation. It wasn't until I read

---

1. Alfred Rehwinkel, *The Flood in the Light of the Bible, Geology, and Archaeology* (St. Louis, MO: Concordia Publ. House, 1957).

Rehwinkel's book *The Flood* that this topic began to come together. By this time I had graduated from college (Michigan State University, 1964), had a family of four children, and was in the midst of moving along in my chosen career in radio broadcasting.

It wasn't long after working my way through *The Flood* that other materials began to find their way into my hands. I recall attending a seminar given by Dr. Henry Morris and others. Later I read his book *The Genesis Flood*[2] and began receiving Institute for Creation Research materials along with the *Bible-Science Newsletter*. It seemed that the floodgates had been opened to a whole new world, and I found myself drinking it all in.

Eventually, given my background in radio, I felt it a good idea to attempt some sort of radio program. I believe this may have even pre-dated the present-day radio efforts of ICR and also before the Bible-Science Association instituted *Creation Moments*. I constructed a small studio in our home and began putting together a 15-minute radio program, *The Creation Report*, which eventually found its way onto several stations. It was largely a program of comments by others in the creationist movement. Little sound bites were aired, as one might use video clips in television. It was well received and even today, I still receive favorable comments about it though I discontinued production more than 15 years ago.

This program prompted several speaking invitations. Perhaps the greatest honor was to address the 1992 Creation Conference at St. Paul, Minnesota, with my paper on *The Origin of Language*, a paper that remains uncontested to this day.

As I look back over the several years of being involved in this area of science, I can only be amazed. One reason is that I am not a scientist. I view myself as being mostly a reporter, someone who gathers information from various sources and sends it along to others so they may understand the material.

It was also in about the early 1970s that I felt it was a good idea to send letters to the editor of the local newspaper expounding on the important issues of the day, especially those related to evolution. Little did I know that this would open yet another door. These letters seemed

---

2. Henry M. Morris, *The Genesis Flood* (Philadelphia, PA: Presbyterian and Reformed Publ. Co., 1961).

to fill a niche in the community, and I began receiving good responses, though not everyone was happy with my ideas. Over the years, the Lord has seen fit to allow me to write and have published some 600 letters, and the list continues to grow. Outside of His leading, I cannot explain these things.

I believe, however, that the key to understanding this is a prayer request made some years ago and one that continues to be in my prayers, that I be able to comprehend things and have the wisdom/ability to share with others. Given my educational background, I should not be able to do the things I have accomplished in my life. God gets the credit; I am only along for the ride.

If I were to travel back through the years of thinking about evolution, it seems the one thing I have found most striking is the power of ideas. *What is it,* I have often thought, *that makes the concept of evolution so inviting to so many people? Why do people buy into such an idea so full of nonsense?* In the end, I've concluded one simple answer: a desire to avoid God in their thinking and in their lives.

There are probably many reasons why people have had a change of mind on this issue. One of the more powerful for me has been to realize that unless God has the interest and ability to communicate important truths of the past, how can He be trusted to tell me about the future? Our understanding of the distant past rests on God telling us what took place. This telling of history relies on straightforward understanding of the words He used. Trusting Him to give us all the necessary information to understand His Word has encouraged me in my walk with Him. Since God holds the responsibility for the whole Bible, from start to finish, and since this communication is to be read and understood as a clear communication, who am I to change the words to mean something different? This was my concern and continues to be the basis for looking at Scripture in ways that would not destroy the plain teaching of the Author. God is in the business of communication. This being the case, I have to be careful that I don't substitute a word or words in order to accommodate a passing thought from those who may have little regard for God. Taken in a straightforward manner and comparing the text to what is actually known about the world in which we live, I have yet to find even one error.

The Inspiration of Being Human

Chapter 11
Chard Berndt

My earliest awareness of the creationist perspective came before I knew I was a creationist.

I grew up in Hong Kong, where my parents served as missionaries and my dad eventually became a seminary president. At age seven, not far from the high-rises and shantytowns of Kowloon Tong, I developed a love for capturing huge, vibrant butterflies in regenerated woodlands. Their flitting motion and graceful pauses delighted me, and I remember feeling inspired. I knew that God had created these. At one point, I wondered what it would be like if I had come out of a cocoon. I also remember thinking that this was an irrelevant question, because if "I" had been one of them, then I wouldn't have been me. Now I understand the biblical reason — the soul of man is incomparable to that of a butterfly, or any other kind of creature. I also recall once freezing in my tracks, net in hand, as the sun backlit a monstrous, perfectly spun web, with its black and brightly colored engineer in the center. Though afraid, I was also awestruck, and my marvel outlasted my trepidation. I knew that God had built the builder as well as the web.

Not all my pursuits of God's works were that reflective, though. I also found myself scaling a concrete house from its flat roof, hanging from the upstairs neighbors' barred windows, attempting to wire up lightbulbs for the next lightning strike. My Franklin-Edison adventure amounted to nothing, but I was always on the lookout for a good typhoon, if not for its meteorological value, at least to stay home from school.

We came to the United States when I was nine. My dad served as a pastor, but I don't remember our church addressing Genesis much, other than to emphasize man's fall. In retrospect, my theology of creation was framed largely by powerful hymns that I sang each week. My education outside of the church never seemed to address the creation/evolution conflict either, but a *C* in zoology in public high school suggests to me that I may not have listened much then. In those years, the only creation/evolution argument I engaged in was on a bus ride while returning from an athletic event, in which I used a brief defense that might be called a "First Cause" argument. I later learned the amazing significance of God's self-proclaimed personal name, YHWH, the "I Am," and it was a breakthrough for me when I saw the connection between Genesis 1:1 "In the beginning God created," and John 1:1 "In the beginning was the Word." I also found it significant that the acts of creation are referred to multiple times in the Bible, not just in Genesis 1 and 2, and that Jesus Christ himself validated the Genesis account.

The value of a creationist perspective came further to light when I ministered as a camp counselor and program director for over five summers. I began taking intense backcountry excursions on my days off with Rob Moore (now a professional oil artist). On our hikes and scrambles, he spoke pensively of patterns of light, and of capturing on canvas their true created relationships. He sounded strangely enthusiastic beneath his quiet, deliberate drawl, speaking more of God as the Artist than he. It was also evident that he had listened to some radio teaching on creation and the Flood and had made the connections between science and Scripture and between his livelihood and his life's philosophy. He had me thinking again.

I had begun writing songs for guitar during that time and sparked by our discussions, I penned "The Artist." This song reminds us that, although we are fallen humans, we are, nonetheless, the crown of His creation, created in His image, and the only kind for whom He gave His Son. And without much of an awareness of how far-reaching the creation/evolution controversy was, I continued writing songs with such a theme. I recall one that read:

> People may say,
> we came from the slime
> It was just a matter of time.

I noticed that young people were hungry to hear something other than the depressing "survival" mantra of evolution. They were already surviving, but knew that human life had to have a much higher and brighter purpose than survival alone. They wanted to *thrive*.

I suppose if I were to identify specifically what I was learning from my friend Rob, from the Bible, and from my own experiences of serving others, it was that the creation was replete with *meaningful discontinuity* and purpose. I noticed that Christians were set apart from the world, not just in moral degree but also in a new nature and destiny. From this, I concluded that if humankind was not itself discontinuous from the rest of creation, then there would be no basis for God laying claim to His people, and that the gospel message would be irrelevant. I realized that I, and each young person committing his life to Christ, was exercising a wonderful, unique attribute: a volitional responsibility that dictated a vital relationship with our Maker.

Toward the end of this time of my life (the late '80s) I was completing my electrical engineering degree at the University of Colorado–Boulder. Because I spoke fairly openly about my Christian faith, I became known as the "philosophical one." I suppose this probably said more about my dry, calculator-punching peers than about me. Nonetheless, unlike most other engineering students, I wasn't satisfied with finding canned topics for the required "Writing in Science and Society" course, but instead dug deeper. My professor, an eloquent sage-type, noticed my theistic worldview, and invited me to coffee on "The Hill." I was astonished at how urgently he tried to dissolve my worldview with talk of enlightened Eastern mysticism. He seemed to think that I, when exposed to such new and fresh ideas, would surely start down a new path of thinking. Meanwhile, I was also surprised to realize that I had a deep enough conviction to return the favor and try persuading him. When all was said and done, I earned his respect, an *A* in the course, and a new appreciation for how pivotal the issue of origins was to virtually any philosophical discussion.

In tandem with that experience, I was struck by the inconsistency of a controversy that dominated the school campus for a time. Fetal pig research was being blasted as a moral evil, while at the same time pro-abortion sentiment ran high. At this point, I recognized that this was about much more than a belief in a blurred continuity of life — it was actually a convoluted misapprehension of the value of humankind. This was not just about the broad assumptions of the evolutionary hypothesis, but also about a strategy of Satan himself to render the gospel irrelevant. Students weren't looking for a Savior, nor were they interested in thinking rationally. Absolute values were being swallowed up in postmodernism, and I realized that this was what my generation was all about.

Seven years later, after five years as a youth pastor and a couple years into my calling as a Christian schoolteacher (I never used my engineering degree directly), I had the opportunity to evaluate our science curriculum. I had attended a seminar on using the days of creation as a framework to introduce middle-school level science units, and this resonated with me. However, when it came time to apply the sequence of creation to my biology units, I realized that I was up against a notable conflict: prevailing taxonomy was completely at odds with the biblical discontinuity of the kind, and with the biblical criteria by which those kinds were grouped when they were created. More than anything, a fresh biblical look at systematics (which eventually became my book *Biblical Classification of Life*) led me to appreciate the observable realities of creation, and to abhor the dogmatic assumptions of evolutionism. Biosystematics is riddled with confusion and inconsistencies today because it is based on a lie.

In addition to biosystematics, I have found a remarkable appreciation for the wonders of God as Designer in the emerging "information science." Having always appreciated mathematics and codes, I found Dr. Werner Gitt's *In the Beginning Was Information*[1] a fascinating eye-opener. DNA is much more than complex, it is *meaningfully* complex — not merely a language, but a message. My God is no mere watchmaker, and He is certainly not a blind one.

Again and again, as I reflect on the ongoing creation/evolution dialogues, I am reminded that it is not about science vsersus religion, but about whether scientists comprehend the whole of reality or not. Materialism gives birth to an empty science that must eventually look the other way when faced with its many shortcomings. This type of "science" worships man's ideas while, strangely, denigrating his very existence. Biblical creationism, in contrast, inspires men and glorifies God.

---

1. Werner Gitt, *In the Beginning Was Information* (Green Forest, AR: Master Books, 2006).

On occasion, I've become quite frustrated with some parents of students enrolled in my classes. Though they have enrolled their children in a Christian school, because they were trained in a world-pleasing theistic evolutionist environment, they have little tolerance for the instruction of science within a six-day creation framework. I've noticed that they are seldom open to dialogue on the matter, and typically, I discover their opposition through the grapevine or a diatribe written on a survey. Interestingly, I've consistently seen spiritual stagnation, lackluster parenting, and even hypocrisy among those parents who make profession of a God who "created" this way. Though already persuaded in my conscience as to the real truth of special creation, I'm further reinforced in the spiritual significance of this belief when I see such beliefs borne out in their fruit, as Drs. Henry Morris and John Morris detail in *The Modern Creation Triology, Volume 3: Society & Creation.*[2]

As I pursue further studies in science education and biology, I do not fear what scientists will find in years to come. There is no research that needs to be censored; only assumptions (and the conclusions they foster) that need to be exposed.

On the other hand, while recognizing the need to distinguish between the observable and the unobservable, both of which have their place in science, I am confident in my biblical presuppositions.

---

2. Henry M. Morris and John D. Morris, *The Modern Creation Trilogy, Volume 3: Society & Creation* (Green Forest, AR: Master Books, 1996).

Accuracy of Radioisotope Dating Doubtful

Chapter 12
Curt Sewell

When I was in school in the 1930s and early '40s, I never heard of anyone with an interest in science who actually believed Genesis was more than a myth. I was raised in church and believed the Bible — except for Genesis — but my church was "liberal," and I hadn't yet become a born-again Christian. Since I had an active interest in science, I believed in evolution and an ancient age for the earth. That belief was reinforced when the army put me on the Manhattan Project (developing the first atomic bomb), where I met a number of scientists whose names you all have heard.

Later, in the 1960s, while I was chief engineer of Isotopes Incorporated, several of our top staff members were PhDs, including one who was also professor of geochemistry at Columbia University. He and a few others were Wheaton College graduates, and Christians who believed in progressive creation. This professor, who was generally recognized as one of the world's experts on geochronology, gave testimony before Congress on that subject. He was also a true gentleman who tried to answer my queries honestly. We often had lunch together, and the subject of origins was one of our favorite "arguing points." By that time I had become a born-again Christian and studied the Bible regularly. I asked many questions — about radioactivity, dating methods, and so on. My questions kept getting back to, "Well, how do you really know?" on various aspects of the foundations of radioisotope dating. Our lunchtime group were all quite knowledgeable about dating procedures, which were part of one of our company's products. But I kept feeling subtle doubts about the foundational accuracy of radiometric dating.

Yet I had never met any scientist who accepted the young-earth creationist viewpoint — that God miraculously created the earth and its inhabitants in a six-day period, no more than some thousands of years ago, not millions or billions, and destroyed it in the worldwide devastating flood described in Genesis 6–9 — so I didn't either.

I kept studying technical journals and books, and finally became convinced that circular logic and faith in prior beliefs played a strong part in radiometric dating — in other words, it wasn't a "scientific fact, provable by scientific methods." There was too much unproved belief involved. By this time I was a dedicated Christian, but I was constantly bothered by this dichotomy in my own beliefs. I became open to considering a young-earth creationist worldview but still had never encountered a "scientific creationist" who believed in young-earth creation.

When I finally met one, he gave me one of the early copies of a *Bible-Science Newsletter,* and I finally discovered that there were scientists who really believed in the early chapters of Genesis. I subscribed and quickly became an active "scientific creationist," as we were known in those days — a term I still don't really like.

When someone asks me why I'm a young-earth creationist now, one facet of my answer always includes the closer relationship to God the Creator, and the comfort that gives. It is often said that you don't need to believe in young-earth creationism to be born again. That may well be true, but I have found that the simple acceptance of God's Word at face value — which means acceptance of the literalness of the first 11 chapters of Genesis — certainly helps one's relationship with God.

Missing Links in the Ape-Men Story

Chapter 13
Dr. Hennie Mouton

I was brought up in a Christian home and heard all the Bible stories from a children's Bible a number of times. I even started reading my own "grown-up" Bible at the age of eight. My reading schedule has always been to read from Genesis right through to Revelation, and then to start all over again at Genesis. This resulted in my having a good understanding of what the Bible was telling us.

I was not taught any direct evolutionistic material in school, or at the university where I studied electrical engineering. Engineers are taught practical things, so the chance of evolution having some bearing there is extremely remote. Engineers learn to design and to appreciate design (and never leave matter or energy on its own to develop into something useful by chance). Technology (and the real world) simply does not think like Darwinists.

While working at Kentron, Pretoria, a missile-developing company in South Africa, I obtained a second BS, this time in applied mathematics and astronomy. Later on, I completed a PhD in engineering. In some of the astronomy subjects, millions of years were mentioned, but not realizing that the Bible stipulated only thousands of years for all of creation, it did not add to my doubts at that stage.

I always liked reading, and articles on the science of origins, apemen, and the like especially interested me. Because I knew the Bible and the history portrayed in it, the stories of claimed human predecessors (and other evolutionary claims) worried me, as I could not reconcile them with the Bible. This led me to wonder if what I was reading in the Bible really was true. Thanks to the grace of the Lord, I never completely lost my faith in Jesus Christ as my Savior, but I often ended up with more questions than answers after reading Scripture.

My wife and I joined a Bible study group some 13 years ago and are still participating. These studies concentrate on "spiritual" matters and never on biblical history, origins, and so on. They were of great value in building and strengthening my Christian faith, but never answered my original questions about reconciling the Bible and evolutionary claims.

Kentron has a Christian association that often invites speakers to give talks during lunch. Professor McMurtry from the United States was invited on a particular occasion some seven years ago, as he was in South Africa on invitation from a Christian pro-creation group, *Deus Dixit*. I did not attend many of these lunchtime talks, but this one interested me tremendously: he was going to speak on the age of the earth.

His talk opened a new world for me — there was really strong evidence for the earth to be only a few thousand years old! He also mentioned that the AiG magazine *Creation Ex Nihilo* could be obtained through Joshua Gilbert, a Christian brother from Durban. A few colleagues, Koos van der Westhuyzen, and myself immediately ordered the magazine. We wanted to know more. Professor McMurtry had also spoken that evening at the University of Pretoria. I asked him some questions on ape-men that he easily answered to my satisfaction. When I learned about the many frauds and missing links, ape-men were shifted in my mind from reality to Hollywood, and they don't even belong there!

I still had many questions, and they were answered one after the other by articles in *Creation Ex Nihilo* magazine. The realization that there could not have been death before Adam's sin according to the Bible, because death is the result of sin, is probably the main aspect that accelerated my mindset toward creationism in the full sense.

On the initiative of Koos van der Westhuyzen, we started a creation group in Kentron, showing creation videos during lunchtime once a week. We also decided to start preparing material for possible presentations in the future wherever the Lord would lead us. We purchased a number of books and videos, and the book on so-called hominid fossils, *Bones of Contention*, by Professor Marvin L. Lubenow.

This book started a new chapter in my life. After reading it, I wanted to summarize it — this was a convenient way for me to prepare myself to be able to talk to others about it. Once I had summarized it, I thought the next question would be, "What about radiometric dating?" And so the Afrikaans book *Evolusie: die onwetenskaplike leuen* was born. A few English-speaking and black people in South Africa asked me to translate the book and *Evolution: The Unscientific Lie* was published about 18 months later. The 500 copies of the Afrikaans version were sold out in less than two years.

Rudolf Steinberg, another creationist in Pretoria, started the presentation ministry for both Koos and me. He is a retired electrical engineer and personal friend of Dr. Werner Gitt. After seeing my book, he contacted me to do a presentation at "The Wonder of Creation" series he was planning to start at his church in Garsfontein, Pretoria. I proposed to him that Koos and I would each speak for half an hour. After this presentation, I thought Rudolf would have had other speakers lined up for the rest of the year, but Koos and I turned out to be the most frequent visitors.

The creation group at Kentron has now grown to about 30 people. We have creation presentation material for about five hours and have completed about 15 presentations at Kentron, at churches and schools, and as far away as Cape Town.

Probably the most disappointing aspect of my involvement in the creation ministry is the lack of real support from my own church. My own pastors are not against what I am doing, but they don't see the real value of it, either. Some of them seem to be quite content with a type of theistic evolutionary view, and some simply don't really want to talk about this matter. My denomination is actually strongly biased toward theistic evolution — no wonder they are nowadays debating the authority of the Bible!

The most satisfying aspect of creationism for me is the growing realization that the Bible is the Word of God. Science, when viewed properly, vindicates the Bible in very exciting ways. Salvation through Jesus Christ is taught in the Bible, and as such is probably the single most important teaching. It is a privilege to also be able to understand so much more of what we see around us regarding all of creation. Our Creator God is omnipotent, eternal, and there is none other like Him! And how much easier it is to believe in Jesus Christ as written about in the Bible if all of the Bible can be trusted to be the truth.

Evolution Is Faulty Moral Theory

Chapter 14
Jeffrey Stueber

When did I become convinced of the truth of the creationist account presented in the Bible? I don't know of a particular date one might normally remember, such as a birthday or anniversary. I do remember it was around the year 2000, after I had spent an enormous amount of time philosophizing about my Christian faith.

I had come to realize that the atheist really has no answer to the question of why one ought to be moral. I was reminded of this dilemma when viewing the movie *Terminator 2: Judgment Day*. The terminator is about to kill two men and Connor stops him. He explains to Schwarzenegger's robotic character that it is wrong to kill, in response to which the robot asks why this is so. John Connor has no answer except the standard response, "You just can't."

The character Connor is not dumb and ably represents the thoroughly modern, secularized, civilized man. He had no answer to that most profound question. A Christian would suppose that one must not kill because God forbids it. One who is thoroughly secularized can only find reasons based on self-interest or other faulty philosophical constructs, or dodge the issue, as John Connor does.

Clearly, humanity has an ethical compass that defies naturalistic efforts to reduce it to mere remnants of biological processes and instincts. Peter Kreeft and Ronald Tacelli, in their 1994 *Handbook of Christian Apologetics*,[1] argue that real moral obligations are incompatible with atheist beliefs. The religious view of moral obligations does not state that a few people believe that we ought to do certain things, or

---

1. Peter Kreeft and Ronald Tacelli, *Handbook of Christian Apologetics* (Downers Grove, IL: InterVarsity Press, 1994), p. 72–75.

believe that they are obligated to behave a certain way. They believe that people act as if they have moral obligations because of objective beliefs. Atheists tell us we are blind products of chance, but moral obligations do not square with a worldview that tells us we are products of chance. Moral obligations cannot spring from something less than us, for who could be obligated to a lesser form of life? Nor can they spring from a purposeless or inanimate natural force. They cannot spring from human beings, because we feel obligated to deny ourselves and act in accord with a law outside our own wishes. We do not wish to be obligated to society, for we judge society by our knowledge of what is right and what is wrong. Therefore, the only thing humanity can be obligated to is a law handed down to us from an intelligent source greater than man.

Humanists and atheists are deft in their attempts to explain the moral sense humans possess. Frank Zindler, an atheist who has debated William Lane Craig, leans heavily on the newest version of the "devil made me do it" theme. We are obligated to feel moral and act on our moral feelings, but it is not the devil that imbues these feelings in us. Rather, nature has given us this sense.

> As human beings, we are social animals. Our sociality is the result of evolution, not choice. Natural selection has equipped us with nervous systems which are peculiarly sensitive to the emotional status of our fellows.[2]

Thus, over millions of years, we have evolved to love chocolate, movies, and ice cream just as we have evolved to like treating others unfairly or even engaging in hate speech. Our cultural elite might consider banning eating chocolate if it is to the detriment of society as a whole, just as it might punish hate speech if it hurts people. According to atheism, the only source of moral sense is culture and the only characteristic that defines an act as wrong is its destructive or nondestructive effect on culture. It is not a remnant of a divine or semi-divine command to do (or not to do) something.

According to Judeo-Christian precepts, some actions, even desires, are sins that we are always obligated not to do (or feel) regardless of

---

2. Frank Zindler in David Bender, ed., *Constructing a Life Philosophy: Opposing Viewpoints* (San Diego, CA: Greenhaven Press, 1993), p. 171.

whether society tells us to do or to not do these things, or feel these emotions. Even though society may not be able to punish you, you are still obligated not to do them. God's demands trump all social commands.

Zindler proposes a natural explanation for the desire to do good, but mankind does not recognize such desire as an instinct alone. Such desires are actually part of a larger cultural hierarchy of acts people are obligated to do (or not do). Secularized society recognizes no such absolutes, though. This is why John Connor can require the Terminator not to kill, though he cannot explain why. Thus, atheists find themselves on the horns of a dilemma — they must recognize the validity of some absolutes while denying their essential existence.

Zindler proposes an *explanation* for our moral feelings that would work if we were motivated by instinct alone. However, he omits entirely the required *justification* for the moral judgments we make: we don't do moral acts because of how they make us feel; we do them because there is a quality about them defined by their relationship to a transcendent rule of law that we sense, but possibly cannot explain, which nevertheless exists and is not instinct alone, but part of our designed humanity. Such judging, which we seemed enabled to do, requires a supreme judge, like God, who creates a set of rules that we must obey — as much as a snowman requires a snowman-maker. A theistic explanation fits the facts better than Zindler's explanation does.

I am always watching closely for faulty moral theory that, when put to the test, harms society instead of helping it. When Zindler debated Lane Craig, Zindler claimed enlightened self-interest could give us a clue as to how to act and avoid evils like genocide.[3] The danger here is in trusting our self-interest in the first place. Zindler supposes our self-interest is our best guide to correct actions and believes that it is seldom wrong. Such a focus on self-interest can be a sure ticket to selfishness, acting for oneself at the expense of others and society. In the end, in Zindler's world, the only reason to be moral is to benefit one's self.

According to Christian theism, man has a moral sense but a sinful body (or predisposition). The moral sense will tell one what to do, but that sense is polluted by mankind's depravity. Only by yielding to the will of God can mankind do well. Humanity is moral not only for self-preservation but because we wish to praise God with our actions. The

---

3. *Atheism Versus Christianity* (videotape) (Grand Rapids, MI: Zondervan, 1994).

ultimate payoff comes in the afterlife. I find the Judeo-Christian explanation for mankind's moral sense, and the punishment/reward mechanism of it, more powerful than Zindler's. Under Christian theism, enlightened self-interest is not an option.

Edward Wilson follows Zindler's line of thinking, favoring a naturalistic explanation for our moral sense. Many theists believe there is no way to translate an *ought* to an *is*, but Wilson disavows this claim. Translating an *ought* to an *is*, he says, makes sense if we attend to the objective meaning of ethical precepts. "They are very unlikely to be ethereal messages awaiting revelation, or independent truths vibrating in a nonmaterial dimension of the mind," he says, and adds:

> They are more likely to be products of the brain and the culture. From the consilient perspective of the natural sciences, they are no more than principles of the social contract hardened into rules and dictates — the behavioral codes that members of a society fervently wish others to follow and are themselves willing to accept for the common good. Precepts are the extreme on a scale of agreements that range from casual assent, to law, to that part of the canon considered sacred and unalterable.[4]

Wilson demonstrates how an ethical code of not committing adultery may originate. Two people might say committing adultery doesn't "feel right" and then, later, conclude that not only does it not feel proper, but that society should condemn it. Then they leap to the conclusion that God condemns it. There is, however, a difficulty inherent in Wilson's reasoning. In order for the second step (the conclusion that society should condemn an act) to occur, a large proportion of people comprising the society must have gone through a similar chain of reasoning. But how can they when, at each step, they must infer that society condemns an act that it clearly hasn't until society has actually run through such a chain of logic? This is a strange chicken-and-egg scenario that seems appealing until you start to ask questions about its plausibility. How can people claim that society condemns an act before society has condemned it when the respective people are themselves

---

4. Edward Wilson, "The Biological Basis of Morality," *Atlantic Monthly*, April 1998.

members of society waiting to making the judgment that society condemns their act? Here, the evolutionary claim (or at least Wilson's) rests on belief in a critical accident: somehow, a large chunk of society spontaneously began thinking adultery was wrong. Then they began to think that God condemned adultery.

Wilson supposes that humans ascribe to God the moral qualms they have about adultery. This raises several familiar questions. Why would humans *want* to attribute to God any desire on their part to conform to moral requirements? Zindler reminds us that even animals are moral, to some extent, without resorting to oracles from God.[5] Of course, animals don't ascribe their moral urgings to God; the concept of God would be as alien to animals as any other human concept. Why, then, do humans need a concept of God to explain their restraint regarding committing adultery? Most atheists I have read say that the concept of God is an accidental construct to explain natural phenomena and desires. Yet, for such conceptions of the Divine to take hold on human culture, a prerequisite would be for a "critical mass" of pre-humans or newly evolved humans to embrace religion simultaneously. I find this highly unlikely. What is more likely is that God created us with a desire for the divine and a concept of God that can become polluted over time. We ascribe to God the source of our sense of moral absolutes because we are created to know moral absolutes and God's intentions for them, although our conceptions of this become polluted by our sinful desires.

I came to the conviction that Christian theism was correct when I read Michael Ruse's book, trying to get us to "take Darwin seriously" (as the title of his book suggests).[6] Ruse explores numerous options for wedding morality to naturalism. He begins his discussion of evolutionary ethics with extreme bluntness. "Morality is about guides to life: obligations. What you should do and what you should not do." Morality is about obligations that apply to all people, like the obligation to not rape little girls (an example he uses). Ruse is clear on this, and when I first read him, I expected him to lapse into a discussion of who (or what) the agent was that obligated us. It would seem to require some kind of intelligent agent, like a god who never changed, like the God of Judaism and Christianity, who could hold us accountable for our actions. Ruse

---

5. Zindler, *Constructing a Life Philosophy: Opposing Viewpoints*, p. 172.
6. Michael Ruse, *Taking Darwin Seriously* (New York: Basil Blackwell, 1986).

provides no such agent. Instead, he leaps into a discussion of Herbert Spencer's beliefs, moral Darwinism, utilitarianism, and so forth. What I found as I read his book is that he continuously seems to seek to provide answers to the question of who the agent is that we are obligated to without ever really getting there. It seems that he debunks every suggestion he provides. I find this a sign that his system of ethics is deeply flawed because it does not demonstrate the coherence required to be viable.

Evolutionists are in agreement on the origins of morality. Paul Kurtz says, "Moral codes thus have an adaptive function; one can postulate that those groups which had some effective regulation for conduct were better able to survive."[7] From Corliss Lamont we read, "Moral standards, like the categories of mind, originate and evolve in the course of human association. Hence morality, too, is a social product."[8] Daniel Dennett quotes Michael Ruse and Edward Wilson as saying, "Morality, or more strictly our belief in morality, is merely an adaptation put in place to further our reproductive ends." Dennett himself locates the "ought" we get from our moral sense in "an appreciation of human nature — on a sense of what a human being is or might be, and on what a human being might want to have or want to be." He does not locate it in the divine will of God.[9]

These theories share the faults I have outlined and raise doubt that atheists and evolutionists can successfully account for all the known facets of human morality. There exists an inborn sense that we are obligated to do (or not to do) certain actions, but atheism has no explanation for why we are *absolutely* obligated to perform (or refrain from) certain actions. There is no explanation for how we can judge past societies either, as we do when we judge them for racial injustices, for to do so requires a supreme eternal law we must know by which we *can* judge others. The moral sense we have could only maintain its hold on people if it had developed in mankind spontaneously and simultaneously, as if by divine creation. Such a sense, under divine creation, would not be

---

7. Paul Kurtz, *Forbidden Fruit: The Ethics of Humanism* (Buffalo, NY: Prometheus, 1988), p. 67–68.

8. Corliss Lamont, *The Philosophy of Humanism* (New York: Frederick Ungar Publishing, 1949–1965), p. 89.

9. Daniel Dennett, *Darwin's Dangerous Idea: Evolution and the Meanings of Life* (New York: Simon & Schuster, 1995).

subject to disregard or oversight, deliberate or otherwise, but would have staying power — as our consciences do. I find that only a theistic creationist picture of humanity's origins, such as that outlined in the Bible, presents a coherent explanation of our moral sense and a guide for us to follow. There is also evidence that our physical and emotional health depends on a link with the divine:[10] we were created to *need* that link. This explains why we ascribe dissatisfaction with our deeds to the divine. Humans live successfully when knowing God and following His will.

My confidence comes not so much from a study of biology, the fossil record, or a study of ancient documents. I am sure of my faith because there is something unique about humanity for which atheists have no answer. That something is the moral sense that we have and the purpose of life we seek that can only be found within, and explained by the context of a life centered on the God of the Bible.

---

10. Patrick Glynn, *God: The Evidence: The Reconciliation of Faith and Reason in a Post-secular World* (Rocklin, CA: Prima Publishing, 1997).

The Message of Creation Finds its Way to India

Chapter 15
Jyoti P. Chakravartty

My conversion was not a Damascus Road experience. The Lord had chosen me before the world was formed, and I obeyed His call when I was a young high school student. I was born into a Christian family; my father comes from a Hindu high caste Brahmin family, and he came to know the Lord by reading Mark's Gospel, which he bought from a group of foreigners who were selling Gospels on the streets of Calcutta. My parents left their vocation to serve the Lord when I was very young, as full-time Christian workers with the Brethren Assemblies.

From my childhood, I was interested in science and used to experiment with various science projects. I became a Christian in my childhood when my mum told me Bible stories. When I was 14 years old, I obeyed the Lord and went through the waters of baptism. Beside my studies, I was active in sharing my faith with my friends and also helping my parents in the ministry among the lepers, street children, and Bible correspondence course students.

While I was getting my bachelors degree in biological science at Serampore College of Calcutta University, I was confronted with the issue of evolution and creation. My fellow students and professors had questions like, "How can you, being a student of science, believe in God?" or "As a biological science student, how can you believe in the Virgin Birth?" and "After studying Darwin's *Origin of Species,* will you still believe in the creation account of the Bible?"

I was puzzled and didn't have any good answers. As a result, my faith was shaken. I had my friends and professors on one side, and on the other side, the elders of the Brethren Assembly church. The church was busy with doctrinal issues and issues such as which version of the

Bible was most accurate, the language we should use in prayer, whether musical instruments should be used in the worship service, and so forth. When I approached them with my concern, they were not very helpful. I, as a youngster, was battling the world alone. I began to question God, the authenticity of the Bible, and the miracles of the Lord Jesus Christ that He performed while He was in the world.

I was also interested in ham and short-wave radio. In those days, my hobby was listening to short-wave radio stations around the world and sending technical reception reports to get a QSL verification card from the short-wave station. I had a good short-wave radio, which I received as a gift from my parents after finishing high school.

On a hot summer Saturday afternoon, I was scanning my radio dial to catch a distant radio signal. While scanning the dial, I came across a short-wave religious station from the United States: Family Radio (WYFR). The announcer invited the listeners to stay tuned for the next 15 minutes to listen to the "Science, Scripture, and Salvation" program featuring Dr. Henry Morris, president of Institute for Creation Research at that time. I listened to the whole program, jotted down the address of the ICR, and sent a letter addressed to Dr. Henry Morris. To my surprise, after a few weeks I received a reply, personally signed by him, with some literature.

I began to search for books on this issue. The local Christian book distributor didn't have any on the subject, but I obtained a copy of *Science Speaks* (a very old Moody Press publication) in an old stack of books that had been left behind by a missionary when he left India. Meanwhile, I met one of our family friends from the United Kingdom who introduced me to Dr. John C. Whitcomb's *Origin* series. I listened to this series over and over. I was also in touch with Family Radio; they gave me the addresses of a few churches in the United States who graciously sent me some tapes on the evolution/creation debate and on the subject of science and the Bible. This literature satisfactorily answered my many questions, and I became involved in a creation ministry.

Later, another friend of my parents gave us a six-part series of videotapes by Professor A.E. Wilder-Smith, along with a VCR as a gift from Australia. He also gave me a subscription to *Creation Magazine*, published by Creation Science Foundation in Australia. I started lending out these magazines and the few tapes I had and also started showing these videos to my friends. Many of them who were not interested in religion did take time to watch these videos, since the gospel was shared by people who were scientists or from a scientific background.

I had a burning passion to reach my friends and people who had studied science, and after graduation I was called to serve the Lord full time. I joined a Christian publisher engaged in distribution of Christian literature for personal evangelism. Literature and other materials on creation science were scarce in India, and the few items that were available were very costly. There were times when a book on creation cost me almost a month's salary.

I married Sushmita in the year 1995, and as our wedding present, we decided to get a few more books, tapes, and videos on creation science. This was also when I met Paul Barnes from the United Kingdom, who was visiting India. I discovered that much had been done for the poor and needy people, yet very little effort was expended to reach the educated and elite of Indian society. The 250 million educated middle class are the least evangelized group in India. Paul encouraged me to think seriously along the lines of starting a creation ministry with a few other friends of like mind.

I got in touch with Dr. Andrew Snelling, Mr. Malcolm Bowden, and a few other creationists who have given their wise counsel to form the Creation Science Association of India. In 1999, we registered in India as a religious educational trust. In the same year, I visited the United Kingdom and I had the joy of meeting with several creationist groups there. Many of them very graciously donated books, tapes, and CDs for our ministry here.

I resigned in March 2001 from the Christian publishing house where I had been working since 1988 to devote myself full time to creation ministry in India. As far as I know, we are the only creationist group here in India. Our challenge is immense: to bring the issue of creation and evolution to the churches, teaching people to uphold the authority of the Bible and defend the Bible from the very first verse as well as to extend the gospel to the educated and the elite of India.

The Science Fiction of Primordial Soup

Chapter 16
Dr. Peter Line

In 1986, I was at a stage in my life where I deeply wondered about the purpose of life. I had a superficial belief in God, but deep down there was uncertainty about whether He really existed. I said the Lord's Prayer nearly every night but rarely got more religious than that. I did not know about being born again, and I certainly did not know Jesus. I knew some Bible stories, but my knowledge of Scripture was poor. However, I did know that God had said He created Adam from the dust of the ground, and Eve from Adam's rib. I also believed that God did not lie, and so it logically followed that one could separate Him from the gods of other religions and cults if His Word contained absolute truth.

This sort of reasoning was also a stumbling block for me. In Western society, the educational system and media, through magazines, books, TV, radio, etc., teach and promote (or brainwash, rather) people into believing a very different creation story than that taught in the Bible. This other creation story is called the theory of evolution and it says that life evolved by time, natural law, and chance from nonliving matter into a simple cell, then eventually fish, reptiles, mammals, apes, and humans. All this was supposed to have happened through natural selection working on random mutations.

A person's window to the world is very much influenced by the environment, culture, media, educational process, political correctness, etc., of the society in which he or she lives. I was no different from anyone else then, and at the time, I assumed that evolution was true — after all, the scientists said so, and the society I lived in reinforced that belief with its one-sided propaganda (although back then I did not realize it was propaganda). Origins was not a subject I had thought much about up to then, but that was about to change.

I was in my mid-twenties at the time and about to start a bachelor degree at a university (a bit later than most students, but that is another story). Back then it seemed logical to me that life progressed from a simple cell to a fish, reptile, mammal, ape, and humans in an evolutionary way. However, *I did not know much about evolutionary theory* beyond the classical and superficial textbook arguments; consequently, I was dependent on the views handed down by the so-called scientific "experts" in forming my superficial opinion on the subject. It had not yet occurred to me that all those supposedly objective and unbiased scientists could be wrong, or worse, that people with an agenda of their own were putting a misleading evolutionary spin on the scientific evidence, consistent with their philosophical worldview and often in direct contradiction to the real implications of the evidence.

Although my knowledge of the subject was limited at the time, I did know enough to realize that the theory of evolution was incompatible with what the Bible said about how God created matter, and life itself. In fact, it would be hard to find a more contradictory version to the Genesis account of creation than the theory of evolution. If the creation story in the Book of Genesis was wrong, how could I trust anything else in the Bible, or believe that it was God's Word? Although the Bible is not a textbook of science or history, if it is the inspired Word of God — it must be correct when it deals with these subjects. Scientific or historical evidence that clearly contradicts what the Bible says would throw great doubt on the authenticity of the author that is said to have inspired it. After all, a Being who claims to know everything, to always have existed, to be all powerful, and to be the way of truth (and not a liar) would surely remember, for example, how He created everything in the universe! He would also be able to communicate that information to those He desired to have that knowledge.

At the time, I could not conceive how the two mutually exclusive accounts of origins could be reconciled. One day, while out riding on my bicycle and thinking about this, I got to talking to God. "If You are there, God," I said, "then You have the power to solve this problem for me." Then I shoved the matter to the back of my mind. It didn't stay there for long, however.

A month or so passed and I began studying science at college. I soon developed an interest in the origin of life and found that very different views were held among evolutionist scientists on some issues, such as the origin of the first cell. Some scientists suggested the first cell had originated from comets, or had been sent here by alien beings; others insisted that it had somehow developed in a primordial soup on earth. This divergence of opinion started to make me wonder about the "obvious fact" of evolution. I also wondered why the possibility of God creating the first cell was not mentioned — was He being deliberately excluded from consideration? While evolutionary scientists affirm that the first cell ultimately happened by chance, nobody seems to know just how, aside from the almost endless and factless speculations. The prebiotic soup theory, so effectively used to indoctrinate people into believing evolution, is in reality science fiction rather than science fact.

Around this time, a series of documentaries on origins were shown at the university I was attending, and halfway through the film series I attended one of the screenings, in the belief that it was on evolution. (I learned later that some Christian lecturers at the university had arranged the screening of the "Origins" film series.) In the documentary, it was discussed whether natural selection and mutations could explain how life evolved. To my surprise, I learned that it could not explain the evolution of life, and I then listened to Dr. Wilder-Smith explaining why the supposed mechanism enabling evolution to occur was wrong. From this moment on, it was as if God had removed the blindfold from my eyes, and the problem I asked Him to solve for me months ago had been resolved. The answer was clearly that God had created just as He said in Genesis, and that the theory of evolution was a lie. I felt cheated that I had never before been told about the immense difficulties of evolution and that I had never been presented with scientific evidence for the alternative creationist explanation. This exposure of the lack of real evidence for evolution, and the realization that an alternative, and more feasible, creation viewpoint existed, is why I became a creationist. After all, there are not that many alternatives to chose from once you reject evolution!

Believing that an intelligent designer created life does not imply that someone is of a particular religious persuasion. For example, many Christians, Muslims, and Jews subscribe to a creationist belief. Presented with evidence that God's Word in the Bible could stand the test when dealing with the subjects of history and science, however, I gained a new confidence that God did exist, and that the Old and New Testaments of the Christian Bible were true and could hence be trusted when it dealt with other subjects, such as salvation. I became a Christian some months later after doing some reading and giving careful thought to, and consideration of, what such a decision involved. I knew by then that I was a sinner on my way to hell, but also that Jesus Christ had provided a way out through His death on the cross for our sins. By believing in Him, the free gift of eternal life was mine. Nothing in this life was worth passing up for such an opportunity. At the time of my decision to accept Christ into my life I was not attending any church, nor did I know any other Christians. I made the decision on my own and really did not know what would happen next. Ironically, in one of the first church services I later attended, I heard the minister, in his sermon, speak favorably about Charles Darwin as a Christian!

I conclude by saying that the reason I took seriously what the Bible says about the gospel of salvation through Jesus Christ was my confidence in God's Word being true. This confidence in God's Word came as a result of being exposed to evidence for creation and against evolution. Before this, belief in evolution had given me reason to doubt God's Word and His very existence. Becoming a Christian involved other issues, but I would never have converted if I believed the Bible was false. Although I had always had some sort of belief in God before this, it was a belief filled with uncertainty, and lacking substance, commitment, and hope. Knowing the facts about creation makes it intellectually satisfying for me to believe and trust in the Bible. In other words, I do not have to go through the mental torture of dissociating my mind from the real world, or "spiritualizing" passages of Scripture, if my religious beliefs contradict the current "evolutionary wisdom" or "evolutionary spin" on observations in the real world. Such freedom is priceless.

Doubts about Punctuated Equilibrium

Chapter 17
Dr. Roger W. Sanders

For almost 30 years, like most natural scientists, creationist materials repelled me. As a theistic evolutionist, I maintained a belief in God and the Judeo-Christian ethic, but I took the Scriptures for spiritual truth, while truth about the physical world was to be discovered by the scientific method only.

How did I get to that point?

I was raised in a Christian home and accepted Christ as a youngster. The churches my family attended were not only fundamentalist but also somewhat anti-intellectual. The prevalent attitude that I perceived there was that all scientists were atheists and believed in evolution. Being dispensational in outlook, they were strongly influenced by Schofield and the gap theory. They didn't know how to answer the geological claim of long ages and dinosaur fossils, but were determined to accept the biblical view about the creation of life. I really liked science but believed that I would have to choose between my faith and becoming a scientist.

College brought me into a new world of learning and contact with Christian professors who had dealt with the same conflicting issues of biblical revelation and evolutionary science. Because they had not been intimidated by science as were those of my family's church culture, they had found a different solution — theistic evolution. To their credit, they had resolved this conflict in their mind before the body of writings by professionally trained neo-creationists had developed. It was an enormous relief to me to know that I could be a Christian and still think logically, accepting evolutionary mechanisms as God's means of creating. Thence, readily accepting the dogma as taught in graduate schools, I earned advanced degrees from the University of

Michigan and the University of Texas in the field of plant taxonomy and evolution.

Even before completing my doctorate, doubts began to nag at me about the ability of natural selection to reorganize coordinated structures. These uncertainties grew as I continued to follow the debate between evolutionists who believed in constant, gradual evolutionary change and the fossil experts who championed rapid, striking changes followed by stasis (punctuated equilibrium). I comforted myself with the thought that someone would work out the real mechanisms sooner or later — and I had to busy myself with research and journal reading to keep up professionally.

After 12 years in a permanent research position, I felt God was working on me to let go of some of the aspects of my career that I valued highly. During this time, my wife and I began homeschooling our children. As I wanted more time to help with our children's education and to get the family into a safer environment, I resigned my job in Miami, Florida, and moved to a small town outside Forth Worth, Texas. There, I attempted to secure enough consulting contracts and adjunct teaching to provide for my family. God graciously provided, and our faith in His provision grew. Homeschooling exposed me to more and better quality creationist materials. Particularly, I was impacted by videos by Ken Ham and Gary Parker explaining how the loss of the biblical foundation destroys the Christian culture and how data can be interpreted in a creationist framework. And ever since I married, my wife had been praying for me to give up evolutionism.

Increasingly, my personal philosophy and understanding of nature conflicted, and the dualist compromise became apparent to me. In 1999, the need for an integrated life confronted me at a Worldview Weekend seminar led by Bill Jack. Keeping in mind that a number of problems with evolutionary theory had come to my attention during my career, I began studying technical publications by scientists with a young-earth creation view, as well as critically reading graduate texts on radiometric dating. I agreed to let God have all of my life, including the possibility of losing my professional position and respect of academic peers, if He could show me that evolutionary theory was wrong.

I set up a test to investigate: Could I reinterpret, in creationist terms, the fossil data I had always believed showed transitions from ancestor to descendant? Looking back, I now realize that I had set up the wrong test. Under a creationist interpretation, the supposed ancestor, transitions, and descendants were all different species within a created kind; they were just from different ecological zones. The correlation was not between rock strata and age, but between rock strata and pre-Flood biogeography.

My evolutionary thinking was finally breached when I learned about the unfounded assumptions underlying old-earth interpretations of radiometric dating. Then, I was intrigued by how geological evidence was more consistent with interpretation of a global year-long catastrophe involving massive flooding and volcanism than with uniformitarian geology, which assumed that current processes and rates of those processes were the key to the past. Suddenly, creationist geology seemed straightforward.

The real challenge to my acceptance of creationism was to grasp how all those species within kinds could appear so rapidly after the Flood. After all, the science of genetics had shown that for only three or four closely related species to diverge, one after the other would take multiple thousands, if not millions, of years. This is because adequate time is needed for sufficient mutations to arise and spread through the incipient species to make it distinguishable from its antecedent species. Yet, creation biologists talk about tens, hundreds, or even thousands of new species having descended from the Flood survivors of each kind just a few thousand years ago.

Everything fell into place when I realized that all the genetic information was designed and stored in latent form at creation for later expression, primarily in the centuries following the Flood. Rapid diversification would be simply the genetic consequences of rapid population growth, fragmentation, and isolation in and exposure to the myriad of newly formed, diverse habitats.

Ultimately, what convinced me was the *fact* that real scientific evidence was *more* consistent with creationist interpretations. This was proof to me that God was real and His Word on creation was to be taken as historical fact. Grasping this concept was very liberating for me. I finally understood that uniformitarian-evolutionary logic and interpretations were not based on provable assumptions. The logic and assumptions of creation-Flood interpretations were just as sound, though perhaps beyond absolute proof. However, the reality of creation and the Flood catastrophe have been provided to us by eyewitness accounts — something evolutionary proponents cannot claim. I no longer fear being accused of being illogical for believing in creation instead of evolution.

Furthermore, the complete inconsistency of the theistic evolution position became clear to me. Although some theistic evolutionists allow for direct divine intervention at the "big bang," origin of life, and imparting of God's image to humans, the cause-and-effect thinking is based on the same assumptions as atheistic evolution: natural laws and processes as directly observed today are the only valid explanations for unobservable origins. In other words, existence or influence of the supernatural is strictly excluded. If we deny the supernatural for science, then there is no objective basis for accepting a supernatural God who has revealed spiritual truth to us in the Bible. A very sobering thought, indeed, is that God anticipated the encroachment of uniformitarian thinking into the Church when, as the Holy Spirit, He inspired Peter (2 Pet. 3:4) to write: "They will say, 'Where is this "coming" he promised? Ever since our fathers died, everything goes on as it has since the *beginning* of creation' " (NIV, emphasis added).

I praise God that He has integrated my spiritual life with my intellectual life. I no longer have to compartmentalize my behavior, pretending to be one person to church friends and another person to professional colleagues. Throughout this worldview pilgrimage, God has continued to provide for my family and me; I still have a job in a respected botanical organization, and the colleagues who know of my creation position have been respectful and curious, rather than belligerent. Furthermore, the creation biologists with whom I have become acquainted during the last few years have encouraged me greatly, both spiritually and professionally. I now have a confidence in the Word, and I pray that this confidence will make me a bolder witness for the gospel.

Jesus replied, "Love the Lord your God with all your heart
and with all your soul and with all your mind." This is the first
and greatest commandment (Matt. 22:37; NIV).

More Complicated than Rocket Science

Chapter 18
Dawid Janse van Rensberg

I am an electronics engineer involved in the design and development of rocket guidance and control systems. I used to think that God used evolution to create — that He made "primitive man" in the same way in which man makes an experimental design model (XDM), advanced design model (ADM), or an engineering design model (EDM), until I read a book by Solly Ozrovech titled *Think of Your Creator*.

Revisiting the Genesis account of creation made me realize the foolishness of my own thinking. Just as it is impossible for an electronic apparatus to understand the process through which engineers "created" it, it is impossible for God's creation to understand fully the process through which He created. I cannot, from my vantage point, fully understand my Creator, because He is far above me. The reality we are experiencing is contained within His reality, which is far greater than we can imagine. I realized that I once wanted to reduce God to my level — wanting to put Him in a box that I could handle and manipulate to my own advantage. From Genesis 3, I understood that this desire to obtain knowledge with which to manipulate God is nothing less than the original sin of which Adam and Eve were guilty.

> "For God knows that in the day you eat of it your eyes will be opened, and you will be like God, knowing good and evil." So when the woman saw that the tree was good for food, that it was pleasant to the eyes, and a tree desirable to make one wise, she took of its fruit and ate. She also gave to her husband with her, and he ate (Gen. 3:5–6; NKJV).

After repenting of this sin, I started reading the Bible with new understanding. I came to the conclusion that the whole of creation did not come about through death and struggle (XDM, ADM, EDM), but that everything came to pass through the word He spoke, and that it was *very* good (Gen. 1:31).

Videotapes by Gary Parker and Ken Ham from Answers in Genesis (AiG) strengthened my belief that everything that exists came about through creative design and organization. Engineers and technicians use similar methods to design and produce complex systems that do not nearly match the complexity of God's creation, which He *spoke* into existence. When looking at the diversity and complexity of creation, and seeing that it all fits so well together, it is clear to me that God carefully designed and planned everything. I realized that, as the products we develop do not have any choice about what is installed in them, we, as God's creatures, do not have any say as to the mechanisms that He has put in place to control us. This fact has some important implications.

Just as the mission of a rocket is to fly to a designated point, the mission of man is to glorify his Creator and to enjoy glorifying Him forever. If the rocket fails in its mission, those who are controlling it destroy it. In control systems, the controller who is capable of optimally controlling an aircraft, for instance, is the one who is capable of sensing what is happening to the aircraft and has a priori knowledge on how the aircraft will react to control commands. (We call it *actuating forces.*)

Not only did Jesus Christ create us, but He also became a man who experienced life and death on our behalf. After being resurrected from the grave and ascending to heaven to the right hand of the Father, He sent the Holy Spirit through whom He senses and controls everything that happens in (and around) the people He redeemed. He can even control the thoughts of people who do not believe in Him (e.g., Pharaoh in Exodus) — all for the sake of His glory!

Through the evidence of creation it is very clear that God the Father, Son, and Holy Spirit is in full control of the universe — Jesus will one day return to judge all people in terms of what they have done during their lifetimes. Those who are not in Christ and who did not glorify their Creator will be condemned — forever separated from His care. All people who acknowledge their Creator and lived lives to glorify Him on earth will enter His rest to be with Him forever.

"Just Believe" Wasn't Enough

Chapter 19
Eric Armbrustmacher

When I was young, my parents took me to church from time to time. Then my mother went to church one day with a friend and met Jesus. She attended a Bible study with that friend to find out even more about Him. I would sit with them and wish that they would "get over this phase." Nonetheless, I started in a Sunday school program, and made some new friends that I enjoyed spending time with.

About a year and a half later, I had a chance to go to Camp Barakel, a Christian camp in northern Lower Michigan. The counselor for my group spoke of several things that God had done with his life and some of the other camp staff spoke of things that God had done at the camp. At that time the counselor took me aside and prayed with me, but nothing of any significance happened.

The following fall came around, school started, and I was back at church with my mother. The public school that I was attending had a good science teacher who sparked an interest within me to learn as much science as I could. Because it was a public school, however, the science program had an atheistic evolutionary emphasis.

I knew enough about the Bible (and heard enough from school) to know that evolution and the Bible did not (and could not) both be correct. The two couldn't be mixed with any sort of credibility. I started asking my mother and her friend, as well as the Sunday school teacher and even the public school teacher, about the Bible and evolution. My mom just said, "We don't believe evolution" and left it at that. The Sunday school teacher said that the two could be merged together, but that answer made no sense to me. I thought God either made everything the way He said and the Bible was right, or everything evolved and the entire Bible was wrong. My science teacher said that, as far as he was concerned, only one was correct. He believed evolution and showed what he believed to be the supporting evidence for evolution. Having no answers, my faith was shaken. As school continued, I could find no answers from Sunday school or other sources. So, though I continued to go to church, I started walking away from the Bible — and God.

Then, when I started attending high school, I met Doug Sharp at church. He had gone to Michigan State University and earned a degree in physical science. He told me how he believed the Bible when God said that everything was created, and he gave examples of evidence that pointed to a Creator. I started asking more questions at both Sunday school and the public school. I even questioned myself: How could the biological make-up of things have realistically gotten started? How could something as complex as the human body have evolved, especially the human brain, which scientists believe to be the most complex thing in the universe? How could these things have arisen by random acts of chance? I also asked if it was possible for this process to happen now, or with something less complex than a human or human brain, such as with a car, or computer. The answers that I found all proved that the evolutionary process that had created the human being was no longer operating in that direction, at least not detectably. I learned that mutations do more harm than good and that it is stupid to say that something as complex as cars or computers didn't have a creator. Who put the information in them?

I took Doug Sharp's class at the Mount Hope Bible Training Institute to find out more. I was not doing too well in school at the time, and I found the material to be over my head. I am afraid that I flunked. But I was so motivated by what I heard that I took it again, and the second time I aced the class. In fact, the grades in all of my classes went up after that, too.

I learned in Genesis that, because sin entered the world, things took a turn for the worse. In addition, the Book of Romans speaks of sin (disobedience to God) entering the world by the first man. Sin was passed on to all of mankind and as a result, death came into the world. Romans also said that one man, Jesus, has paid the price for our sins. The Book of John also speaks of God sending His Son to give everlasting life to those who believe in Him. I believe that it is important to use my talents in whatever way God wants me to, and I have assisted the *Revolution Against Evolution* as a studio technician for their television program. Having the answers to my questions concerning creation and evolution has provided a foundation for my faith in Jesus Christ and has added stability in my life and boldness in sharing my faith with others.

A few years ago, I had the opportunity to accompany Ken Ham, Buddy Davis, and Carl Wieland on their Australian tour. This tour helped to sharpen my beliefs in creation, as did the *Revolution Against Evolution* adventure tour to the Grand Canyon.

Is Man a Perfect Animal, or Is He the Image of God Spoiled?

Chapter 20
Dr. Paul Back

I was born in South Africa into a happy, churchgoing family and educated in a school that required chapel every day and twice on Sundays. In spite of this exposure to formal Christianity, I had no idea what it meant to be a Christian — I simply assumed that I was one.

In my early teens, I began to develop an interest in science and often read books on science. I came across an article on evolution and the writer excitedly explained that, with the finding of the Piltdown skull, all arguments against our evolutionary links to apes had been settled. This article left me with two clear thoughts. First, evolution is true and second, that only an unscientific fool could possibly think otherwise. Once I reached university, I no longer went to church and decided that Christianity was irrelevant to life. I graduated from Cape Town University with an honors degree in engineering and won a Rhodes scholarship to Oxford University to continue my studies there. I eventually obtained a doctorate of philosophy (DPhil) in engineering science from Oxford.

At Oxford, I became even more convinced that Christianity was intellectually untenable and that science had shown it to be devoid of any credibility. I enjoyed mocking my Christian friends and showing them how science (and especially evolution) had undermined the foundations of their faith. For some years after leaving Oxford, I continued to hold such views. I was doing well in my professional career as a consulting engineer and felt no need for the "prop" of religion. But then, through a series of happenstances (another story), I found myself at a Sunday school birthday party for ten year olds. I had driven the speaker, a friend of mine, to the party, and although I had intended to drop him off and return to pick him up afterward, on arrival, I was embraced by the pastor and very unwillingly led into the meeting. I was converted at that meeting and my intellectual world (of which I was so proud) was turned upside-down. Here I was — a doctor of philosophy from Oxford University being brought to my knees by a simple talk about Jesus to ten year olds.

I immediately developed a thirst for the Bible and became involved in Christian youth work in a deprived area of London (where I was to meet my future wife, who also was involved in the work). All this time I continued to believe that evolution was the scientific truth about our origins, but the more I read the Bible, the more uncomfortable I became about the discrepancy between what the Bible taught and what science appeared to demonstrate. I found I was putting my mind into two compartments. I believed that the Bible was the Word of God when dealing with sin, salvation, and the birth, death, and resurrection of Jesus, but not when it impinged on such matters as origins. I preferred just not to think about the biblical account of creation in Genesis.

One day I was asked to join a so-called "expert" panel at a Christian youth club to answer questions from the floor. One question that caused me much embarrassment was, "If the Bible is the inerrant Word of God, how do we reconcile Genesis with the theory of evolution?" I squirmed. I had no answer.

I made some lame comment about truth being indivisible, but I was being incomprehensible. From that moment, I knew I had to get to grips with the conflict between the creation stories in Genesis in contrast to evolution, as described by Darwin.

I began to explore the available literature on the subject of creation and evolution. (This was well before the advent of the Internet and the powerful search engines available today.) I came across a small booklet reproducing the substance of a lecture given by the Reverend Richard Acworth at Westminster Chapel, London, in 1969 on the subject of creation, evolution, and the Christian faith. One line in his lecture particularly struck me. It was the simple question, "Is man a perfected animal, or is he the image of God spoiled?" Put like that, it was abundantly evident that there is a world of difference between the two concepts and no amount of smooth talk or gloss about the Genesis account enshrining spiritual truths (but not physical reality) could disguise the gulf that separates the two accounts about the origins of life. To believe, as some do after the school of Teilhard de Chardin, that God used the processes of evolution to bring about first primitive life (and ultimately human-kind as the pinnacle of the evolutionary process) is to stand Christianity on its head. The Bible declares unequivocally that the world was created good, but has fallen since into disorder, corruption, and death by human sin. According to Teilhard de Chardin, sin was a necessary instrument of evolutionism used by God to drive the process onward and upward via death and survival of the fittest and ultimately, reaching its fulfill-ment in humans. What then, one may ask, was the purpose of Jesus and the cross?

About this time I came across a book by Whitcomb and Morris titled *The Genesis Flood*[1] that, in my mind, began to unravel the seem-ingly impregnable fortress of evolutionary dogma. Evolutionism was not the only explanation. The book inspired me to dig deeply into the whole edifice of evolutionism, and the more I dug, the more it seemed that it was built on sand — on wishful thinking, on gross extrapolations of observations that could better be interpreted from a creation world-view. The other significant thing I noticed was the *anger and animosity of evolutionists that was directed against those who dared to challenge their viewpoint*. My studies led me to the ever greater conviction that evo-lutionism was a deeply flawed theory sustained not by science, but by those who were determined to find any explanation — no matter how absurd — that banished God from the scene.

Once I had come to realize the bankruptcy of evolutionism as a scientific account of origins, I began to explore the subject of time. A straight reading of Genesis appeared to indicate that creation was a rela-tively recent event and had been accomplished in six literal days. I strug-gled with the usual arguments about the meaning of *yom* — whether it referred to the usual meaning of a day, or whether it could be periods of time, possibly millions of years. By this time, I had come to the view that, unless there were compelling and good reasons otherwise (such as when the words were meant to be understood figuratively — such as "the four corners of the earth") then the words should be taken literally. Nothing in the Genesis account implied that the creation days were meant to be

---

1. John C. Whitcomb and Henry M. Morris, *The Genesis Flood* (Philadelphia, PA: Presbyterian and Reformed Publ. Co., 1966).

understood as other than literal days. In addition, after reading about the scientific basis of dating, it was evident that there were numerous assumptions and extrapolations that cast considerable doubt on the credibility of the technology and the resulting millions, if not billions, of years assigned by scientists to past events. The blanket assumption of "uniformitarianism" was the major peg on which evolutionists appeared to hang everything — and if that assumption is flawed, as indeed it appears to be, then many of their conclusions could also be flawed.

Ultimately, belief in the young-earth creation position is a matter of faith — faith that the Word of God is true and to be trusted above any ideas of fallen fallible man ("Let God be true, and every man a liar" [Rom. 3:4; NIV]). Having reached that position, it was my experience that more and more factors emerged that gave support to a young creation. We all know that there are still huge areas of ignorance in cosmology (only a fool would claim otherwise), but the more that is being discovered, the more doubt is being thrown on the earlier confident claims of scientists concerning the so-called big bang and the emergence of an unbounded universe claimed to be 15 to 20 billion years old. The work of Russell Humphreys on "white-hole" cosmology and a bounded universe (*Starlight & Time*[2]) and of Barry Setterfield on the decay of the speed of light have both demonstrated that there are possible explanations of a young universe not yet dreamt of in the philosophies of most scientists.

The journey from initial unbelief in the God of creation to my present position has been a journey of increasing wonder and amazement as I have seen the evidence of science and the Word of God come together in a breathtaking harmony to which, perhaps, the only possible response can be that of doubting Thomas when he encountered the risen Christ — "My Lord and my God!" (John 20:28; NIV).

---

2. D. Russell Humphreys, *Starlight & Time* (Green Forest, AR: Master Books, 1994).

Evolution Was Unwelcome Baggage

Chapter 21
Rick Lanser

I have had a profound hearing loss since age seven, the result of an attack of spinal meningitis. However, by the grace of God, I was able to develop decent lip-reading ability and thus was able to continue with a normal high school education, rather than attending a school for the deaf.

Intensely interested in science and technology as a child, I did well academically in both of those areas, taking honors courses in biology and physics during high school. Wishing to build on that success and at the same time to avoid a career with too much public contact — lipreading is hard work, and not infallible — I opted to study medical technology with a microbiology minor at Penn State (they didn't know they were getting a deaf student when they accepted me!). I figured a career in lab work would provide a safe haven from that enemy of mine — the telephone.

My sophomore year at PSU saw me drawn by God into His kingdom, the end result of years of exposure to the gospel and a praying grandmother. Reading the Book of Daniel, and recognizing Christ for the first time in the Old Testament, sealed the matter. Thereafter, knowing that the Bible was God's book, I filtered what I learned in my various classes through that sieve of truth. His Word told me, quite simply, that He had created all of the animals and man fully formed from the outset, which was enough to make me an unsophisticated creationist. Isn't that what *any* true Christian should be as an infant believer?

To backtrack a little . . . as was the case with most of my generation, we were given a generous helping of evolution in high school. I still remember studying imaginary creatures called "caminalcules" in Biology

2. They were basically drawings of little beasties with fine nuances of difference between them, and we students were expected to sort them according to an evolutionary tree, thereby "proving" the reasonableness of evolution. It was fun, but not a very real-world exercise. We also did the Drosophila thing, raising mutants, which purported to demonstrate that evolution happened. I cannot remember reflecting on these and similar projects at the time and questioning whether they truly proved evolution happened; not having learned anything else about origins, except the Bible's stories I learned as a kid and which carried no weight with a sophisticated teenager, I accepted the concept as delivered.

That unquestioning acceptance all changed following my conversion. I began to harbor suspicions that the whole evolutionary edifice could not be true, notwithstanding the repeated heavy emphasis on it delivered by my genetics professor, whom I self-righteously considered to be deluded. I was probably right, but I could not give good reason, outside of the Bible, for thinking so. Not knowing any clear scientific reasons against it, I felt like I had to carry the evolution idea along with me as unwelcome baggage, relegated to a mental niche to await the missing information that would help me sweep it out, and thus finally reconcile my faith in God as Creator with my scientific bent.

At the right moment, I finally found that long-sought information. It started with my purchase of *The Genesis Flood*[1] by John Whitcomb and Henry Morris; absorbing that book was an experience that truly opened my eyes to the reasonableness of my faith. This was followed by some of Morris's other books on scientific creationism, which began giving me the mental equipment to sweep some mental baggage out of the attic and into the trash.

A year or so after reading *The Genesis Flood*, the Lord called me out of my hospital microbiology lab job to attend seminary. This was the time when I was first exposed to the old-earth creationist (OEC) viewpoint, but it was not overly emphasized — it was just part of the background of an overall solid, conservative course of study that I am deeply grateful God gave me. Having been first exposed as a Christian to a young-earth creationist (YEC) perspective through Morris's books, I was never thereafter able to find the OEC arguments very persuasive.

---

1. John C. Whitcomb and Henry M. Morris, *The Genesis Flood* (Philadelphia, PA: Presbyterian and Reformed Publ. Co., 1966).

They were so much more complicated and did not reflect the plain sense of the Scriptures, which was emphasized in all other parts of my studies, that this perspective never "took" with me.

To summarize, I began as an unquestioning, ignorant accepter of evolution in its popularized form, then became a simple Christian who felt it was traitorous to hold to evolution, yet I then had no clear reasons to discard it. This dichotomy eventually was resolved, giving way to a comfortably informed faith that finds biblical revelation and science fully compatible with one another. By starting from the position that God says what He means and means what He says in the Scriptures, I never needed to jump through the theological hoops, which are the apparent burden of those holding to an old-earth perspective.

Discovering the Truth about Evolution

Chapter 22
Dr. Sean Pitman

G rowing up in a strong Christian home as the son of a pastor, I knew about God and the Genesis story from my earliest years. As I grew older, I became more and more interested in nature and science, always assuming, "God just made it that way." Of course, I saw some serious problems in nature, such as pain, suffering, and death. These problems just did not fit my idea of God. How could a good God intentionally make such a place? This question was explained to me as being the result of a moral fall. The evilness of pain and death was not originally part of God's plan for humanity or the universe, but it came into existence because of the rebellion of humans against God's plan. As part of this confrontation between good and evil, God took on the nature of mankind in the person of Jesus. Jesus then suffered the consequences of rebellion for each one of us.

This is the standard Christian position used to explain the nature of the world around us and the existence of evil in this world. It all seemed to make sense to me. The story of the great controversy between God and Satan or evil really did strike a chord. However, during my first year of grade school, I was presented with the idea of evolution. I was told that man evolved from monkeys and monkeys from smaller animals that evolved from fish and that these fish evolved from tiny little creatures in the ocean that evolved from the ocean sludge, millions and even billions of years ago. I asked my parents about this evolution. They, of course, said that it was not true; man was created in God's image, "in the beginning." They said that we did not evolve from monkeys and that those who said so didn't know any different.

For several years, such answers from my parents satisfied me. However, I soon noticed that not just a few, but many people believed in evolution. It was all over the news, in my textbooks, and in popular magazines. All the smart people I knew seemed to believe in evolution, even within the church and the church schools that I attended. There were, of course, teachers and professors who did not believe in evolution, but they didn't know exactly why Darwinism was wrong. Aside from the fact that it disagreed with what the Bible had to say, my parents also could not explain to me why it was wrong. Often they would tell me, "Microevolution happens, but macroevolution doesn't." When asked to explain exactly what the differences between these two types of evolution were, they would say something like, "Microevolution is a change within a species, but macroevolution would require a change between different species, such as a lizard turning into a bird." I would press the issue and ask why all the small changes couldn't add up to turn a lizard into a bird. At this point, the creationists I knew would turn a little red and say something to the effect of, "We just don't know." The creationist books that I was referred to were not much better at answering this question.

This question plagued me through academy and college, and even through medical school. No one could explain to me why evolution was wrong, and yet these same people held that Christianity and the Bible were true. As I saw it, there was a major problem here. I clearly saw that if evolution turned out to be true, then Christianity was a lie. There are many Christians who also believe in evolution, but for me this was an irreconcilable dichotomy of belief. It seemed that the Christian *must* believe in the moral fall of man, which requires supernatural help in the form of a divine Savior, and without this help, the destiny of humanity is destruction and death. Yet, if evolution were true and man evolved from an amoral animal through a process of natural selection (survival of the fittest), then morality was not a gift from God, but a process of natural law. If true, humanity does not need a supernatural Savior since "in the beginning" morality came through natural law. Also, death is not a result of rebellion from moral law but was always here as a natural process of evolution. The cruelty of evolution is obvious in that it is dependent upon selfishness, suffering, and death. In fact, without death, evolution is impossible. Evolution is all about the "survival of the fittest." And yet,

Christianity claims, "We who are strong ought to bear with the failings of the weak" (Rom. 15:1; NIV). The Christian also believes that in the new heavens and earth, "The wolf will live with the lamb" (Isa. 11:6; NIV).

If anything seemed clear to me, it was that either evolution or Christianity was wrong. Both could not exist together, as they were diametrically opposed to the ideas that each held to be true. However, it was not until after medical school that I made up my mind to determine exactly which one was true and why. Since no one seemed able to explain the details to me, I was determined to figure out for myself if evolution really could work or not, regardless of what my discoveries might say about, "The faith of my fathers."

What I learned stunned me. I found only examples of what I would call microevolution or variation within the Genesis kinds! Almost every example of evolution that I read about in the textbooks was not really an example of true Darwinian evolution. By this time, I had learned a fair amount of information about DNA and genetics. The changes that Darwin noted in finch beaks and the like were not really the formation of anything new but were simply a variation in the expression of genes or traits from a common gene pool of options. Gregor Mendel first described such nonmutation dependent changes in allelic variations during Darwin's time, but Darwin was never made aware of such possibilities. Other examples of evolution in action such as bacterial antibiotic resistance, cave fish without eyes, flightless birds on windy islands, and the like are the result of mutational changes to individual genes. Often these phenotypic or expressed changes are the result of the up-regulation, down-regulation, or complete inactivation of existing genes. In such cases, no new function is gained. An old function of a gene is simply changed as far as its degree of function, but the actual function itself remains the same (or is even deleted altogether). So where is the evolution of anything new as far as a unique genetic function is concerned?

As these thoughts floated around in my mind, I soon came upon an idea that, for me, sealed the lid on evolution's coffin. Often genetics is compared to language systems, such as the English language. I clearly saw the relevance of such a concept. The information contained in DNA is a coded language. It has all the same structure and function as any other language system. The information is written with the use of symbols, just like the letters of the alphabet in the English language. Such symbols mean nothing in the language system except as they are given meaning by a code or dictionary. As with the English language, there are many more possible symbolic arrangements in a given genome than there are definitions for these various arrangements within a given life form. For example, there are vastly more possible words or combinations of letters of a given length in the English language than there are definitions in the English dictionary.

The same is true of genetic sequences in a given life form. This means that, within a given life form, the functional genes are separated from each other by vast numbers of nondefined or potential genes. Without definition, they have no function in the cell. If they have no function in the cell, they cannot be selected for (or against) by nature. Without the ability to select, nature is blind and cannot guide any further genetic changes until, by sheer random chance, something evolves that does, in fact, have a function. A few simple calculations will dramatically demonstrate that the crossing of such statistically large functionally neutral gaps between recognized genes is impossible. In fact, the crossing of a functionally neutral gap that is wider than one or two point mutations has never been documented.

Some people quote professor B.G. Hall's experiment with *E. coli* and the evolution of the lacZ genes that he deleted from these bacteria, but this study is not convincing. Hall did delete the gene that produced galactosidase (an enzyme that breaks down lactose), but there was a second gene (ebgA) that required only a single point mutation to give it full lactase activity. Such a single point mutation can easily be achieved through the process of random chance alone, without the guidance of natural selection. This involves the crossing of a gap in function that is only one mutation wide. It is not a neutral gap at all, since the very first mutation achieved new function.

But what if neutral gaps in function exist that are wider than one mutation? Hall determined that a neutral gap in function just two mutations wide would take around 100,000 years to cross in nature. He achieved such a double mutation in just a few days in the lab, but he never documented the crossing of anything wider than this double mutation. Hall went further in his experiment by deleting the second gene that gave rise to lactase activity with just one point mutation. He then attempted to "evolve" lactase ability in *E. coli* without either lacZ or ebgA genes present. It never happened, and to my knowledge, it still has not happened since the very first of such experiments was done in 1973. Hall finally concluded that these colonies had "limited evolutionary potential."

Through my study of genetics, I have come to believe that all living things have very "limited evolutionary potential." In my research, I have not found anyone who has successfully theorized how such a process of genetic evolution might cross gaps of neutral function in a genetic language code. Natural selection is helpless here since it is dependent upon changes in actual phenotypic function each and every step of the way. These apparently small gaps are, for me, the signature of deliberate design. In all other such language systems, the ideas came before the symbolic representation of those ideas. I see that the same holds true for the genetic language system beyond very low levels of functional complexity.

I am convinced that the discovery of the arbitrary nature of genetic symbols and language systems reveals the signature of God himself. To fail to see the deliberate purpose and design in nature, though fallen from perfection, is inexcusable in this modern age. The handwriting of the Designer is written all over it. This should give all those who recognize it a strong hope for a better future. For those who do not recognize the designed character of nature, all that is left is the evil reality of evolution and the fact that pain, suffering, and death are here to stay.

I hope my experience brings comfort to those who are in need of good news. No one should be afraid of science. Science is a powerful force in our common search for truth. If God is truth, then a scientific investigation of His nature will lead us to Him. That certainly has been the case for me.

A Geologist's Story — My Journey from Evolutionist to Creationist

Chapter 23
Roger G. Sigler II

I was raised in the Roman Catholic Church and never had trouble believing in God — that He existed and created all things. While young, I became very interested in rocks, fossils, and dinosaurs. I remember my first *Tyrannosaurus Rex* (*T. rex*) kit. I put the model skeleton together and was in awe of this fascinating creature. My dinosaur booklet explained that *T. rex* was about 20 feet tall and up to 50 feet long — amazing! This was the first time I learned about the Triassic, Jurassic, and Cretaceous periods of the Mesozoic and learned that these animals became extinct 65 to 70 million years ago. This bothered me because I could not understand why God would make certain creatures that went extinct and the Church never discussed these issues. The only time creation was mentioned in church was during recitals of the Apostle's Creed.

Growing up in Pennsylvania gave me plenty of opportunity to observe nature — the woods was my second home. I remember examining leaves that fell from the trees. The support structure that held the leaf together had obvious design. In creeks, I found salamanders, crayfish, and snakes. There was also a wonderful waterfall and other rock formations nearby. As I wondered about the rocks as a child, I made a discovery along one of the talus (loose rock debris) slopes. The rocks were being eroded from layers in the cliff just above the talus. There I discovered beautiful and perfect impressions of what appeared to be ferns. I tried burying leaves in mud to see if I could make my own fossils and quickly found that this idea was not going to work.

I don't recall the subject of evolution ever being discussed during high school (1975–78). However, some of my school friends and I considered "Negroes" to be lesser humans and we referred to them as "human apes." Evidently (and much to my shame now), I must have learned this "evolutionary concept" somewhere. I do remember someone explaining to me that blacks had long arms because they used to swing in the trees.

At college (1978–82), the theory of evolution was the underlying philosophy for many of my courses (my major was geology). Mention of the theory occurred regularly in physical geology, historical geology, anthropology, and sociology. In anthropology, I was shown the typical monkey-to-man icon depicting the supposed transitional forms. It was taught as fact that no one questioned. In one sociology class, the professor made derogatory remarks about women — that they had smaller brains and therefore were not as intelligent as men. Remarkably, no one, not even the women in the class, questioned these claims. Later, I learned that this colossal ignorance stemmed from the earlier 19th-century evolutionary beliefs. As I understand it now, brain size in humans has little or nothing to do with intelligence.

I will never forget my first day in geology class. The professor mentioned the Bible, which immediately got my attention. He then proceeded to explain that Bishop Ussher (I had never heard of him before) had studied the Bible and determined that the earth was created in 4004 B.C. He went on to say that we now know that the earth is much older than 6,000 years; that it is really approximately 4 to 5 billion years old. Everyone agreed, including me — all in the class already knew that the earth was billions of years old. We were already prepped by our dinosaur stories from childhood.

The very first question on my first test in my first geology class went something like this: Which of the following numbers is closest to the age of the earth: (A) 6,000 years; (B) 60,000 years; (C) 600,000 years; (D) 6,000,000 years; or (E) 6,000,000,000 years? I circled E and earned full credit. I do not remember *anyone* getting the answer wrong; that is the answer the professor wanted.

This particular professor was my advisor and taught many of my geology courses. He did not seem overbearing or too prideful and emphasized on more than one occasion that evolution is just a theory. I never learned what his religious views were. One time he showed us a picture of two fossil fish (complete with scale imprints from head to fin).

One big fish was in the process of swallowing a smaller fish when they apparently became fossilized. We were all astonished by this and the professor thought it remarkable that this event became a fossil — but he did not elaborate.

At this time, I had never read the Bible but had heard that God made the earth in six days. Later, as I pondered the professor's comments, a lightbulb went on in my head. I came up with the idea that the six-day creation I heard about must represent six geologic periods of time.

During (and after) college, I was convinced that humans evolved from cavemen and that Negroes were a lower form of human. Sometimes I observed the hair on my arms and wondered if body hair was a leftover feature after we evolved from animals. Did facial hair mean that we evolved from apes? I did not know where God fit in, but I still continued to attend the Catholic church. In 1982, I graduated (with honors) with a bachelor of science (BS) degree in geology. After graduation, I moved straight to Houston, Texas, because this is where many geologists are hired. At this time, I was a theistic evolutionist, although I never heard this term until later in life. (I never became an atheist because this worldview never seemed logical to me.)

From the time I was 15 years old until I was 26 years of age, nearly all I cared about was girls and parties. Sometime after I turned 24 years old, I stopped attending church altogether, because I felt that I was being a hypocrite. But this all began to change in the fall of 1986.

I was sitting with my remote control in hand and came across a popular televangelist at the time. He was preaching against abortion, and he did so with great passion. This really caught my attention because I had never heard anyone preach against abortion — he actually spoke up and claimed that it was a horrible sin and spoke of God's coming judgment. Even though I had attended church twice every weekend while at college (the Catholic church and my girlfriend's Methodist church), I didn't remember anything of relevance or substance being preached. Something caused me to send the preacher a donation. I had always known abortion was murder but had never heard it preached against.

Another interesting event occurred around this time. I was on a date (with my future wife) and had some car trouble. A man on a bicycle stopped to help us. After we pushed the vehicle out of the way, I asked him if there was anything I could do for him. He said no, not for him personally; however, he asked us to send a donation to KSBJ, a popular local Christian radio station. I agreed and followed through with the donation. I never saw him again but now know that he must have prayed for us.

I began to receive a plethora of information from the evangelist. At the beginning of 1987, I began traveling for my job and was gone for three to six weeks at a time. To pass the time alone, I took to reading. One book I read, *The Seduction of Christianity* by Dave Hunt,[1] proved to be seminal in my life. In this book, Mr. Hunt contrasts what modern preachers claim with what the Bible says. I began checking the Gideon's Bible (in the hotel rooms) to see for myself if what I was reading was true. I became convinced that someone was wrong — and I did not believe it was the Bible.

So, in May–June 1987, it all came together for me. In a hotel room in Indiana, I began to ask God through prayer if the Bible was true. While reading in the Book of Revelation, I dropped to my knees beside the bed and asked Jesus to come into my life and make me the kind of person that He wanted me to be.

Being born again was a powerful experience for me. I repented and told God I was sorry for my sins. For the first time in my life, I realized that I was a sinner and that I had hurt God and other people. By this stage of my life (I was nearly 27 years old) my sins had piled up to heaven. I was on my knees for days confessing past sins. I quickly learned that the Bible spoke about all of life's issues — everything. I would ask God a question one night and soon receive the answer through the Holy Scriptures.

During these days I realized churches, the media, and college had lied to me. I was quite upset about this — why hadn't anyone told me the truth about hell, why I needed a Savior, and the truth about creation? Through my prayers after being born again, I knew immediately that the theory of evolution was a lie. I realized that body hair was part of God's artwork and that God had created men to have beards.

My whole life turned around. I began to see all things in a totally new way — I was a new creature. I was very excited and began sharing Bible verses with my girlfriend over the telephone. About one month

---

1. Dave Hunt, *The Seduction of Christianity* (Eugene, OR: Harvest House, 1985).

later, she gave her life to Christ. A month after that, we were engaged. We were married the following month.

I was still traveling and receiving more studies from the evangelist. He had a study called *God's Plan for the Ages*. In it he espoused the gap theory. I thought it was the greatest thing I'd ever heard; it seemed to solve all the problems about evolution, particularly the fossil record. Although I now knew evolution was wrong, I still maintained that the earth was quite old.

In 1988, we joined a local nondenominational Bible church and later in the year I began to serve as a junior high leader. I taught various subjects, but the issue of evolution kept coming up. Although I fell into the gap theory, I also knew that some in the church believed that the earth was young. I tried to avoid the subject at first because I knew it was going to take substantial study to tackle this issue from all angles. At this time I started receiving catalogs from the Institute for Creation Research (ICR). Some of Henry Morris's relatives went to this church and someone had put me on the ICR mailing list.

The book that caught my eye first was *The Lie: Evolution*[2] by Ken Ham. Back then, this book had an intriguing cover: an evil serpent's head with the word evolution written on the forbidden fruit underneath. After staring at the book cover in the ICR brochures for about two months, I eventually bought it. Even though I was 28, I still judged a book by its cover — males need more radical ways (like hard-hitting book covers) to be reached. (Unfortunately, the cover has now been changed.)

This book opened my eyes to what's really going on. Then I read *The World That Perished*[3] by John Whitcomb. After reading these books, I went back to Scripture to review the passages that were used to support the gap theory. I immediately discovered that verses were being pulled out of context: verses used to support the hypothetical Lucifer's flood actually were speaking about Noah's flood.

The fossil record now made *more* sense. It was catastrophic deposition that was a primary requirement for most fossils. How could the event itself (and scale imprints) of the "big fish swallowing the small fish"

---

2. Ken Ham, *The Lie: Evolution* (Green Forest, AR: Master Books, 1987).

3. John Whitcomb, *The World That Perished* (Grand Rapids, MI: Baker Book House, 1988).

become a fossil? To preserve fossil fish requires extraordinary geologic processes. In normal, everyday geologic processes, fish do not become fossils. They just die, float around, slowly sink, decay, and are torn apart by scavengers. Everything was now beginning to make more sense. Over about two years I shook off the gap theory and became a young-earth creationist. But it was a struggle for me.

During one of those years, Henry Morris spoke at a nearby church. When I heard that he believed the earth was no more than 10,000 years old, I began to mock him. I said to my pastor, "How can anyone believe the earth is so young?" The pastor replied that it was "possible" — and this was all he said.

But God was working on me. During my early years as a Christian, I had put limits on God's power. Eventually, I came to believe the earth is young and that scientists are the ones who are limited in knowledge and power, not God.

Then I began teaching the youth and adults of the church all the things I was learning. They were astounded to learn that the Bible mentions extremely large beasts and that some type of dinosaur best fits this description. During this time (1989–91), I started attending the yearly Bay Area Creation Conferences south of Houston, Texas. Some of this group worked at NASA. This was the first time I personally saw and heard well-known creationists in person. I heard Drs. Duane Gish and Steve Austin of the Institute for Creation Research (ICR) and Don Chittick. During one of these events, I picked up an ICR Graduate School catalog.

After much thought and prayer, and with my wife's encouragement, I applied and was accepted in ICR's geology program. The Lord opened these doors wide for me. I was working a full-time job in the groundwater-control business in Houston and explained to my boss (who is also the owner of the company) what I wanted to do. He asked if I had looked into the local universities, so I would not have to be as far away as San Diego, California. I explained to him that I had deep religious convictions about attending ICR. He said okay and gave me the time off — with pay! Since ICR teaches their courses in the summer, I was gone six to seven weeks each summer for the next three years. I began my course work in 1993 and graduated in 1998 with a master of science (MS) degree in geology.

While at the groundwater company, my boss never gave me problems due to my beliefs. I was in a pretty high-level position (I reported directly to the owner). However, I would tell my peers little by little about creation and the Flood. I did receive some resistance, but I was persistent in showing them the evidence, such as the archaeological evidence for the co-existence of humans and dinosaurs. I showed them the cave carvings of dinosaurs from secular books. When one fellow geologist saw this, he said, "You're going to make creationists out of all of us."

In the fall of 1999, I started in a new position with a start-up geothermal energy provider. I was the sixth person hired. At this new company, I hung the same posters I had hung on the wall of the previous firm. Everything was fine until the company began to grow and secular corporate types were hired. Shortly after the new CEO arrived, I was called into his office. He told me that someone had objected to my creationist posters: the spiritual battle was on. He asked me why I had them, so I explained the born-again concept to him and how I no longer believed in evolution. He then proceed to tell me that evolution was the traditional view — then he caught himself and realized that it was not always the traditional view. He felt that office surroundings should be secular.

Everyone in the office knows what I believe. The posters have always been good conversation starters with people. I show them the maps and explain things in the light of creation and the Flood. Thankfully, there is another strong believer at work who is a great encouragement to me (but I still meet with constant resistance).

Other than my witnessing at work, I also now speak to churches and Christian schools about creation and the Flood. I have also been involved in research, writing, and presenting technical papers at the International Conference on Creationism in the Pittsburgh, Pennsylvania, area. I was the main author of a Flood geology paper in 1998, which was based on my thesis at ICR. In 2003, I co-authored a paper with a Hebrew scholar on a detailed chronology of the Flood. From 1997–2001, I was the president of the Greater Houston Creation Association, and a board member at the present. This is evidence that a person can be a practicing geologist without compromising his belief in the Bible.

On the Sixth Day, God Created . . . Creationists!

Chapter 24
Scott Hanson, DVM

Isat frozen in my seat as our first-year zoology professor detonated his bomb. Up to that point, it had been a rather mundane lecture on Galapagos finches and whatnot. There certainly had been no clue as to the surprise that lurked inside Dr. Middleton's slide carousel, and perhaps that was his strategy. But we need to go back more than a decade to the beginning of this story.

From my earliest recollection, I have soaked up science like a sponge and although surprising to some, faith has never been an obstacle to my scientific endeavors. On the contrary, life makes sense *because* of the rock-solid foundation provided by God's Word. Over the years it has become apparent that the true history of the Bible is completely intertwined and inseparable from the spiritual ramifications of that history. For example, we can trust in the finished work of Christ because He literally lived, died, and rose again in history about two thousand years ago. In my experience, most, if not all, of the so-called scientific attacks used to discredit the Bible have been based upon a misunderstanding of either what the text says or what true science really is. My life has been no exception.

The first provocation between faith and science that comes to mind was in my neighbor's backyard. Dennis reveled in getting a rise out of me all of the time. Looking back, perhaps God was using him to get me thinking about *why* I believed what I believed. At any rate, somehow we got on the topic of Adam and Eve, at which point he airily inquired, "How do you know that Adam and Eve weren't apes?"

That was a novel idea to me because at that time I knew nothing about evolutionary ideas and ape-men. If asked, I would have thought that australopithecine was a country. Undeterred, I shot back that the

Bible said differently and that Adam and Eve were most definitely human. He wasn't much impressed.

As a youth, my experience was that the media did not inundate delicate minds with evolutionary ideas as it certainly does today. Even professional wrestling had a smidgen of honesty in it, and *Leave it to Beaver* was all the rage then. Nonetheless, I had many different questions about the Bible, and nobody, including my parents or Sunday school teachers, seemed to have any credible answers. Without being disrespectful, it appeared that the only correct answers to Bible-related questions were either God or Jesus. Perhaps that was why I was so unsettled in Sunday school. But a major turning point was to come.

Mel Stevens was the director of a Christian camp that my parents would send me to for a couple of weeks out of each summer. Mel had godly wisdom and was always approachable. I'll never forget one morning after breakfast, when I asked him a question that had been annoying me for a long time. "Mel," I asked, "how could Adam, Methuselah, Noah, and all those others have lived nearly a thousand years each?" He explained to me that the world had been absolutely perfect before sin and that there had been no death. Even after God cursed the world with death and decay at the time of Adam and Eve's disobedience, planet Earth would have continued to be a pretty incredible place in which to live. He proceeded to explain that, over time, sin grew along with its consequences: death, disease, and suffering. Over time, the world became a far less ideal place, leading to shorter life spans.

His answer made sense. Mel might not have had the facts that creationists now have about mutations, longevity genes, and changes in the post-Flood environment, but it didn't matter, because he provided a reasonable answer from the Bible. Looking back, I believe that was the moment in which I became a creationist.

When I was 14, a speaker named Josh McDowell from Campus Crusade for Christ was invited by our youth pastor to speak at a Sunday evening service. Josh went to university an atheist and despised the way Christian students on campus would be so kind to him. He set out to show them that the Bible was hogwash. However, in his personal studies he came face to face with the conclusion that the Bible was truly what it claimed to be: the accurate, historical Word of God. Through this experience, he accepted Christ and set out to defend the Bible's authority on campuses all over the world. I listened as he explained that Christ's resurrection was an undeniable fact of history. The Bible was real history that could be proven beyond a reasonable doubt. My heart was pounding! After the service, I coerced my mother into purchasing Josh McDowell's entire tape series at the book table. She retorted that she did not want to invest all that money into something that I would never use. But I persisted, and she bought all the tapes. Twenty-five years later, I am still using those tapes to witness and teach others that the Bible is trustworthy. God was getting me ready for something — if nothing else, at least to believe His Word.

At about that time, I came across a small booklet on evolution that covered some of the common arguments used to support evolution and then answered them biblically and scientifically. For weeks on end, I would read that booklet almost every night. It was clear that evolution was the enemy of God's Word, and I needed to know more about it.

A critical event concerning the Bible and evolution occurred several years later in high school. It was the first day of grade 13 physics class and Mr. Smythe was laying down the law. His basic thesis was that the Bible (Genesis in particular) fell into the realm of "truth" and was ultimately not open to observation or repeatability. On the other hand, science could be observed, repeated, and falsified, and could properly be termed the "fact" of science. Looking back, I believe that his ultimate design in this discussion was to eliminate any discussion over the Genesis account of creation in class.

Writing this now, I can see a couple of critical flaws in his reasoning. First, if Genesis 1–11 was true history, then observational science should be able to confirm (or deny) that history to some degree. Moreover, he subsequently put forward Darwinism as a fact of science, which it obviously is not: it is a faith and, as such, is not subject to direct observation.

His next step was to explain how the second law of thermodynamics (entropy) was not actually opposed to macroevolution at all. The amusing fact was that nobody in the class had asked if it was! I vividly remember him rapidly drawing a circle on the chalkboard to represent the earth followed by a sun and then a squiggly line from the sun to the earth. Pulling the chalk away, he turned quickly on his heels to face us, gazing up with nearly closed eyes (as was his habit when something of great significance was imparted to us). "The earth is an open system," he said. "The ultraviolet radiation from the sun allows evolution to occur."

I knew that there was a serious flaw to his argument, but it would be several years later before I had an answer.

Now let me take you back to the opening story about my zoology class. The bomb that I mentioned was when Dr. Middleton projected an artist's conception of Noah's ark and then started jeering at it. He told us that the event was purely fictitious, obviously not something that an academic would ever believe. "After all," he said, "how could Noah have chased down and lassoed all those thousands of species of animals and insects? It's impossible."

At the time I didn't know what the answer was. It was like a sudden cold shower on my understanding of the Bible. Yet the doubt bomb seemed to have a positive impact, at least on me, because it forced me to do my homework — to get more serious about why I believed what I believed. Over time and Bible study, I realized that a straightforward reading of Genesis and a basic understanding of "created kinds" and rapid post-Flood speciation would have explained the apparent problem of Noah's ark. Indeed, biology and genetics are friends of Genesis! Noah needed far fewer animals than my professor asserted. Besides, abundant physical evidence existed that showed there *had* been a global catastrophic flood, whether he believed it or not. When I look back at that day, I am reminded of what Peter wrote two thousand years ago:

> For this they willingly are ignorant of, that by the word
> of God the heavens were of old, and the earth standing out of
> the water and in the water: Whereby the world that then was,
> being overflowed with water, perished (2 Pet. 3:5–6; KJV).

In the same course, this professor also publicly attacked the reliability of Archbishop James Ussher's chronology of history and made him out to be a bumbling idiot. But later I learned that Ussher was a brilliant and well-educated scholar who carefully researched and integrated biblical and secular history to come up with a date for creation. Personally, I don't think that my professor had any evidence to substantiate his claims. Ussher's well-known chronology simply didn't fit with the billions of years his worldview demanded.

The last two years have taught me much about radioisotope dating, purported to be a rock-solid case against a recent creation. However, these methods only measure concentrations of isotopes — the time aspect is only an inference based on a number of assumptions that cannot be proved (i.e., decay rates, original conditions, and closed system). Through careful reading, it became evident that different methods used to date the same rocks often yielded very disparate dates or disagreed with the corresponding geological age previously assigned. Furthermore, the dating of rocks of known recent ages has often yielded absurd ages such as a 45,000-year-old piece of wood based on carbon-14 dating inside of 45-million-year-old basalt! What would Bishop Ussher think if he were alive today?

We don't need to fear those who attack the Bible. Every attack is an opportunity to share the hope that is within us, the hope of knowing the Lord Jesus Christ as our Savior. Furthermore, we can show people how reasonable and sensible God's Word really is — how it is foundational to everything. It is *not* the enemy of science. The world desperately needs Christians to lovingly teach the truth of Christ through His Word and interpret the evidence of creation and the Flood through "biblical glasses."

Throughout my undergraduate training in veterinary medicine, I became increasingly awed by the infinite creativity of our Creator. By studying the complexity of living systems in physiology and anatomy, and the incredible repeatability of the laws of nature, I wondered how anybody could doubt creationism. I learned how wounds and fractured bones healed and blood clotted with unbelievable intricacy and precision. God had made His invisible qualities glaringly obvious through His visible creation (Rom. 1:20). No Christian college could have ever done for me what my university education in science did to completely and utterly convince me of the truth of the Bible, and Genesis in particular. Later I would learn that James Watson, co-discoverer of the double helix configuration of DNA, was an atheist. And of all people, he *should* be a believer!

In my genetics courses, especially medical genetics, I observed that mutations were destructive in nature and certainly not the creative forces that were purported to turn bacteria into baboons. In zoology, we were taught that natural selection was a magical force that catalyzed the creative progress of macroevolution. However, it didn't take long for me to realize that this observable "microevolutionary" process could only redistribute, corrupt, and eliminate *existing* information. A student asked one of our genetics professors why macroevolution was not being observed today if it had happened in the past. His answer was that it was too slow to observe. That reasoning was rather vexing. How could a lack of evidence be used as proof of something happening? He confidently reassured us that mutations we observed in his fruit fly (*Drosophila melanogaster*) colony were clear evidence of evolution, even going to the point of giving us a tour of his lab so that we could see them. We were given pictures of fruit flies missing a wing or having an antenna in the wrong place, but nothing that would support the development of new, unique features or that would turn a fruit fly into anything other than a fruit fly.

I was intrigued that my zoology textbook contained a chapter entitled *Lesser Proteostomes and Lophophorates*, which might as well have been called *Invertebrates That Just Don't Fit Neatly into the Evolutionary Tree!* The chapter contained a hodgepodge of all sorts of fascinating but misfit organisms sharing similar traits with a number of phyla but not falling into any neat category within the Darwinian phylogenetic tree of life. As a creationist, this didn't bother me in the least. It was clear evidence that God had made such an extensive array of creatures that some were bound to not fit into our somewhat arbitrary and rigid classifications. I noticed many stippled lines that ran from an unknown common ancestor to the nodes of the tree, indicating that the evolutionary sequence had not been discovered. Neither did the idea of a flying mammal (bat) seem to make sense within the evolutionary picture — but there they were, emitting sonar at 30,000 to 100,000 cycles per second and creating mental images with sound that are equivalent to sight.

Recently, my wife and I were chatting in the living room while our daughter Jamie was organizing her seashells on the floor for the millionth time. I mentioned the misfit chapter in my zoology text when she directed my attention to our daughter playing on the floor, only to make a most astute observation. Jamie had all of her shells neatly laid out and organized according to size and shape. However, she had constructed a little container that read "Miscellaneous" on the side, where she kept all of the shells that didn't fit into any of her rows. It dawned on me that we humans love to fit our observations into neat categories, whether child or adult, regardless of whether those presuppositions contain significant inaccuracies. Just like Jamie and her shells, the uniformitarian geologist sees order in his interpretation of the geological column and the evolutionary biologist takes comfort in her Darwinian tree of life — even if those interpretations are awkward and introduce inconsistencies. We can always just create a miscellaneous file into which we put inconsistent observations.

Precious little in my formal science training advanced the logic of the evolutionary proposition, in my mind at least. It was clear that God's hand was written all over the universe, from the enormous spiral galaxies to subatomic particles to the unimaginable complexity of the simplest living creature. What was also fascinating to me was the anthropic principle; an idea advanced by non-Christians that, at its core, states the universe appears to be designed for human life. However, I struggled with the age of the earth. Both Christians and professors were saying that the universe was billions of years old. This obviously disagreed with the Bible, which seemed so clear on the subject.

After my graduation, a creationist geologist from Australia was invited by our church to speak at a local high school. It was then that I began to realize the very real spiritual implications of secular thinking on society and the Church. He explained how evolutionary and millions-of-years ideas were not only contrary to the Bible, but also had devastating consequences on the doctrines of God, sin, death, and salvation, as well as the trustworthiness of a historical rendering of the text itself. I, in time, learned that the evidence from geology in the rocks and fossils (the supposed hard evidence for vast ages) was more consistent with the events surrounding the global flood of Genesis. Most Christians do not appear to be aware that there are many limitations to the uniformitarian view of geology. Because of that, many very good Christian leaders have given up on the historical value of Genesis and swallowed the doctrine of an ancient earth because "science" has proven it to be ancient — or so they think.

As I continued to study the geologic column, I recognized that it could be interpreted as the result of creation week (the land being lifted out of the water on day 3) as well as the events surrounding a global catastrophic flood. I have come to the conclusion that the evidence for catastrophic burial is overwhelming and everywhere! However, I cautioned the students in church that the Flood was a supernatural event — as supernatural as God sending manna to the Israelites, Elijah calling down fire from heaven, or the parting of the Red Sea.

When I think about one to two miles of sedimentary strata in most places, mountain ranges rising for thousands of feet, vast burial of vegetation to form coal and oil deposits, or the Grand Canyon, I am amazed.

This was an event on a scale and proportion that truly boggles the mind — a miraculous act of judgment on mankind by a Holy God. The magnitude of this worldwide judgment by God, as recorded in Genesis 6 to 9, is absolutely ghastly. Although the physical evidence of a global catastrophic flood is abundantly clear, we have to keep in mind that the immensity of it all cannot be understood by the slow rates of present geological processes. As Dr. Steven A. Austin (Institute for Creation Research) has discussed, perhaps God used the events of Mount St. Helens to give us a small taste of the type of geological processes behind Noah's flood.

One of my favorite places in the world is Centennial Park. This sanctuary has become very special to me over the past years. Centennial Park, as we used to think, was just an ordinary picnic stop on the south shore of Colpoy's Bay, a pretty shoreline along the Bruce Peninsula in Wiarton, Ontario. We frequent the park because my wife's parents live in the area. Having discovered the place a couple of years ago, we didn't think much about the interesting layers of shale and limestone that lined the shore in a steplike fashion. All that our two children wanted to do was sculpt the clay from the water's edge into little balls! However, last fall we started looking closely at these rocks and noticed enormous quantities of marine fossils crammed into them. Then we began realizing what we were looking at: direct evidence of the flood of Noah—a veritable fossil graveyard. We have subsequently been able to identify brachiopods (marine animals that superficially resemble clams and other mollusks), bryozoans or "moss animals" (spongelike creatures that grow in colonies), and crinoids (commonly known as "sea lilies"). Although these are all ocean-dwelling fauna, there is no ocean around! Obviously, the source and mechanism for these fossils had nothing to do with Georgian Bay.

I've been thinking that this could be the ultimate witnessing tool! Imagine bringing people to this park and opening the Bible to Genesis 6 and reading the Flood account. The devotional could be followed by a brief description of how fossils form and then a fossil hunt, with interpretive books available so that people can identify the fossils that they find. I have found it almost sad to observe families visit the shoreline who never realize the incredible story behind the rocks: the testimony to God's watery judgment of sin and provision of an ark of salvation — a picture of Jesus Christ.

I remember one particular young lad who was tagging behind his father. He asked his dad what all those things in the stones were, to which his father replied something like, "They *are* neat, son. I don't know what they are." They got in their car and left. That father and son missed the "message in the fossils." This past summer, we had the opportunity to show some people the various types of fossils in the shale, marl, and limestone at Centennial Park. I explained to them what I had learned about how formation of fossils like these marine creatures is an extremely rare occurrence associated with rapid burial, such as what would be expected with catastrophic flooding conditions. Finally, I mentioned that this evidence could be seen as plain evidence for the Genesis account of Noah's flood. Areas with fossils make great witnessing tools for nonbelievers to prove the true history of the Bible and the message of the gospel of Jesus Christ!

Three people have made a tremendous impact on my life recently. I met Drs. Danny Faulkner (University of South Carolina), Emil Silvestru (Answers in Genesis, Canada), and Jerry Bergman (Northwest State College, Ohio) at the Fifth International Conference for Creation at Geneva College in Beaverton, Pennsylvania. They individually counseled me not to engage in evolution bashing, but to take a more positive approach to evangelism by showing people how the physical evidence agrees with the Bible. In fact, this is how Dr. Silvestru, a geologist from Romania, became convinced of the truth of the Bible. A number of concerned creation researchers patiently showed him how the geological evidence fit better with a global flood than with a uniformitarian interpretation. This resolved a difficulty that he had as a geologist with the Bible early on. Dr. Silvestru also explained to me that there are difficulties in geology that have not been fully resolved by the creationist interpretation, such as worm burrows and animal homes found within certain sedimentary strata (catastrophic upheaval and deposition would have destroyed any prior structures such as this). As creationists, we shouldn't ignore these issues or put them into our own miscellaneous file. If the Flood account is true, as I believe it to be, then further research should give insight into interesting features such as this. If the Bible is true, there is nothing to fear.

Dr. Faulkner mentioned his frustration with the way that some creationists misrepresent what evolutionists actually believe, particularly in the areas of cosmology and geology. He admitted that many creationists vehemently attack concepts like the big-bang theory and the geological column without really knowing what these interpretations of the evidence teach. This demonstrates a lack of respect for scientists with a different worldview and diminishes our credibility in their eyes. Moreover, some creationists deny that there is a definite order to the sequence of fossils in the geological column. However, it's the *interpretation* as to how that order occurred (i.e., vast evolutionary eras versus the events surrounding a global flood). The evidence is all the same.

Finally, Dr. Bergman talked to me about how important it was to genuinely care about lost souls as opposed to ramming information down their throats and then smugly walking away. As Christians, we should abound in truth *and* love. Dr. Bergman's academic qualifications are almost embarrassing in their plenitude. He could argue circles around the most ardent anti-creationist, but that is not his style. His demeanor is quiet and genuine, more concerned about winning his students' and colleagues' hearts for Christ than simply winning a fight over creation/evolution. When Dr. Bergman later asked me if I would write a chapter in this book, I initially hesitated. What could I offer? Then I realized how God had been leading me throughout my life through His Word and creation. His purposes are always right!

I have no idea as to what lies ahead in my creation ministry. Currently, a number of us are teaching the curriculum *It All Begins with Genesis* (Answers in Genesis) in our Sunday school program. Our students seem to be really enjoying it, and from discussions with the parents, the students are sharing the information with their family and friends. I cannot think of a better goal than to see this generation of Christian youth being equipped to defend their faith boldly in a godless world. We have also had the opportunity to use creation evangelism to strike up conversations with nonbelievers and those seeking to know more about Christianity. Many people have a foundation that is very different from ours, and we as Christians need to start right at the beginning. Is that surprising? As the title of my story reads, God created us to be creationists! Every Christian should be thrilled about God's creation and how the evidence fits so well with His written revelation — there is no excuse to miss it. This is not just for PhDs. We all need to share this message on many levels with those who need Jesus Christ so desperately. This is the ultimate challenge for every Christian in this dark world.

The Making and Unmaking of an Evolutionary Atheist

Chapter 25
Dr. John Sanford

Editor's note: *John Sanford has been a Cornell University professor for more than 25 years. He received his PhD from the University of Wisconsin, in the area of plant breeding and plant genetics. While at Cornell, he conducted agricultural research at the New York State Agricultural Experiment Station in Geneva, New York, and trained graduate students. His research first involved breeding new crop varieties using conventional breeding methods, and he soon became heavily involved in the newly emerging field of plant genetic engineering. While at Cornell he published more than 70 scientific publications, and he now holds more than 20 patents. His most significant scientific contributions involved three inventions — the biolistic ("gene gun") process, pathogen-derived (PDR) disease resistance, and "genetic immunization." Most transgenic crops used in the world today incorporate one or more of his inventions. He also started two successful businesses derived from his research — Biolistics, Inc. and Sanford Scientific, Inc. John now devotes his time to Christian service in three main areas: the creation/evolution controversy, the issue of "spiritual nutrition" (entertainment), and general evangelism.*

I was brought up believing in Darwinism. From my earliest children's books about dinosaurs, through all my primary and secondary education, I was taught that evolution was a fact, not a theory. The liberal church I was raised in never questioned evolution, nor did my parents, nor, to my recollection, did any person I knew (or anyone else in the world). The strong evolutionary teaching of my high school soon made it clear to me that the weak religious teaching of my church was negated by evolution, was powerless, and was actually absurd. In college, virtually every class I took started from the premise of evolution and built from there. Absolutely everything I learned was in the context of evolution. Even the books where I read about religion (pagan and Christian) were always built on the cornerstone of evolution. *Evolution was the ultimate fact.*

As a godless youth in college, I had no foundation for my life, and I was very empty. My spiritual hunger led me to worship pretty women, experiment with drugs, try out exotic religions, and be fascinated with magic. I then became a socialist/communist. I dropped out of school and hitchhiked through Mexico — looking for all the wrong things. I was headed nowhere fast. If ever there was a lost and hungry soul, I was one. As I look back, I shudder at the spiritual danger I was in during that period in my life and how close I strayed toward utter darkness. I marvel at God's grace, which let me come through all that darkness without being destroyed.

In spite of all this, I do not feel I was ever entirely "Godless." From my earliest memories, I remember a presence I felt — in my mother's lap, in the love of my family, when I looked at clouds, when I felt the wind on my face or heard the thunder. Even when I was the most lost, being close to family and nature made me think of the Creator (but not by that name). And I always spent much time alone — seeking. In a sense, I came simply to worship nature and kindness (I know, and love, many who still do this). Because I did not know the Maker, I could only worship His works. But one can never know a tree like one can know God — as a result it was an extremely lonely and sad sort of worship. And of course, to worship a tree is a perversion — it is idolatry.

During those days, I knew a girl who talked to me about her belief in a personal God. Although not a Christian, she gave me a hope that there might be, not just a "Force" out there, but a "Somebody." The possibility of a personal God really touched something inside me — but this seed would lie dormant in my life for many years.

Not long after this, I entered into agricultural research within a university, which I thought would allow me to work closer to nature. I was training to be a scientist. I met another young student of science, who had a profound influence in my life. He was an extremely romantic evolutionist. Up until that time, evolution was just a cold fact of science to me — like the fact that the world is round, or that all people must die. This friend's vision was so much better. Evolution was not just random changes through time, filtered by selection. Instead, it was essentially a purpose-driven process of self-creation — the one and only noble thing — which must be continued at all cost. Evolution was leading us toward the cosmic destiny of the universe, and humans were a stepping-stone toward ultimate intelligence, self-understanding, and power. In the end, man (or whatever evolved from him) would eventually reverse entropy, death, and cosmic degeneration, resulting in a perfected, immortal universe. And scientists (like us) would help lead the way!

Although my friend did not use these exact words, his view was essentially that, through evolution, we were on our way to evolving into God, and heaven would come about via the evolutionary progress. I bought into this, hook, line, and sinker! For the next ten years of my life, this romantic version of evolution became my religion. It was my hope and my purpose, and defined all my other values. I owe my success in the field of science to this vision — which motivated and inspired me to think big and push hard. During those years, I never dreamed that I would ever become a Christian. The idea that I might ever reject evolution as historical fact and a future hope would have been the most ludicrous idea imaginable. The thought that I would ever believe the biblical view of creation, the Fall, and the Flood was unthinkable.

The Making of a Christian and a Creationist

While I was experiencing success in my research at Cornell University, and was thinking very highly of my success, my marriage was falling apart. When our marriage reached a gut-wrenching crisis, Helen asked that we attend church. I consented to this, and we found a humble little church that we began to attend. As I learned more about Jesus, I realized that even though it was impossible for me to believe in miracles or heaven or hell, I could at least see that Jesus was somehow profoundly good, and that He had something I really wanted. I also began to realize there was something real and alive within that church, which I was drawn to — the love of Christ. And so very reluctantly, very slowly, I began to be changed. I realized that if I wanted to know the love and righteousness of Jesus, I needed to come to terms with His claims. One by one, after much thought and study, the claims of Christ began to sink in. Did He really die for my sins? Did I really need to repent? Did I really need to choose sides — to be either *for* Him or *against* Him?

After several years, Helen decided she wanted to be baptized and asked me if I wanted to be baptized also. To my own surprise, I said yes — I was finally ready to get off the fence. When I stepped into the baptismal basin and the preacher asked me if I accepted Jesus as my *Lord and Savior*, I suddenly realized the meaning of that expression. He could not be my Savior if He was not first my Lord. In that moment I realized that, at last, I could enthusiastically receive Him as my Master. I even sensed at that moment that He might command me to believe and profess things that would destroy my very respectable scientific career. He might overthrow my earthly understandings. For me, when I went under the water, something in me really did die, and when I came up again, something else really was born within me. That was one of the happiest and most beautiful days of my life. That was more than 15 years ago, and I have never been the same. From that point onward, I began a meaningful and progressive walk with Christ. At that point, I still could not imagine a literal creation, and in fact, I still felt heaven was simply too good to hope for. My choice was neither in the hope of heaven, nor the fear of hell. It certainly was not based on any deep understanding of God's Word. It was really based primarily on the love of Christ. That is not such a bad place to start.

In the years that followed, our church asked Helen and me to start teaching. Since they thought we were knowledgeable about certain earthly things, they thought we would be qualified to teach about heavenly things. What a terrible mistake! Given what the Bible says about the grave consequences of being a false teacher, I realize how my first teachings must have grieved God. I consistently molded the Bible to fit my own personal, earthly understandings. I thought the Bible had to be taught from a theistic-evolution perspective. I consistently twisted the truth — teaching my own earthly understandings as an overlay of God's revelation. Yet God in His awesome grace used this time to help me. Our teaching put Helen and me in regular contact with God's Word, and so we gradually began to grow and came to know and respect the Bible more and more. Even as God brought our teaching more and more into alignment with His teaching, we began to see that our church had not really surrendered to biblical truth. Truth was not consistently taught from the pulpit — instead, we heard mostly worldly wise teachings. The day came when we sadly left that little church, which had given us so much, and where we had first encountered Jesus, the family of Christ, and His Holy Spirit. But God wanted us to keep moving forward, and our children needed a firmer foundation than that church was providing. Yet, for all that growth, I still struggled with Genesis 1–11.

In the coming years, precept by precept, line by line, I gradually came to understand and accept the teachings of Christ, and the truth of His Word. Although my mind and self-will resisted this process, I realized I was being called to be faithful to Him. I often surrendered begrudgingly. Often I surrendered without full understanding, believing by faith alone. Yet God later rewarded this submission of faith with genuine understanding and a growing awe for the truth and integrity of the Bible. I would say, "Lord, show me the evidence and I will believe." God always seemed to answer, "Believe, and I will show you the evidence." This applies to believing in Christ, and it likewise applies to accepting creation. Ever since I became a creationist by faith, God has poured out for me evidences to support my faith. So, what begins as blind faith eventually becomes faith supported by evidence.

Strangely, I accepted the hope of heaven only gradually, although it is clearly presented by Jesus and is the most awesome promise we can receive from the Lord. I felt unworthy and did not want to be selfish or vain in claiming such an incredible personal gift. How strange that we are so quick to believe the bad, but remain so skeptical of the good!

Genesis 1–11 was a great challenge to my faith. Creation, the Fall, and the Flood seemed impossible — and it stood in direct defiance of my old religion, evolution. If there were a miraculous creation, a Fall, and a global flood in the recent past, then everything I had ever been taught had to be rejected (or radically restructured). To accept this would result in a total overthrow of my entire mental framework. It would mean that the whole story of evolution, which had come to permeate every field of knowledge, was a lie — a monumental deception. Not a lie concocted by men, but a lie birthed from the Fall and from Satan. To accept the creation/Fall/Flood seemed to me to require the complete negation of all my scientific training and all my earthly understanding. I felt I would have to just close my eyes and turn off my brain!

Ironically, after becoming a creationist (by faith, not by knowledge), my mind has been renewed. An overthrow of my old mind was exactly what was needed to make room for a new mind and a new understanding. I have *not* had to turn off my mind — indeed, the challenge of understanding and defending Genesis has been the most exciting and stimulating phase of my entire scientific career. The diverse issues have not only become more vital because they address profound spiritual truths, but now there are also a host of new and amazing mysteries to unravel and great new discoveries to be made. This is after a long period in my life when I felt science had become progressively more boring and routine — scrutinizing more and more trivial variations of the same old story. Now that I have become a creationist, I have experienced a renaissance of my interest in all the sciences, including cosmology, astronomy, geophysics, geology, biology, genetics, paleontology, linguistics, and more. Imagine the intellectual excitement of taking the deeply entrenched doctrines of the scientific establishment and rethinking them from a totally different angle — looking at them in a radically new way!

More important than providing scientific excitement, accepting creation has given me new spiritual eyes to see with. I can now see the Bible as the only reliable source of deep truth in a world filled with so much deception and false teaching. I now see God's creation around me in a totally different light. The creation now speaks to me of a God who is very immediate, very personal, very supernatural, and very powerful. The ugly parts of this world now speak to me of the tragedy and corruption associated with a very literal and relatively recent Fall. Evidences of the Flood speak to me powerfully of the impending Final Judgment, and of the new heaven and earth that will soon be re-created.

When I was coming to Christ, I was embarrassed, and even fearful, to admit it. Likewise, when I was coming to accept creation, I was both embarrassed and ashamed to admit it publicly. My culture at that time (i.e., Cornell) would view all such things as profound ignorance! In that culture, it would have seemed more respectable to say I was homosexual or practiced witchcraft. I felt that to admit such Christian beliefs would invite many hard questions, for which I then had no answers. When I would first confess to being a Christian (and later a creationist), I would literally *choke* on my words! My face would flush; my heart would skip a beat. I felt the perfect fool and wanted to hide. Even after the fear of personal humiliation began to pass, I remained fearful that I could not adequately explain my faith to skeptics, thereby failing my obligation to defend God's truth. Before I was baptized, if someone asked me if I was a Christian, I would try to explain that I was — *sort of*. After I was baptized, I was liberated to this extent: if someone asked, I could answer confidently that I was a Christian, with no qualification. But I was still basically hiding — afraid of the hard questions that I feared might come. I certainly did not openly proclaim the good news!

Accepting Genesis 1–11 has put into place for me those foundational principles that I had been lacking to defend my faith. Rather than making it harder for me to defend my faith, the acceptance of Genesis 1–11 has actually given me more confidence and boldness. Now, finally, I have come to the point where I am eager to tell people I am a Christian. This is not because I am *proud* to be a Christian (how can a man who was drowning be proud that he was rescued?), but because I am eager to acknowledge the One who saved me. If someone is a believer, we can share a common joy. If someone is an unbeliever, I have an opportunity to share this joy with him or her, in case he or she is ready to receive it. In the very same way, I have come to the point where I am unashamed and grateful to say that I believe Genesis 1–11 (even those parts I do not fully understand). I am ready to proclaim from the highest hill, "We have a Creator, a Judge, and a Savior — let all heaven and earth praise Him!"

Dinosaurs Capture the Imagination

Chapter 26
Donald D. Ensign

"Brrroarrrrr!" A vast herd of great and unusual creatures instantly glanced toward the direction of this horrifying sound. The source of this loud, guttural noise was a huge reptilian creature standing on two massive hind legs. Its gigantic head sported a gaping mouth filled with long, daggerlike teeth. This amazing creature fearlessly charged into the herd, which scattered before him like so many leaves in the wind. One large, four-footed monster with large plates going down its spine and tail proved too slow to escape the pursuit of the relentless attacker. Thus ensued a tremendous duel to the death between the peaceful spike-tailed plant eater and the awesome predator. Eventually the aggressor overcame the vegetarian's defenses. The victor (a *T. rex*) stood over his kill (a stegosaur) bellowing triumphantly to this "prehistoric" world.

This mighty battle was done to the background of classical music. Disney studios produced this vignette as part of their 1942 animated film *Fantasia*. As a second grader in 1955, like many of my contemporaries, I faithfully watched the Walt Disney TV program. In the midst of Mickey Mouse, Donald Duck, and numerous nature programs, this cartoon sequence stood out. "Wow, what are those things?"

Thus began a fascination — a boyhood love affair with dinosaurs. I became one of those annoying pint-sized dinosaur know-it-alls. I read everything on dinosaurs the school and public library had to offer. I remember being impressed with the children's dinosaur books by Herbert Zim and especially Roy Chapman Andrew's *All about Dinosaurs*. I could tell you how long they were, how much they weighed, what they ate, when they supposedly lived, and I could even pronounce many of their names. Shortly after this I came across a comic book in a supermarket called *Turok: Son of Stone.* This comic told the adventures of two American Indians who entered "the lost valley" where dinosaurs, ape-men, and other prehistoric creatures still lived. A feature of this periodical was a comic strip called the "Young Earth." One story in this series showed small dinosaurs sprouting feathers and over long periods of time, they became birds; a virtual primer for evolution. This coupled with the books I was reading with their dinosaur family tree illustrations were my first introduction to evolution. When adults asked me what I wanted to do when I grew up, I immediately responded, "I want to be a paleontologist!" thinking that most everyone else wanted to be a paleontologist, too! This early passion of dinosaurs culminated in a 1962 trip to the Dinosaur National Monument and a 1965 journey to Drumheller, Alberta, the site of extremely rich dinosaur fossil mass kill graveyards.

Along with this fascination with dinosaurs, I developed a love for insects. I had the privilege of being raised on a small farm in northwest Washington State, surrounded by fields, wooded forests, streams, ponds, swamps, and mountains that contained sandstone leaf fossils. It was a great place for a boy to grow up, especially one with an interest in animals and "creeping things." I spent many Saturday afternoons searching for the creatures that inhabited the neighborhood swamps and ponds. Along with the usual frog tadpoles and salamanders were such aquatic denizens as dragonflies, damselfly nymphs, water boatmen, backswimmers, whirligig beetles, water striders, water tigers of various kinds, diving beetles, the sticklike water scorpions, and the furious giant water bug. I captured these creatures and observed their habits. I especially became very interested in the praying mantis and (with the county agent's permission) made an early unsuccessful attempt to introduce them into the area. This interest culminated in organizing, compiling, illustrating, and writing a 40-page one-of-a-kind publication modestly titled *Ensign's Encyclopedia of Praying Mantids,* which eventually was turned in as a school project.

I was born into a Bible-believing, churchgoing home. From a very young age I heard the gospel that Jesus, the Son of God, had lived a perfect and sinless life and died as a sacrifice for my sins. He then was raised from the dead as a sign of His victory over sin and death. I believed and accepted Christ as my personal Savior at a young age and faithfully went to church. Years later, as a young teen, I began to realize that there were problems with the biblical account of creation in

Genesis and the evolutionary origin stories that I was receiving from the popular media. Both couldn't be true.

On a visit to a Christian bookstore, I came across a book that seemed to give me an answer to this question. It was *Evolution and Christian Thought Today*[1] (edited by Russell L. Mixter). This book contained essays by several Christian scholars in a number of sciences. I purchased it and read it. It attempted to bring biblical Christianity and evolutionary thinking together. This book was published at the time of the 1959 Darwinian centenary. This book influenced my thinking for several years on the subject of origins. Much later I came to realize that it mainly contained the writings of advocates of what I now recognize as compromise positions, such as progressive creationism and theistic evolution.

During my freshman year of college, I discovered another scholarly volume called *The Genesis Flood*,[2] by John Whitcomb and Henry Morris. These men took seriously the biblical record of the worldwide flood as a historical event (and also the Genesis creation account) and proceeded to lay out the theological, historical, and scientific reasons for this contention. This book resonated in my spirit. I began to realize that biblical Christian faith and evolutionary thinking were not compatible. God did not need millions of years or a bloody, cruel, and inefficient process like evolution to accomplish His creative purposes.

In college, I took a number of biology courses (all taught from an evolutionary perspective), which stimulated even more interest in the creation/evolution debate. During this time, I met my first creationist author, Donald W. Patten, who wrote *The Biblical Flood and the Ice Epoch*.[3] Patten spoke at my church on his "astral catastrophism" theory, which was then (and now) controversial in creationist circles.

After college, I joined the staff of Campus Crusade for Christ and was assigned to work at their then headquarters at Arrowhead Springs just outside of San Bernardino, California. There I met another staff member who had a similar interest in the creation/evolution debate. In 1973, we decided to attend the summer seminar at the Institute for

1. Russell L. Mixter, ed., *Evolution and Christian Thought Today* (Grand Rapids, MI: Eerdmans, 1959).
2. John C. Whitcomb and Henry M. Morris, *The Genesis Flood* (Philadelphia, PA: Presbyterian and Reformed Publ. Co., 1961).
3. Donald W. Patten, *The Biblical Flood and the Ice Epoch* (Seattle, WA: Pacific Meridian Pub. Co., 1966).

Creation Research at Christian Heritage College in El Cajon, California. There we met and heard lectures from Duane Gish, Harold Slusher, a very young Steve Austin, and Richard Bliss (not yet on ICR staff). This was very heady stuff, and my friend and I came back and began a short-lived creation study group with several other CCC staff members. During the rest of the 1970s and 1980s, I followed the work of ICR and returned in 1993 for another summer seminar.

In the late 1980s, I began attending a church in Sierra Madre, California. The church's minister of apologetics was in the process of forming his own ministry. He was a former Cal Tech astrophysicist who looked and sounded like the stereotypical college professor. This, of course, was Dr. Hugh Ross, who is perhaps currently the foremost progressive creationist. While I was still connected to ICR, I began to wonder if my positions on creationist issues were correct. I started reading Dr. Ross's books and listened to him speak, and compared it with the young-earth creationist perspectives that I had accepted for many years. At the end of this review process, I became convinced, more than ever, that the young-earth viewpoint was the biblically correct position and was scientifically tenable. During that time, I became involved with a nearby Bible science group. At one of their meetings, Dr. George Howe spoke and presented a challenge to his audience to become actively involved in the creation science movement. He suggested that everyone could do something to further the cause of creation. This prompted me to move beyond just giving financially to creationist organizations to writing book reviews for creation publications like *Creation Research Science Quarterly*.

During these later years, my dormant interest in dinosaurs had revived. In 1997, while working as a volunteer at an archaeological dig in Israel, a student volunteer asked me what I would like to do next. I mentioned that I would enjoy being involved in a dinosaur dig. After arriving home, I found out that a friend who I was involved with in pro-life activities at the Sierra Madre church years earlier was also interested in fossils. He had since moved to Colorado Springs, Colorado. The next summer we met in western Colorado to participate in a one-day dinosaur dig sponsored by a secular museum. We enjoyed the experience so much we planned to do something similar the next year. This time we chose a creationist dig on the Paluxy River near Glen Rose, Texas. My friend was very skeptical because of the adverse publicity about the dinosaur tracks and what looked like human footprints in the same riverbed strata. However, we decided to give it a three-day shot and were encouraged at what we found. We uncovered new dinosaur tracks by sandbagging sections of the river and pumping out the water and removing the bottom mud sediments. We also found some tracks that didn't fit the usual dinosaur mold. My friend even placed his foot into one of the tracks. It was a very good fit.

At that time, we met a creationist fossil digger named Joe Taylor. He, along with several friends, was ensconced in a nearby motel filled with computer equipment, writing and designing a book he would later publish. My friend, a professional writer, would later get in contact with Taylor for an interview. This interview formed the basis for an article in *New Man* magazine. In early 2000, I visited Taylor at his museum in Crosbyton, Texas. Later, we struck up an e-mail correspondence that resulted in my moving to Texas for a two-year stint as associate manager for the Mt. Blanco Fossil Museum. This time was like a childhood dream come true. I was actually doing the work of a paleontologist (and a lot more besides).

During that time, I had many opportunities to do field excavation in mammoth and dinosaur digs in Texas and Colorado. One exciting excavation occurred when we were hired by a small west Texas museum to excavate mammoth remains. This event garnered much local press and television coverage. Many public schools brought their classes to the dig site, and Taylor did a splendid job of presenting a creationist view of what may have happened to the animal we were excavating. Also, I worked as an assistant in fossil preparation work and helped revise Taylor's book *Fossils: Facts & Fantasies*,[4] and designed and edited two other smaller books. One of these books was *Man, Dinosaurs and Mammals Together* by John A. Watson.[5] This book contained reports from 19th-century sources of dinosaur, mammal, and human bones mixed together in the South Carolina phosphate beds. I was also involved in planning several museum seminars and did other administrative tasks. Another highlight was going to the 2001 annual meeting of the Society of Vertebrate Paleontology in Bozeman, Montana, and writing a report for CRS's *Creation Matters* newsletter.

4. Joe Taylor, *Fossils: Facts & Fantasies* (Green Forest, AR: Master Books, 1998).
5. John A. Watson, *Man, Dinosaurs and Mammals Together* (Crosbyton, TX: Mt. Blanco Fossil Museum, 2001).

I have found that many people who are fascinated by creation science are interested in many other areas. While I have never married, I developed a strong interest in genealogy that stimulated several family reunions, as well as my writing a biography. This biography dealt with a great, great uncle who had the distinction of being one of the family doctors for the C.P. Ingalls family of *Little House on the Prairie* fame. I am also currently working with the Stonecroft Ministries (the Christian Women's Clubs of America) as supervisor of their book and media department. This is a challenging position in which my fellow workers and I try to keep up with the Christian publishing industry and how we can chose resources to best advance the evangelistic and discipleship goals of Stonecroft.

As Christians and creationists, we should see our lives as the wonderful adventure God, in His loving providence, has meant them to be. I see the importance not only for creation science to be grounded in scholarly excellence, but to be also firmly and lovingly spiritually based and exciting to the popular imagination. Truth is worth defending for its own sake, but especially truth that is connected to one's eternal destiny. Creationists need to be constantly reminded that we are in a spiritual struggle and that praying in love for the soul of that atheist college professor or the mind of that Genesis-compromising Christian is of supreme importance. As a young-earth creationist who was in a church dominated by progressive creationist thinking, I know the need for real compassion (without compromising the truth) for those who disagree with us.

Also, we need to realize that deeply held beliefs are often embedded in a person's mind by the mass media, such as adventure movies, children's books, popular fiction, and even comic books. As a graphic designer and cartoonist, I have helped produce comic books that have shared the truth of creation and the gospel message. It is heartening over the years to learn that others in the movement have produced similar tools in many forms that appeal to the popular imagination. Also, the adventure of creation-based fossil hunts, dinosaur digs, or outings of similar nature help to cement the truth of Genesis in my heart and mind in a very tangible way. I look forward to the continuing adventure, as a Christian who takes the Bible and Genesis seriously, that God has for me in the future.

From New Age to New Creation

Chapter 27
Victor Marshall

Though baptized into the "Christian church" as a young man, my father's defining philosophical experience occurred during his college days at the University of Texas in the late 1940s. His study for a bachelor's degree in physics, with a minor in geophysics, changed his life. His geology and paleontology classes especially influenced him to embrace the prevalent uniformitarian/materialistic view of life, grounded in classical Darwinism.

Ironically, the one event that actually precipitated his abandoning Christianity was a college Bible course on the Gospels. The superficial differences in these four evangelists' testimonies led him to distrust both them and the Bible. Having adopted a commonly held skeptical view of Scripture and embracing the conventional scientific wisdom of a long-aged earth, a "spontaneously generated" proto-cell, and trans-phyla evolution, he took a stand on the platform of agnosticism.

My mother grew up in a large Appalachian family amid the Blue Ridge Mountains of Virginia. With two of her older sisters, she used to walk several miles to church. My parents were married in a Christian service. In 1953 (a good year!), DNA was discovered, and I was born. As I groped through my formative years, my mother sought to instill the faith of her childhood in her children. Without overt opposition from my father, she took my siblings and me to a mainline church for religious instruction and worship. However, discussion of God was nonexistent in our household, and my father stayed at home on Sundays. His aversion to Christianity did little to encourage my love for church. My memories of church were not all negative, however. While walking home from church service one day, I remember singing the well-known song "Jesus Loves Me." Suddenly, hovering at eye level next to me, was a beautiful hummingbird keeping pace with me for what seemed like a marvelously long time before flying off. This simple experience is still with me today. By the time I was 11 years old, my parents moved to a contemporary house they built in a new development, miles from the nearest church. This time of transition represented the last time I would attend a church for nearly two decades.

During this time, my father bought my siblings and me the recently published Life Science Library books (the books titled *Evolution* and *The Universe* were my favorites). A trip to the Natural History Museum in Washington, D.C., and my father's regular subscriptions to *National Geographic* and *Scientific American* rounded out my science education at home. The photographs and artwork of the *National Geographic* played a unique role in the formation of my childhood aspirations. Having cultivated a love for visual art, I was engrossed by the magazine's depictions of prehistoric landscapes inhabited by saber-toothed tigers, *T. rexes*, giant sloths, and hair-covered constructs of early "ape-men." The television program *What in the World*, broadcast from the University of Pennsylvania in Philadelphia (only 30 minutes from our home in Valley Forge), also contributed to my love of things ancient.

This long-running program pitted a panel of archaeological experts against an enigmatic artifact, with nothing but their powers of educated deduction to determine its age, origin, and author. I developed a fascination for antiquities and anything prehistoric. Long before the cinematic exploits of *Indiana Jones* or close encounters of *Jurassic Park*, I dreamed of finding a pre-Columbian artifact or the long-forgotten fingers of some pterodactyl. When asked the proverbial question, "What do you want to be when you grow up?" I would proudly answer, "An archaeologisst."

In my high school freshman year, I ran headlong into one of the most influential evolutionary polemics ever devised — the dramatization of the famous Scopes trial, *Inherit the Wind*. Hidden away in the preface to the play was this disclaimer by its authors: "*Inherit the Wind* does not pretend to be journalism. It is theater." However, plastered all over the cover of the book were misleading contradictions to this statement. In a marquis at the top of the book were the words "The tense drama of the most explosive trial of the century." On the back cover was written "The legal battle of the century," "At stake was the freedom of every American," and "One of the most moving and meaningful plays of our generation."

Little did I, my fellow students, or probably our teacher know that this play really had very little to do with the actual events that took place during America's first great media circus that fateful summer in Dayton, Tennessee. John T. Scopes volunteered in response to a general invitation by the ACLU for anyone to play the role of the accused. By his own testimony, he could not even remember if he had ever actually taught evolution. He was never in danger of incarceration. The defense asked the jury to return a guilty charge and the prosecution offered to pay the defendant's fine. In the famous movie based on the play of the same name, the town's inhabitants are portrayed as an effigy-burning lynch mob. However, Clarence Darrow would write of the real people of Dayton, "I came here a perfect stranger and I can say that I have not found upon anybody's part any citizen here in this town or outside the slightest discourtesy."[1] This is a far cry from the melodramatic misrepresentation of "the most explosive trial of the century" that we were assigned to read out loud in class. As our class worked through the script of the play, we often moved back and forth between laughter and righteous indignation at the black-and-white descriptions of good-guy materialists and bad-guy creationists. The only conclusion that could be drawn was that most Christians (and southerners) were the worst type of ignoramuses and half-possessed bigots.

In high school biology class, we learned of the laughable medieval superstition of "spontaneous generation." Little did we know that Stanley Miller's unsuccessful "intelligent intervention" effort to create the right- and left-handed amino acids necessary for life in the 1950s was based upon just this unbelievable premise — that nonliving matter could spontaneously generate into living matter!

In 1964, a little more than 3 percent of American households owned a color television. When my family joined that minority, "the Tube" consumed my visually dominant Baby Boomer attention. The perennial television experience that began in 1959 and continued through the 1960s like clockwork every year was the playing of the 1939 classic *The Wizard of Oz*. It provided an annual escape from the monochromatic drudgery

---

1. Trial transcript from the Scopes trial, p. 225–226.

of our mundane life with a masterful work of cinematic magic. Though we repeated the mantra, "There's no place like home," who really believed that Kansas was better than Oz? By my high school sophomore year, I began a search for my own Oz. The Beatles' *Sgt. Pepper's* album, released in 1967, contained a photograph of the band, their eyes bloodshot from marijuana. My generation would take a deadly detour into a poppy field of substance abuse. Many of our heroes would end up dead from the extremes of hedonism. The Beatles made their journey through drugs and Hinduism, and so eventually, would I. From 1970 to 1983, I was immersed in a longhaired culture of psychedelic rock, drugs, New Age theosophy, Eastern religion, pseudo-science, UFOs, and the occult.

When *Time* magazine asked in 1966 the rhetorical question, "Is God Dead?" the implication was that the monotheistic God of Western Christianity had succumbed to atheism. With the discovery of Eastern philosophy, the "gods" of the Orient would smile down Buddha-like upon the West's conversion: not to atheism, but to Eastern mysticism.

After my high school graduation, I hitchhiked to a Tibetan Buddhist commune whose "enlightened" leader made provisions for the use of intoxicating substances, contrary to the widely accepted fifth precept of the Buddhist faith. Meditating for three hours a day did much to calm my metabolism but little to still my troubled soul. I longed for a personal peace that seemed all the more elusive the deeper I delved into drugs. Knocked over the head with injurious substances, I eventually awoke amid the shards of a broken and twisted reality; no Auntie Em or friendly farmhands to comfort me — my mind seriously afflicted with chronic paranoia. Psychotropic substances, like the forbidden fruit, promised an enlightened revelation of my "god" nature. Instead, it only produced a terrible nakedness of the soul. Following Shirley MacLaine's lead, I yelled at the top of my lungs in the middle of the wilderness, "I am God!" The frightful acid face staring back at me from a mind-altered mirror looked like anything but God. Those who have experienced only the euphoric effects of high-grade marijuana can never fully appreciate its deleterious downside.

Once, the trauma of a bad trip on mescaline landed me in the ER with a kidney stone and crippling depression. My neighbor's first acid trip was her last. She entered a mental hospital and left seriously mentally ill. One of my friends (a record-breaking high school halfback), high on magic mushrooms, leaped headfirst from the highest tree in Hawaii, breaking his neck — only to survive as a quadriplegic.

In college, I gravitated toward the bohemian subculture — a colony of artistic camaraderie. My favorite professors were those who were cool — meaning favorably disposed toward illicit substances. My BS degree in art education required me to take a number of science courses, including a general course in anthropology. During this course, I learned about the paleo-anthropological belief in an unbroken evolutionary line from ape to man. Each new discovery of a fossil primate promised to be another missing link. However, it has become increasingly evident that the participants in this supposedly unbroken chain of development were actually living side by side as contemporaries. Most recently, fossil bones found in Kenya in 2000 have led to a radical re-assessment of the traditional evolutionary assumptions about human origins. *Homo erectus*, once believed to have descended from *Homo habilis*, is now proclaimed to have been a "sister species" with *habilis*. Furthermore, *erectus*, once believed to be humanlike, is now understood to be far more like the modern-day gorilla.

The closing section of my general anthropology class examined the religious development of man. I undertook a deeper religious search in some of my other college courses. I explored Hinduism, Buddhism, Islam, and the theology of Carlos Castenada. Professors who were either current or former practitioners of these faiths taught the classes in major religions. My Hinduism teacher actually broke his arm during one of TM's much-touted levitation sessions. One of my girlfriends joined a well-known quasi-church that utilized intensive "love bombardment" and "sleep deprivation" sessions — only to later get kidnapped and "deprogrammed."

A study of the Bagavad Gita, the Rig Veda, the Upanishads, the writings of Confucius and Lao Tsu, the sayings of Buddha, the life of Muhammad, I Ching, Tai Chi, Kung Fu, pyramid power, astrology, astral projection, Zen Buddhism, the Egyptian and Tibetan books of the dead, primitive tribal religion, shamanism, spiritualism, Greek mythology, Greek philosophy, and a host of lesser dabblings brought me no closer to peace of mind or health of soul.

My pantheistic "all is one" (drug-induced) view of the universe seemed perfectly compatible with evolution's premises. I did not question my physical ancestors as leading all the way back to nonliving matter. I believed that I had a shared physical and spiritual ancestry with the vegetable kingdom. I engaged in a weeklong tree-hugging session in sub-zero temperatures. I lobbied to save the whales, a species that many felt was superior to our own, perhaps destined to outlive us. One night, while high on LSD, I spent the better part of an evening staring intently at the fossil of a brachiopod found on the highest mountain in Maine, Mount Katahdin. This fossil took on the appearance of living primordial soup, a chunk of Darwin's "warm little pond." I imagined it teeming with proto-biotic life until the rock in my hands took on the appearance of a prehistoric amphibian — having evolved before my eyes into a higher life form.

Then in 1980, PBS came out with the famous 13-part series, *Cosmos*. Carl Sagan had achieved what I had only been able to unconsciously approximate — the synthesis of evolution, Hinduism, history, art, and "psychotropia." As I thrilled to each of the special-effects-laden episodes, it became readily apparent that Dr. Sagan was no stranger to psychoactive inspiration. Metaphors, music, and surreal visual excursions often made *Cosmos* a "trip." A scene incorporating Alice in Wonderland and friends flying high at a tea party was compared to parties that Carl had attended. His last wife, Ann Druyan, would become a vice-chair on the board of the marijuana legalization advocacy group NORML. In his Pulitzer Prize–winning book *Dragons of Eden*, he postulated that cannabis might have been the first plant cultivated by Stone Age man. "It would be wryly interesting if in human history the cultivation of marijuana led generally to the invention of agriculture, and thereby civilization."[2]

Sagan also speculated that the effect of marijuana on the brain could be the same as that of Oriental meditative states — to suppress the left hemisphere of the brain, thus pronouncing the right. Describing the right hemisphere of the brain he related, "These experiments showed a remarkable tendency for the right hemisphere to view the world as more unpleasant, hostile, and even disgusting than the left hemisphere . . . a dark and suspicious emotional tone seems to lurk in the right hemisphere."[3] Dr. Sagan even theorized that psychedelic substances may induce uterine contractions in the birthing process, and that adult use of similar substances could produce a flashback to the birth event. "Perhaps it is therefore not so implausible that, much later in life under the influence of a psychedelic

2. Carl Sagan, *Dragons of Eden* (New York: Random House, 1977), p. 191.
3. Ibid., p. 180.

drug, we recall the birth experience — the event during which we first experienced psychedelic drugs."[4]

Though he never came out of the "psychedelic closet," he would posthumously receive notoriety for developing many of his ideas while "under the influence." In retrospect, some of his pronouncements in *Cosmos* seem like drug-induced "profundity": "We owe the existence of our world to random collisions in a long vanished cloud." "We are star stuff which has taken its destiny into its own hands." "Sex was stumbled upon by the microbes." "The Universe made us."[5]

It also is no coincidence that Hinduism, the religion that *Cosmos* favored to be "the only one of the world's great faiths" that fit the "scientific" view of the universe, would be based in a psychoactive theology. In the Vedas (some of Hinduism's earliest writings), much praise is given to a psychotropic drink made with *soma* — a plant also deified as a god. It was used by the Brahmins in their mysteries and rites and purported to impart deific enlightenment. "We have drunk soma and become immortal; we have attained the light, the gods discovered."[6] "LSD induces a sense of union with the universe, as in the identification of Brahman with Atman in Hindu religious belief."[7]

Episode 2 of *Cosmos* dealt most specifically with organic evolution. Technology made it possible to visually witness the imaginary process of evolution from single cell to upright man. The contour drawing metamorphosis was convincing to my impressionable mind. Creature after creature morphing from one to the next in effortless evolutionary movement; surely this was a time-lapse snapshot of what brought us from the pond to politics.

Yet behind the smoke and mirrors were insurmountable difficulties. A multitude of missing links were pulled out of a nonobservable hat; none of them witnessed in life or geology — only a chimera of the mind. Untold organ systems and unfathomably complex living machinery developed by time and mutational chance, preserved by natural selection while still nonfunctioning, all of which developed toward an

4. Carl Sagan, *Broca's Brain* (New York: Random House, 1974), p. 359.
5. Carl Sagan, *Cosmos*. Original release, Carl Sagan Productions, KCET, Los Angeles, CA, 1980 (remastered DVD, Cosmos Studios, 2002).
6. Rig Veda 8.48.3.
7. Sagan, *Broca's Brain*, p. 356.

unseen yet highly specified functional purpose that neither species nor system could envision. All of this took place with no known mechanism capable of adding the necessary new information into the DNA data bank. What was Sagan's "just so" explanation for the evolutionary emperor's missing new clothes? "The reason that evolution is not immediately obvious to everybody is because it moves so slow and takes so long."[8] Evolution must be slow — so slow that it is not observed in life or geology.

The famous evolutionists Stephen Jay Gould and Niles Eldredge had the courage to boldly proclaim the nakedness of paleontology with the announcement of their "punctuated equilibria" theory in 1972. Harvard professor Gould declared in 1977, "The extreme rarity of transitional forms in the fossil record persists as the trade secret of paleontology."[9] Eldredge, curator at the American Museum of Natural History, stated more recently, "No wonder paleontologists shied away from evolution for so long. It seems never to happen. . . . Evolution cannot forever be going on somewhere else. Yet that's how the fossil record has struck many a forlorn paleontologist looking to learn something about evolution."[10]

What was their "just so" explanation to this disturbing absence of evidence? Evolution must take place rapidly — so rapidly that it can't be seen in life or geology! Never mind that science is defined as "the study of observable facts." Evolution was still pronounced to be "scientific" fact.

I was totally unaware of the glaringly inadequate paleontological evidence and just accepted the pronouncements of the experts as gospel. I believed that the fossil record was incontrovertible proof of Darwin's theory. In *Cosmos*, Sagan pronounced, "Evolution is a fact, not a theory. It really happened." His proof for this bold claim? The trilobite fossil he held in his hand as he made this declaration.

In my travels through rural New Hampshire, I stumbled upon a small shop that specialized in fossils — an anomaly in the midst of an avenue of antique stores. As I engaged the fossil collector/owner in conversation, he made the most startling statement, "Fossils are proof of

---

8. Sagan, *Cosmos*.
9. Stephen Jay Gould, "Evolution's Erratic Pace," *Natural History* (May 1977): p.14.
10. Niles Eldredge, *Reinventing Darwin: The Great Debate at the High Table of Evolutionary Theory* (New York: John Wiley and Sons, 1995), p. 95.

the biblical flood." I left the store with a fossil in my hand and laughter on my lips. Little did I know that I would eventually adopt his "preposterous" belief. Is it so unbelievable to conclude that a planet covered from head to toe in catastrophic sedimentary layers of fossilized remains (with little or no evidence of inter-layer erosion) may be the result of a universal flood of biblical proportions? Is it so insane to observe marine fossils on all of the mountains of earth and infer that the entire world was once covered with water? The encapsulated impression of a soft-bodied jellyfish and the brachiopod from Mount Katahdin in my own fossil collection are empirical evidence of just such an event.

For me, 1983 was a very eventful year. I celebrated New Year's Eve with a generous cocaine dealer, friends, and a plate filled with "snow." One of the participants at that party would give me my first copy of the Bible. I read it cover to cover. While searching through volumes at a large book sale, I discovered a book titled *The Light of the Nations*,[11] a 700-page volume written in 1884. In this book, the theologian C.F. Deems undertook a "rational examination of the four evangelists, on the grounds that their memoirs are merely human in all respects." Even though he began with an intentionally disinterested method, he concluded the work, "with a love for Jesus deeper and better than that which I feel for any other man dead or living." Ironically, a "scientific" approach to the four Gospels would play a role in instilling my own confidence in the Bible.

Contrary to my father's loss of faith through an encounter with the Gospels, I received a life-transforming experience through their study. I read another 800-page book on the life of Christ and a 700-page book on the history of the Christian church. Though I had consumed all of this material in the span of less than a year, I was still not ready to embrace the Creator God of Christianity. Though the mounting evidence of Scripture and nature appeared overwhelming, prejudiced presuppositions, developed over the span of decades, continued to prevent me from surrendering my philosophical pride. My eclectic gleaning of the "best that philosophy, religion, and science had to offer" had done nothing to heal my wounded life. I clung tenaciously to my intellectual house of cards.

---

11. Charles F. Deems, *The Light of the Nations* (New York: Gay Brothers & Co., 1884?).

Conversion came providentially through close encounters of the third kind with Christians. Though I had no conscious interest in interacting with such people — and up to this point I had no significant contact with Christians during my entire adult life — in the space of this one year, I became the focus in a "harmonic convergence" of no less than eight primary Christian contacts. They came from a variety of denominations and walks of life, all living in a secular part of the country (New England). Lebanese, Puerto Rican, and Anglo; inner city and rural; Protestant and Catholic — they all brought their own personal perspective on the Christian faith. Yes, still human, yet all having a deep spiritual impact upon my life. As my relationship with the drug culture began to inexplicably collapse, God brought these people into my life and gave them the grace to love me in the midst of my own humanity. As mentioned, I met the first of these "gospel witnesses" at an obviously non-Christian gathering.

I also became friends with a born-again Christian woman who I tried to pick up. A co-worker at one of my jobs also had a Christian background. Surprisingly, the fossil dealer I met earlier worked at my second place of employment. Musicians at an open talent night in a bar/club shared their faith and friendship with me. These encounters all snowballed into a conglomerate of Christian acquaintances and friends. Somehow, devoid of any conscious intent, my entire peer group was miraculously transformed from New-Age-believing, drug-ingesting aficionados to professing and practicing Christians. Through the influence of their personal testimonies, and the personal testimonies of the Bible writers, I made a conscious decision to surrender my life to Jesus Christ in December of 1983.

My first real encounter with creationism occurred not long afterward. I reveled in material from the Institute for Creation Research like Howard Carter in King Tut's tomb. What a treasure trove of unearthed truths! My lifelong interest in science now entered a thoroughly new phase. No longer was my knowledge limited to the materialistic biases of scientists seeking to deny God. Every day brought new revelations of how the puzzle pieces of science and nature fit perfectly into the larger biblical picture. Little did I know at the time that I would eventually teach creation science to convicted felons in a state prison system — a privilege that public school teachers do not enjoy.

I developed an implicit trust in the Bible through an open investigation of its claims. This unique revelation is among all the world's sacred scriptures — the one objective standard of religious experience. Numerous prophetic passages, like Isaiah 53, confirmed in the Dead Sea Scrolls and outlining in detail the passion of Christ nearly 700 years before its occurrence have no parallel in any other faith. Its profound influence in my own personal healing and progress in life is without comparison.

I found the Bible to be in many ways like the incarnation of Christ — the union of God and man in an earthly form. Written by imperfect prophets in imperfect human language; conveyed by imperfect scribes and imperfect human translators — yet still God-breathed. Like the burning bush, its divine fire found in humble wooden pages. The Bible's critics crucify its humanity but cannot kill its divine, life-saving power.

My search for truth met its end in a personal encounter with the One who called himself the truth. I found that truth has its ultimate source in the Creator of all things. In the famous words of the Declaration of Independence, "We hold these truths to be self evident. All men were created. . . ." All of creation is a declaration of a Creator. The hundreds of volumes of information downloaded into every cell of our being proclaim a master programmer. The 120 trillion connections in the hard drive of our brain cry out that there must be an Architect behind this supercomputer to end all supercomputers. Far more compelling than broken "choppers" in the Olduvai Gorge, or prime numbers on a SETI (Search for Extraterrestrial Intelligence) screen — life itself is the ultimate argument for design.

The Bible is very clear that the Creator of the universe (Jesus Christ) — the source of all personality, a super-personal Creator and Redeemer — became a man and offered himself as an infinite sacrifice and substitution for every inhabitant of a world gone bad. We are not the product of some amorphous, cosmic nebulosity, "merely indifferent to the concerns of such creatures as we."[12]

Paradoxically, the scientific method also helped me to arrive at these faith-filled conclusions. In the words of the psychiatrist M. Scott Peck, "Science is an anti-narcissistic phenomenon. It assumes a profound human tendency to self deception, employs the scientific method

12. Sagan, *Cosmos*.

to counteract it, and holds truth higher than any personal desire."[13] If only Carl Sagan had taken his own advice, "All assumptions must be critically examined. Arguments from authority are worthless. Whatever is inconsistent with the facts, no matter how fond of it we are, must be discarded and revised. We have learned to value careful observations. We must respect the facts, even when they are disquieting; when they seem to contradict conventional wisdom."[14]

Though the scientific community praises such self-effacing objectivity, the truth is that none of us is fully capable of exercising such an unbiased approach to life. We all bring a priori assumptions to any investigation. If our presuppositions are steeped in an anthropocentric, rather than theocentric, philosophy, our search for truth will be in vain. Without the utter surrender of creature to Creator made possible by divine intervention, without the master programmer counteracting the selfishly biased sin-virus of self-deception in our minds — truth will always remain elusive. Only through such a supernatural self-denial can the scales fall from our self-centered eyes, allowing the light of truth to illuminate the revelation of nature and Scripture. Every aspect of creation will then become a marvelous hummingbird, providentially sent for our enjoyment and "scientific" observation.

> He has delivered us from the power of darkness and conveyed us into the kingdom of the Son of His love, in whom we have redemption through His blood, the forgiveness of sins. He is the image of the invisible God, the firstborn over all creation. For by Him all things were created that are in heaven and that are on earth, visible and invisible, whether thrones or dominions or principalities or powers. All things were created through Him and for Him. And He is before all things, and in Him all things consist. And He is the head of the body, the church, who is the beginning, the firstborn from the dead, that in all things He may have the preeminence (Col. 1:13–18; NKJV).

---

13. M. Scott Peck, *People of the Lie* (New York: Touchstone, 1983), p. 208–209.
14. Sagan, *Cosmos*.

My Cup Continually Overflows

Chapter 28
Dr. John Doughty

In 2004, I went to my 50th high school class reunion. There I was dramatically confronted with the effects of the second law of thermodynamics for open systems — everyone there showed the effects of aging. As a senior in high school, we were taught that the earth was 3 billion years old, yet there I was 50 years later and the earth had aged by 1.56 billion years! It would seem that geologic clocks and human clocks run at different speeds.

I was raised in a nominal Christian home. My father had left the church before I was born over an argument with the pastor about being re-baptized. My mother recognized the need for Christianity in life and saw to it that my sister and I were baptized and confirmed. At my baptism at the age of seven, I expected some sort of a "God" moment when the minister sprinkled me, but nothing happened — no inner voice, no feelings of joy. I simply got a little wet on my head. I was very disappointed. At the age of 14, I attended confirmation class with a group of other teenagers. I was a bright young boy, and I was good at taking tests. Confirmation was easy; just say the right words and you are in! All I had was head knowledge.

I finished high school and went to the University of New Mexico for my bachelor's degree in mechanical engineering. I was then commissioned in the USAF, who sent me to graduate school at the University of Arizona. In graduate school back in the 1960s, one particular lecture in advanced thermodynamics stuck in my mind. The professor, Dr. Rogers, gave the class the following scenario: You are given all the raw materials to make a Cadillac. You place them inside a protective hemisphere. The hemisphere is filled with a nonreactive noble gas. A shaft is allowed to penetrate the hemisphere to provide mechanical energy. While the hemisphere can exchange heat with its surroundings, the interior remains at essentially a constant temperature. Dr. Rogers then asked the class, "How long will it take for the materials to assemble themselves into a Cadillac?" That was a clever way of asking the question — given enough time and chance, will an ordered state arise on its own? Almost in unison we cried out, "It will never happen!" Dr. Rogers replied strongly, "Give me a scientific reason why you say that it won't happen!" It was quiet for a moment and then several of us said, "It violates the second law, sir." However, at the time I didn't connect the thought problem with the need for a designer, a comprehensive plan, and the right form of energy at the right time, the right amount, and the right place to be able to build that Cadillac. That came much later.

As a young mechanical engineer, I wasn't interested in evolution. The history that I was interested in only went back two hundred years (Carnot, Kelvin, Maxwell, etc.). My friends and colleagues didn't talk about evolution. It appeared on the periphery via dinosaur models for my boys and reading the *National Geographic*. I considered the Leakey discoveries very boring. Digging up old bones was totally the opposite of making new things like rocket engines and chemical lasers. Who cares about the past? Let us press forward into space and the future!

In 1967, I started my PhD program under an air force scholarship. We had to take a foreign language, so I selected French since I was almost fluent in Spanish. Near the end of the course, I happened upon a book in the university library titled (translated) *The Theory of Heat* written in 1877. The author tried to explain the source of fuel for the sun, noting that calculations had shown that hydrogen-oxygen combustion was an insufficient answer because the sun would have burned out eons ago. So he adopted Newton's earlier hypothesis that meteorites fueled it. *Not bad*, I thought to myself. That is a pretty good model considering that the author knew nothing of nuclear processes at that time. This little supposed "rabbit trail" in my French training would be valuable later.

I finished my graduate work in 1970 and moved to Albuquerque to work on chemical lasers at what is now called the Air Force Research Laboratory. It was quite an intellectual privilege to be in the original chemical laser group: we were on the cutting edge of technology. What more could a newly minted PhD ask for?

In 1974, a younger officer had the audacity to ask me if I was a Christian. From my rather pompous response, he knew that I wasn't. Later, he told me that he had put my name before a prayer group that he attended. At the same time, my car-pool friend knew that my wife, Jeanette, and I were only churchgoers. (We were in a socially oriented mainline denomination church.) He and his wife invited my wife and I to a midweek short course on biblical principles and the family. We recognized the need for help, and so we went. As it turned out, the teacher, Dr. Ken Touryan, was a man that I knew professionally, another PhD in mechanical engineering.

At the end of the course, there was social time. My wife commented that we really needed to talk more with Ken about some difficulties we were having with one of our children. I replied huffily, "If God wants us to do that, He will have to arrange it!" About 30 seconds later, Ken came over to us from across the noisy room and said, "I believe the Lord wants us to get together." I was mentally knocked over with a spiritual two-by-four! My wife gave me a look that meant, "What do you do now?" A week later, Ken and his wife, Cheryl, came to our home.

As Cheryl was talking to my wife, Ken asked me, "What happens if you violate one or more of the physical laws?"

I replied, "You can't, that's why they are laws!"

He said, "No, no, what happens if you violate a physical law?"

I answered, "Oh, I see what you mean. You throw the system out of equilibrium and it eventually returns to its equilibrium state."

Then Ken lowered the boom by asking, "And what happens if you violate God's laws?"

I was speechless. He then quoted John 5:24, "I tell you the truth, whoever hears my word and believes him who sent me has eternal life and will not be condemned" (NIV).

I told Ken that I liked the idea of not being condemned because I knew that I was guilty of many violations of God's law, but I didn't become a Christian at that time. However, Jeanette did when she was told that God would accept her just as she was. She didn't have to work up to a level of goodness to be able to approach God. Isaiah 1:18 became very real to her, " 'Come now, let us reason together,' says the LORD. 'Though your sins are like scarlet, they shall be as white as snow; though they are red as crimson, they shall be like wool'" (NIV). Jeanette was sitting there radiating. She had just been saved, trusting in Jesus and His atoning work on the cross.

Some time later, Jeanette attempted to talk to me about salvation, but I put up a barrier that lasted four months. I finally was saved one morning in a motel room while on a business trip after reading two questions. The first was "If I was to die in the next few moments, was I sure that I would go to heaven?" I thought that I would. However, the next question I answered wrong. The question was "How would I answer God, the Father, if He should ask me 'Why should He let me into His heaven.'" I thought, *I've done more good than bad.* When I saw that the answer is Jesus and His atoning death on the cross for me, I repented and asked Jesus to come into my life and take it over. When I returned home that evening, I told Jeanette what happened and she replied, "Oh! Hallelujah! Now we can really talk to each other!"

Upon becoming a Christian, I noticed that I had a strong desire to read the Bible from cover to cover. The Bible clearly was (and is) a book revealing truth. My wife and I had many, many discussions about what I was reading. Those discussions brought us closer together as a married couple. I found that Jesus was a very different type of "macho" man than what the world was popularizing. I lost a significant portion of my vocabulary. I was (and still am) fascinated by the accounts of miracles found throughout the Bible. God feeding and watering about 2 million people for years in the Sinai became even more profound when I actually visited the area in 1983. The orderliness of things that I observed in the physical realm began to make a lot more sense, and I began looking for it more intensively in my own areas of technical expertise.

The next book that I read was the *Battle for the Bible*[1] by Harold Lindsell. Through reading that book, I saw the necessity to hold to the Bible itself and much less to interpretations by liberal theologians. I became a proponent of inerrancy and began to examine some of the so-called myths in the Bible. Genesis became very intriguing, especially the account of the Flood. I noticed that the events were given like I would enter information into a logbook. It had all the hallmarks of a factual narrative. However, even though I had become a Christian, I

---

1. Harold Lindsell, *The Battle for the Bible* (Grand Rapids, MI: Zondervan Pub. House, c1976).

PERSUADED BY THE EVIDENCE

was still dragging along a lot of baggage, such as evolution, from my pre-Christian life. I wondered, *How can I fit evolution into the Bible?* I did go on a detour for a short time when I joined the American Scientific Affiliation (an organization of Christians in science). Their journal was interesting, but somehow the old-earth, theistic evolutionary stance didn't fit well with what I was reading in the Bible. I recalled my previous excursion into the French book *The Theory of Heat*, and thought perhaps the American Scientific Affiliation had a reasonable creation model, but just didn't have enough scientific support yet.

One day, a statement in the local newspaper got my attention. The writer, an evolutionist, stated that the laser takes particles that are moving at random and brings them into a coherent beam of light — order from chaos. To the uninformed, such a statement sounds reasonable, but it is a violation of the second law of thermodynamics. The second law can be stated as follows: The disordered state is more probable than one of complete order. My gas laser research used the scientific laws and theories of quantum physics and chemistry, spectroscopy, optics, fluid dynamics, thermodynamics, and heat transfer, plus a lot of structural engineering in building the laser device and its supporting hardware.

I knew that laser action is produced by a nonequilibrium event, the excitation of an atom or molecule from its usual state. When the atom or molecule returns to its normal state (often referred to as the ground state), the desired photon is normally emitted. If a population inversion (full or partial) can be created inside an optical resonator, stimulated emission will result, but only by very careful design! Is the laser then an example of order coming out of chaos? Most emphatically *no*! Is there chaos? No. A highly ordered nonequilibrium state is produced using the rules of quantum physics and chemistry in a well-engineered device. I started to turn away from Darwinism based on what I knew for a fact from my own work. I began to be like a Berean when it came to evolutionary claims and studied to see if their claims were true.

I remembered that Louis Pasteur had shown that life comes only from life, so how could a living cell evolve from goo by natural forces? Then, being involved in laser optics, I recalled that Pasteur had also noted that molecules from living systems all had the same chirality in molecular structure. As was later shown, all living systems have left-handed optical orientation amino acids (except glycine) from which we humans are constructed. How, then, can a cell be constructed from a racemized mix of amino acids found naturally plus the requisite enzymes, etc.? When I learned that the probability of doing such was effectively zero (to an engineer anything with a chance less than one out of a million is zero), I had yet another reason to look for something better than evolutionism.

When I read in Job 38 where God questioned Job about celestial mechanics, one of the courses I had in grad school, I was amazed. Job 38:31–33 says, "Can you bind the beautiful Pleiades? Can you loose the cords of Orion? Can you bring forth the constellations in their seasons or lead out the Bear with its cubs? Do you know the laws of the heavens?" (NIV). Pleiades is indeed a gravitationally bound constellation whereas Orion is not. The zodiacal constellations appear in a regular, orderly, monthly fashion and Polaris leads around Ursa Major and Minor. Job is one of the oldest books in the Bible. No one but God could have caused such a statement to be written so long ago.

After much more study, my view of inerrancy was strengthened even more. Biblical truth seemed to be spread across a variety of scientific disciplines. Why, then, was evolutionism so strongly held? One answer was that the education establishment had bought into it. That came home very strongly when one of our sons came home with an *F* on an essay written for an astronomy class. He happened to quote a Scripture at the end of the essay. Below a big red *F* on the page was a note from the teacher that said, "The Bible is not true and cannot be used to support any points in modern science and thought." Wow!

In 1976, I read *Scientific Creationism* by Dr. Henry Morris.[2] When I came to the section on thermodynamics, I recalled my graduate thermodynamics class with Dr. Rogers and suddenly things started making a whole lot of sense. I concluded that, even with all my education, I had been cheated. I had never heard or read that there was any other scientific option to evolution. It wasn't mentioned at work or at church other than the theistic evolutionary-based gap theory. By now, the reading of the Bible plus the *Battle for the Bible* and *Scientific Creationism* converged and merged in my mind and spirit. I became a committed young-earth creationist.

---

2. Henry M. Morris, *Scientific Creationism* (Green Forest, AR: Master Books, 1985).

Were all my questions answered? No. However, my position had changed because of the previously noted factors where, if there wasn't a satisfactory scientific answer, I was content to reason, "Not all the data are in yet." Darwin himself said that his theory rested upon the discovery of millions of transitional forms that he presumed existed in the fossil record. *National Geographic* has beautiful photography, but their data (or the lack thereof) simply doesn't stand up to scrutiny.

When I taught a second semester thermodynamics course as an adjunct professor at a local university, I discovered something in the Maxwell Relations that I had missed before in my studies. Basically, for one gram of "stuff," the thermodynamic properties can be fully described by just three things — the trinity of pressure, volume, and temperature. When I commented to the class about the mathematical beauty of what I put on the blackboard, I was met with either the usual glazed eyes or looks of disbelief on the order of "How can you find anything at all beautiful in mathematical formulations?" However, there it was on two blackboards for all to see. Only one student appreciated what I had done (and I learned later that he was a Christian).

When I attended the ICR Summer Institute in 1979, the whole class had questions. The main one was, "How do you explain the long distances to the stars and the young age of the earth?" Drs. Morris and Slusher gave us five possible theories, but they admitted that there was a lot more to be learned. That question now has a much better answer (the best I've seen to date) in Dr. Russ Humphreys's book, *Starlight & Time*[3] and Dr. John Hartnett's (and co-author Alex Williams) book, *Dismantling the Big Bang*.[4]

Now, with the exciting new developments that have come forth from the RATE (**R**adioisotopes and the **A**ge of **T**he **E**arth) project, it is spiritually and intellectually satisfying (and fun) to be involved in the search for scientific truth. My own foray into the world of geochemistry and isotopic analysis has been, and is now, both the most challenging and rewarding work in my 40 years of scientific research.

3. H. Russell Humphreys, *Starlight & Time* (Green Forest, AR: Master Books, 1994).
4. John Hartnett and Alex Williams, *Dismantling the Big Bang* (Green Forest, AR: Master Books, 2005).

A Flood of Evidence

→ **Chapter 29**
Dr. Walt Brown

BIOGRAPHY BY DAVID COPPEDGE

Dr. Walter T. Brown received a PhD in mechanical engineering from MIT (Massachusetts Institute of Technology) while in the military. His career in the army and air force began at West Point and included service as a paratrooper and ranger, directing a 450-person research and development laboratory, teaching mathematics at the Air Force Academy, and teaching science and technology at the Air War College. He is the founder and director of the Center for Scientific Creation, based in Phoenix, Arizona. His story is included in the book Christian Men of Science: Eleven Men Who Changed the World[1] *by George Mulfinger and Julia Mulfinger Orozco, along with those of Kepler, Faraday, Maxwell, Henry Morris, and other Bible-believing scientists.*

Walt Brown received Christ as a teenager, but like many Christians, accepted evolution simply because it permeated secular and educated society. To harmonize evolution with the Bible, he assumed (like many others) that evolution was merely God's way of creating. One day, Walt heard claims that Noah's ark might be on Mount Ararat in Turkey. That piqued his curiosity; was it possible the Genesis flood really was a worldwide event, not just a legend? If so, where did the water come from? Where did it go? Through long and careful study, Walt learned that the scientific evidence for creation and the Flood was overwhelming.

---

1. George Mulfinger and Julia Mulfinger Orozco, *Christian Men of Science: Eleven Men Who Changed the World* (Greenville, SC: Ambassador Emerald International, 2001).

He also began to conclude that the Genesis flood explained most of the characteristics of the earth, including the fossil record that he had earlier supposed supported evolution. Creation science became the passion of his life.

In 1980, after a successful military career, including a year in Vietnam, Walt retired as a full colonel in the air force so he could spend all of his time in creation science research, writing, and teaching. For two years, Walt served as the director of ICR Midwest Center in Chicago. Then, under the direction of his board of directors, the Center for Scientific Creation (CSC) was formed as an independent not-for-profit organization. Though all of creation science interests him, Walt's focus is on scientific arguments for creation and the worldwide flood. Having taught college-level mathematics and physics and leading a major research and development laboratory were all helpful, as were his experiences in scientific research and engineering. To these subjects, he added intense study in geology, biology, and astronomy.

Walt's creation science work began with a great deal of speaking and travel as well as writing. He developed a set of presentations for CSC that could be held on one or two days, called the "In the Beginning Seminars." Before long, he was traveling around the country with a van full of sound and projection equipment. The seven-hour seminar was sometimes followed by a debate, if the local sponsors could find a qualified evolutionist. These seminars were almost always well attended. They usually ended with long and lively question-answer sessions. Most audiences rated the seminars as "a very worthwhile experience" by overwhelming margins.

For more than 20 years, he traveled around the United States and Canada giving seminars. During that time, Walt and his family moved from Chicago to Phoenix, Arizona. There he studied geology at Arizona State University, including private, weekly sessions with Dr. Robert Dietz, a world-renowned geologist. Walt also took a number of trips in and around the Grand Canyon and all over the Colorado Plateau to investigate various aspects of his Flood model. One expedition nearly cost his life. Exploring alone in the Grand Canyon, he became trapped and dehydrated in a box canyon. Due back in one week for the wedding of one of his daughters, he garnered his remaining strength. With sheer grit and determination (and prayer), he managed to swing a 50-foot rope over an overhanging rock and pull himself out. Once safely home with a tale of adventure, his wife was quick to make him promise to never hike alone again.

Walt's research is encapsulated in a book that has gone through multiple revisions and expansions since its fledgling edition: *In the Beginning: Compelling Evidence for Creation and the Flood*.[2] Readers say it is one of the finest comprehensive books on creation science they have found, in both in content and presentation. The encyclopedic 8" x 11" volume, fully indexed and footnoted and profusely illustrated, begins with 135 categories of evidence that support creation and oppose evolution. These include evidences from the biosphere (life sciences), above the biosphere (astronomical and physical sciences), and below the biosphere (earth sciences). Part II discusses the Flood in detail, and Part III provides answers to 30 frequently asked questions about science and the Bible. Readers state that it is the kind of book that once you start leafing through, it's hard to set down. This is partly due to its hundreds of color illustrations and charts that Walt has gathered and developed over the years with the help of a skilled graphic artist. He has also placed the entire book on CSC's website, www.creationscience.com.

Whenever attempting to explain a phenomenon, whether frozen mammoths, the origin of comets, or the death of the dinosaurs, Walt likes to begin by giving a fair and balanced survey of all the leading explanations. After giving an overview and history of the phenomenon, he lists the details needing to be explained and the best explanations put forth by experts, including each theory's predictions of what should be expected if that position is true. Then, Walt systematically evaluates each theory's strengths in explaining the phenomenon and compares them in a table. (Readers are invited to do the same.) Walt tries to be honest in mentioning any weaknesses of his own theory, admitting openly when he feels there is a difficulty requiring more research. Walt has retracted arguments openly if they later proved unsupportable.

The most-developed and original part of the book (Part II), and the most popular subject in his seminars, concerns the Flood and the hydroplate theory. When Walt was an evolutionist, among the hindrances to his acceptance of the Genesis global flood were two questions: Where did

2. Walt Brown, *In the Beginning: Compelling Evidence for Creation and the Flood* (Phoenix, AZ: Center for Scientific Creation, 1995).

the water come from, and where did it go? For years, Walt studied many disciplines as he pondered these questions. The result was a global model of the Flood, faithful to the biblical record, involving physics, math, geology, biology, and astronomy, which Walt believes convincingly answers these two questions. As a bonus, the hydroplate theory explains 24 other geological mysteries around the world that have puzzled geologists since they were discovered. These include submarine canyons, seamounts, salt domes, mid-oceanic ridges, the Ice Age, the origin of comets and asteroids, the fit of the continents to each other, the Grand Canyon, frozen mammoths, and much more.

An insight for Walt came from studying the Bible's description of the "fountains of the great deep," which burst forth on one day at the onset of the Flood, according to Genesis 7:11 (KJV). The location of these fountains, Walt proposed, corresponded to the mid-oceanic ridges that wrap around the earth like the seam of a baseball. Further study showed that all the effects of the Flood, including the rapid drifting of the continents, fell into place from this catastrophic rupture in the earth's crust. The success of this theory in explaining so many disparate phenomena has impressed even some evolutionary geologists. As a result, Walt has become friends with several leading secular geologists. Walt's confidence in the hydroplate theory has been strengthened as other geologists attempt to refute the theory.

Not all creationists accept every aspect of the hydroplate theory, but the theory has one thing going for it that is often lacking in creation models: It includes predictions that allow it to be falsifiable. A number of predictions Walt made in the 1980s have since been confirmed. The hydroplate theory shows the power of offering testable scientific models instead of merely criticizing evolutionary ones. Hopefully, Walt's efforts will inspire young scientists to follow this pattern of creation research.

Walt was also the first to propose a radical new model for the origin of the Grand Canyon, one that has since become the favored model of other creationists. This is the idea that the Grand Canyon was formed from a specific dam breach in a large post-Flood lake that he identified via a number of techniques. When the floodwaters receded, continental basins were filled with water. A breach in the rim of such a post-Flood lake would produce a catastrophic outflow, quickly dumping the entire body of water. Walt has traveled throughout the Colorado

Plateau for years looking at the evidence of a large lake, which he calls Grand Lake. This huge, ancient lake in Utah and parts of Arizona, Colorado, and New Mexico, supported a volume of water exceeding the capacity of all the Great Lakes combined. He has also found what he believes is the breach point where the lake catastrophically dumped to the west, sweeping away thousands of feet of sediments and then rapidly down-cutting into the soft sediments laid down during the Flood. This represents a remarkable shift in thinking about this natural wonder, long considered an icon of uniformitarianism (that is, millions of years of slow, gradual processes).

In the Beginning is on ongoing project. The eighth edition will be published in 2008. Each revision contains new material from Walt's research. In addition, the hydroplate theory continues to mature as more facts come to light. Many readers have found *In the Beginning* a valuable resource, and quite a few have ordered multiple copies to use in pre-evangelism with friends and co-workers. A number of persons have come to Christ by seeing the scientific case for creation presented in detail, breaking down some of their major objections to taking the Bible seriously. Needless to say, such evidences also strengthen the faith of all Christians exposed to evolutionary arguments in college and society.

In 1979, Walt attended a creation symposium in Anaheim, California, where dozens of prominent creationists gave presentations on various aspects of creation science. At this time, Walt was formulating plans for his seminars. On the last day of the symposium, Walt saw, and was very impressed by, a multimedia presentation called *How Big Is God?* It was an audiovisual journey from earth to the farthest ends of the universe, presented with three projectors and more than 700 color slides, all computer-synchronized with narration and music. The gospel, which was presented in the context of the vastness of the universe, brought tears to Walt's eyes. (I had just produced this show, and subsequently took it on the road for 25 years, where more than 300 audiences saw it.) Walt felt this visually rich and thought-provoking program could provide an inspirational aspect to his seminars, bringing the hours of scientific material back to a gospel focus. Walt contacted me to see if he could get a copy of it, and we worked together to make it a reality. I duplicated all the media and helped Walt obtain the needed equipment and learn how to operate it. He always used *How Big Is God?* as the grand finale for his seminars. It was often voted the second most popular presentation after the lecture on the hydroplate theory.

In his book and in his seminars, Walt has made a standing offer to evolutionists. He invites a qualified evolutionist to join him in a written, strictly scientific debate on the scientific case for creation versus evolution. The debate must be restricted to scientific evidence alone — no religious arguments are allowed. Each side would have the opportunity to read the other's arguments and respond with a written rebuttal. All the results would be published. Walt is convinced that a written debate would be superior to the usual live debate format, because it could be more widely disseminated and carefully studied, and each side would have more time to carefully respond in rebuttals. For more than 25 years no one has taken Walt up on his debate challenge. Walt is convinced that any evolutionist restricting himself to strictly scientific evidence would be at a profound disadvantage. Most Darwinists attack creation on religious grounds, ruling it outside of science a priori. They have rarely had to defend evolutionism on the scientific evidence alone.

Walt thanks God for his family, which now includes 4 grown children, their spouses, and 14 grandchildren. He also is grateful for the many opportunities the Lord has given him and the wonderful people he has come in contact with during all these many years of creation science work.

Creation, Science, and Rewards

Chapter 30
Dr. Raymond Damadian

MRI is a household acronym these days; everybody knows somebody who has had one (if not themselves) to help reach a diagnosis for a disease. But in the 1970s, being able to produce a noninvasive image inside a body would have seemed like a device out of *Star Trek*. To see inside a living body in fine detail, without the harm of x-rays, was then one doctor's impossible dream; today it is a reality, thanks to Magnetic Resonance Imaging (MRI). And MRI is even going to revolutionize the operating room.

A biophysicist by training, I took a relatively new discovery in physics called nuclear magnetic resonance (NMR) and applied it to biology. The record is clear: I was the first to document my research on the effects of NMR on biological tissue, and the first to produce a working MRI scanner for medical applications. But recognition of priority for my invention, and being able to capitalize on it, was to prove an uphill battle against doubters and patent thieves. The three stages of the reaction by outsiders to a new invention are, (1) *it is impossible*, (2) *it is possible but impractical*, and (3) *it was not your idea*. I experienced all three. After years of legal hassles and near loss of my livelihood, I was vindicated in court — but denied recognition by the Nobel Prize committee.

Some have likened my case to a Hollywood David-and-Goliath script. It's the common story of the lone entrepreneur against the giant corporations, the optimist with a vision against the skeptics in the establishment. Physicists had been using NMR, first reported in 1938, to study various materials, but I reasoned that hydrogen (in water) within the cells of living tissue might prove responsive to NMR, allowing imaging of water variations (thus, tissue differences). Moreover, I proposed that cancerous tumors or other pathology might respond differently than healthy tissue. Working on borrowed time, I experimented on mice in a makeshift lab and gained confidence that my hunch was right. I published a seminal paper in *Science* in 1971 on these preliminary findings, and then applied for a patent and attempted to obtain a research grant to build a prototype of the invention I had in mind: a device that would flood a human torso with high-energy magnetism and then receive radio emissions from water in body tissues. I included a sketch of such of a device in my published paper. But my academic colleagues said it couldn't be done, because I would have to spin the patient at 10,000 rpm to make it work! Physicists laughed at the idea and the National Institutes of Health refused my request for grants.

Undaunted, I appealed directly to President Nixon, who in 1971 had just declared war on cancer. This resulted in a modest grant, but I soon found myself in a race to produce a working scanner after finding out that others were beginning to infringe on my patents. *Scientific American* wrote, "Damadian pushed himself and his students relentlessly and found private backers to keep research going on a shoestring budget." Finally, in 1977, I was ready to step into the contraption that my graduate students and I had built, which I named "Indomitable." It must have looked like a scene from Frankenstein.

I demonstrated on my own body that the intense magnetic fields did not produce any harm to the human body, but the machine was too small for me. I persuaded a thinner graduate student to agree to be the guinea pig. It worked — we succeeded in getting the first NMR image of a human torso. The press leaped on the story, giving the project some notoriety, but since the image was imprecise (it showed the heart, lungs, and chest, but with low resolution), I could not find venture capital willing to support a larger effort. Convinced that my invention could scan a human body for disease, I decided to go it alone. With a small group of friends and supporters, I started Fonar Corporation to design and build Magnetic Resonance Imaging (MRI) scanners. Others soon realized the importance of my work, and I soon found myself in competition with major corporations, including General Electric, Toshiba, Siemens, and other corporate giants wanting to capitalize on my discovery.

They nearly robbed me of my invention (and I learned firsthand about corporate greed and corruption). Though my patent was legally binding, I had to spend millions of dollars defending it. In 1982, a jury trial vindicated me against international corporations that were manufacturing scanners overseas, but one judge single-handedly reversed their verdict. After years of legal wrangling, Fonar Corporation was eventually awarded more than $128 million in damages (all of the proceeds went to research and development). Unfortunately, much of the profits from my work are going to overseas manufacturers — those who were never involved in the invention. I found that my case was not unique, and became a passionate advocate for lone inventors competing against corporate giants. I lobbied Congress for protection of patents from infringement and warned against the consequences of weakening the patent laws.

In 1988, I was awarded the National Medal of Technology, the nation's highest award for applied science. The following year I was enrolled in the Inventor's Hall of Fame, in company with Thomas Edison, Samuel F.B. Morse, and the Wright Brothers, and many other famous inventors. Today, my prototype scanner "Indomitable" resides in the Smithsonian alongside the first electric lightbulb and the first airplane.

Needless to say, Magnetic Resonance Imaging has swept the medical world. After years of embellishments and refinements by Fonar Corporation and others, thousands of MRI scanners are in daily use around the globe, detecting not only tumors but also many other diseases and ailments. MRI routinely diagnoses bone and ligament injuries with much higher resolution than other imaging technologies, and without the radiation damage of x-rays. Fonar remains a leader in MRI technology. Our new Open MRI scanners are less intimidating to patients and allow more freedom to position the body by the doctor, and our small units can effectively scan individual parts of the body, such as arms and hands. We have stand-up units that allow imaging in true physiological positions. As the imaging time and cost of operation drop, it is now possible to take multiple scans to evaluate the full range of motion of an arm or neck and thereby detect abnormalities previously missed by single scans. Our newest invention takes *Star Trek* to the next generation: a whole operating room MRI. Soon it will be commonplace for an entire surgical team to surround the operating table, unaffected by the intense magnetic field that is being applied to the patient. A projected 3D image will allow the doctors to pinpoint the tumor precisely in real time, giving surgeons unprecedented accuracy in delivering curative agents to the tumor without damaging surrounding tissue.

I again feel, however, a little like I did at the beginning of my work when I could not find backers for the idea. So far, very few hospitals have been willing to test the operating room MRI that is just now coming on the market, but I am confident that they will see the clear advantages to this technology. Since MRI is much safer than chemotherapy and radiation, with their destructive side effects, we can look forward to a day when millions of lives may be saved by this expansion of MRI technology.

Does creation play a part in my philosophy of science? No, it does not play a *part*; it plays the lead role. My greatest single scientific discovery was not a machine or a physical principle. To me, the highest purpose a man can find for life is to serve the will of God. That is what motivates my work as a scientist: exploring and applying the laws of nature and of nature's God for the benefit of mankind.

I am convinced that the Bible is the reason for the advancement of science and the blessings of Western civilization. I feel our country is in great peril if we do not return to biblical principles, including the foundational doctrine of creation. This is a vitally important message for America today. I told *Creation* magazine in 1994 that acceptance of the unqualified Word of God "has been the foundation for Western civilization since the printing of the Gutenberg Bible in the fifteenth century." The Christian worldview has brought centuries of blessing in all aspects of society. But that blessing is now imperiled by greed for the almighty dollar and the widespread teaching of Darwinism. When the spiritual batteries of a country are drained, its bank accounts will become empty. Those batteries are being severely drained by evolutionary thinking. Americans need to wake up to the fact that there is a "Battle for the Beginning," as John MacArthur called it, a cultural clash over our understanding of our origin and purpose for life. The evidence for creation and against neo-Darwinism is overwhelming. Pastors need to learn this evidence and preach it in their churches. The battle for the beginning is not solely the property of the scientists; if America is to be rescued, she must be rescued from the pulpit.

I personally experienced the cost of maintaining a creationist position in a dogmatically evolutionist scientific community. I believe it cost me the Nobel Prize. The record is clear: I had priority on discovering the NMR signal in pathological biological tissue (the discovery that makes MRI possible), was the first to publish this discovery and mention its potential for medical imaging, and I was the first to make a working MRI scanner and produce the first scan on a human body. Historians have called me "the Father of MRI" — but the Nobel Prize for Physiology or Medicine in 2003 for MRI went to two physicists who learned about my discovery from *Science* and made important refinements to the imaging process.

This was to me an outrage and severe disappointment. The committee did not even have the courtesy to mention my contributions in their press release about the award. My company published full-page ads denouncing the unfairness of the decision signed by many eminent scientists and historians, but the protests got nowhere. The rules allow for three winners to share in the prize, but they would not even grant that. Even some evolutionists were surprised and alarmed at the rebuff given me by the Nobel committee.

Although the Nobel committee's deliberations are secret, and will remain so till all the parties involved are long gone, several commentators, including pro-evolution secular sources, have speculated that the committee didn't want their prestigious award to go to an outspoken creationist. This is one of the many outrages in our post-Christian world. Creationism has become so politically incorrect as to disqualify exceptional scientific achievement if the scientist or inventor does not pay homage to Darwinism. It may be the reason that Fritz Schaefer also, though the leader in his field of computational quantum mechanics, has not been awarded the Nobel Prize, even though he has been nominated five times so far.

Unfair and disappointing as it was to me to be passed up by the Nobel judges, I know the more valuable earthly reward is to see millions of lives helped by MRI. And that's just the beginning. Through faith in Christ Jesus, we are promised an inheritance that is incorruptible, undefiled, and will not fade away (2 Pet. 1:4; NKJV), reserved for us in heaven. The epitome of my satisfaction will not be just to be vindicated personally, but to see Jesus Christ glorified, and His will done on earth as it is in heaven. That, to me, is worth more than any temporal reward or fame.

An Evolutionist Becomes a Creationist Parasitologist

Chapter 31
Frank Sherwin

It was in the navy after a year of college that I put my life in proper perspective. In boot camp during Christmas, I read Luke 1 and 2 from the New Testament given to inductees after the swearing-in ceremony in Denver. A year later, I was working on the flight deck of an aircraft carrier as a plane captain. During my first Vietnam tour, I signed up for a Bible study with the Navigators. At this time, a member of my squadron shared his faith with me. I was ready to listen and received Christ during a Sunday service in the ship's chapel while we were docked in the Philippine Islands. I was saved (Rom. 10:9), but was still an evolutionist out of ignorance — I did not know the rest of the scientific story. During my third Vietnam tour I worked in the ship's jet engine repair shop. There I came across a booklet titled *Have You Been Brainwashed?* by biochemist Duane Gish.[1] Reading through it, I was amazed at the scientific data in favor of creation and contrary to Darwinism. After more study, I soon understood the critical importance of taking God at His Word, starting with the first chapters of Genesis.

After completing several college night classes on the Lemoore, California, base, I decided to major in biology following my navy enlistment. Two years later, I was in college in Colorado, fueled with a determination not to repeat my past mistakes; I graduated with a biology degree in three years and was hired in northern Colorado as an EMT/firefighter. I also enrolled in graduate school under one of the foremost parasitologists in the nation, Gerald D. Schmidt. All his graduate students were required to take a 500-level evolution course

---

1. Duane Gish, *Have You Been Brainwashed?* (South Holland, IL: The Bible League, 1986).

(which turned out to be a class in advanced genetics). Three years later, I had a master's in zoology (parasitology). Soon after that, my wife, baby daughter, and I moved to Pensacola, where I taught a variety of college biology classes (and labs) for nine years.

Many scriptural, scientific, and philosophical reasons exist why I remain a creationist. These convictions took me through my undergraduate and graduate studies in a secular college and university, and my certainty has only increased as I continue to complete biology graduate classes in San Diego.

THE FACT OF GOD

For the invisible things of him from the creation of the world are clearly seen, being understood by the things that are made, even his eternal power and Godhead; so that they are without excuse (Rom. 1:20; KJV).

Paul makes it clear in Romans 1 that the fact of God ("His eternal power") and His nature ("and godhead") are "clearly seen" by everyone — including the unbelievers.

Extraordinary claims require extraordinary evidences. The Christian worldview offers transcendental proof — proving something from the impossibility of the contrary — which is the secular worldview that cryptically states, "Everything came from nothing." There must be a *cause* for our existence (called the causal argument). Logicians and scientists constantly think in terms of cause-and-effect connections. As one trained in the sciences, I was taught the basic assumption of causality is to answer the question, "Why is there something, rather than nothing?" Indeed, why should there be anything? What are the compelling evidences and/or reasons for the existence of the universe outside of a personal Creator? Logic dictates that we can extend this causal thinking back to the origin of the universe and a great First Cause. Furthermore, when we look at the physical parameters of earth in relation to our solar system — and the edge of the Milky Way galaxy we inhabit — it is obvious there is a causal (and protective) hand involved.

The universe, with its billions of galaxies, each containing billions of stars, is far from being cold and distant. It is a harmonious revelation of God's glory: "The heavens declare the glory of God" (Ps. 19:1; KJV).

The Psalmist describes the total of God's perfections: His divine energy, magnitude, and precision. Conversely, atheism attempts to avoid the Psalmist's declaration and violates the conditions of rationality. Scientific inference and daily experience point to the God of the Scriptures, and upon examination, I found objections to biblical theology are not legitimate.

Investigating life on this unique planet shows the unmistakable mark of complexity and design according to a plan. The purposeful genetic blueprints within living systems cannot be attributed to time and random forces. Either the doyens of Darwinism are right in their secular musings, or the apostle Paul is. He stated that not only is God's living creation seen, but also it is *clearly* seen. In other words, all who care to look can see the fact that the world is plainly, unmistakably, undoubtedly, and undeniably created. From the Hubble Space Telescope that focuses on a distant wall of galaxies, to electron photomicrographs showing minuscule protein subunits of a flagella motor — God made His creation *clearly* seen.

These analytical procedures presuppose Christian evidences (moral absolutes, human dignity, and the inductive principle) and therefore, the God of the Bible. For example, former longtime atheist Anthony Flew recently described his ascent out of atheism, saying he simply "had to go where the evidence leads."[2] This led Flew to a deist position and to renounce naturalistic evolution theories.

HISTORICAL EVIDENCE AND RELIABILITY OF SCRIPTURE

All scripture is given by inspiration of God, and is profitable for doctrine, for reproof, for correction, for instruction in righteousness (2 Tim. 3:16; KJV).

The Scriptures appeal to us to use our mind to think and reason together. Such analysis gives positive results when tracing the historical reliability of the Bible. Significant numbers of ancient writings contain an amalgamation of religion, mythology, philosophy, and history. For example, the history of Abraham who lived a thousand years before Homer (author of the *Iliad*, containing a jumble of history and

---

2. Interview with Dr. Gary R. Habermas, professor of philosophy and theology, September 9, 2004.

mythology) is detailed and accurate. During Homer's time, the reliable histories of Samuel were dutifully recorded under divine inspiration.

Surviving manuscripts of the "father of history," Greek writer Herodotus, are both few and late. His writings are contemporary with Malachi and Nehemiah, the last of the Old Testament authors. The historical reliability of both the Old and New Testament has been firmly established through principles of historiography and archaeological studies, yet most intellectuals accept the writings of Herodotus, but scorn the biblical record.

Between 58 and 50 B.C., Caesar wrote his history of the Gallic Wars. Only ten manuscript copies survive today — all written ten centuries after his death. Numerous New Testament manuscript copies present clear evidence for the birth, life, death, and resurrection of the Lord Jesus. The detailed research of Dr. John A.T. Robinson forced him to conclude that virtually the entire New Testament was inscribed before the fall of Jerusalem in A.D. 70. Early papyri discoveries validate New Testament manuscripts, such as the Bodmer Papyri II, A.D. 200, and the John Ryland manuscript, A.D. 130. Why is it the agnostic will embrace the historical fact of Julius Caesar while being diffident of the One who lived in the same era — Jesus Christ? Could it be that if the agnostic acknowledges Jesus rose from the dead, as these records clearly state, then biblical miracles (i.e., creation) are possible?

Immanuel Kant (who didn't like Christianity and attempted to erect a wall between religion and science) supposedly delivered the deathblow to the design argument. Both he and Scottish agnostic David Hume allegedly discovered irrevocable flaws in the standard teleological proofs of God. But this was hardly a cause for secular rejoicing. One need only study the works of Richard Swineburne, Richard Taylor, and A.C. Ewing to realize that philosophers continue to use the robust teleological argument.

THE RELIGION OF NATURALISM

The fool hath said in his heart, There is no God (Ps 14:1; KJV).

Naturalism states that God does not exist and that *only* matter exists — that's all there is. Lynn Margulis, Dorion Sagan, and

Jessica H. Whiteside recently stated, "Evolution must be understood by extrapolation from bacteria. Bacteria are neither lower plants nor lower animals. They are not germs; they are our ultimate ancestors." Liberal seminary professor David Jobling of St. Andrew's College, University of Saskatchewan, opined, "We must find some way of facing the fact that Jesus Christ is the product of the same evolutionary process as the rest of us."[3] In contrast, Phillip Johnson concluded:

> Darwinian theory is the creation myth of our culture. It's the officially sponsored, government financed creation myth that the public is supposed to believe in, and that creates the evolutionary scientists as the priesthood. . . . So we have the priesthood of naturalism, which has great cultural authority, and of course has to protect its mystery that gives it that authority — that's why they're so vicious towards critics.[4]

The naturalists have done their work well, convincing many that the Christian worldview has no place in today's pluralistic society. Those who would challenge this need only observe the growing public intolerance of any public Christian expression of Christmas and Easter. Furthermore, they imply that the followers of Christ deserve but a footnote in history. How soon would some forget past intellectual contributions made by men and women of faith. This is certainly true when it comes to the nature of science, and the offerings by the likes of Newton, Kepler, Descartes, Boyle, Cuvier, Maxwell, and Faraday. During my graduate and undergraduate studies, I was not taught *any* of the many contributions made by known believing scientists. How refreshing it was to later read that, "In one of those strange permutations of which history yields occasional rare examples, it is the Christian world which finally gave birth in a clear, articulate fashion to the experimental method of science itself."[5]

Biology, philosophy, physics, mathematics (the "language of God"), and all other scholarly disciplines point to the Creator and His creation. The biblical worldview offers transcendental proof through

---

3. *Enquiry* (September–November 1972).
4. PBS television documentary, "In the Beginning: The Creationist Controversy," May 30–31, 1995.
5. Loren Eisley, *Darwin's Century* (New York: Anchor Books, 1961), p. 62.

the uniformity of nature and the inductive principle. Conversely, the secular worldview is centered on an irrational denial of this uniformity. In addition, naturalists cannot explain the ultimate source of *any* natural (or supernatural!) phenomena. Despite the naturalist's supposed allegiance to empirical research, their macroevolution premise fails to meet even the most basic elements of rational inquiry.

As a zoologist, I had to honestly go where the scientific evidence leads. My field was, and is, parasitology, and it is here (as in all other fields of biology) that the case for macroevolution has simply not been made (e.g., *Journal of Parasitology* 87 [6], p. 1,334). By being able to account for everything by Darwinian edict, macroevolution explains nothing. Using natural selection and random effects such as genetic drift, Darwinian naturalists maintain *any* biological existing phenomena are possible by these laws, from the subtle biochemical cascades to the myriads of ecological associations and interactions. But some evolutionists are surprisingly open about the real limits of Darwinism. Noble, Noble, Schad, and MacInnes said, "Natural selection can act only on those biologic properties that already exist [creation]; it cannot create properties in order to meet the needs of adaptation [Darwinism]."[6]

Wherever one looks, naturally produced units rich in information (complex data) are not to be found. Can natural processes produce those data-intense arrangements (e.g., DNA)? Life clearly is loaded with information that can only be attributed to an Intelligent Agent. As tired as the adage might be, it remains: design means a designer.

THE FAILURE OF NEO-DARWINISM

Ironically, one subject Darwin never discussed in his infamous book *On the Origin of Species* (1859) was the *origin* of species. He spoke much on minor variations, such as varieties of the wild rock pigeon, which modifications are perfectly compatible with the creation model. But what is the explanation of the *origin* of these birds (not to mention the origin of everything else)? Darwin (with only a BA in theology) was silent, as are the proponents of macroevolution today. As recently as 2003, evolutionist A.G. Fisher admitted, "Both the origin of life and the

---

6. Elmer R. Noble and Glenn A. Noble, *Parasitology* (Philadelphia, PA: Lea & Febiger, 1989), p. 516.

origin of the major groups of animals remains unknown."[7] Fisher is well respected in the secular community — evolutionist Bruce Lieberman of the University of Kansas geology department opined that Fisher is a "great paleontologist."[8]

A major evidence for neo-Darwinism is the Galapagos Island finch. Much is made regarding the subtle change (all microevolution or minor variation) their beaks underwent in response to a 1980s drought. But with the return of water in the form of a flood, their beaks returned to "normal." We see only limited change in response to environmental stress. This is easily explained — even predicted — by the creation model, but is hardly evidence for vertical change or macroevolution.

In the 1994 Pulitzer Prize–winning book, *The Beak of the Finch*, author Jonathan Weiner admitted that a male *scadens* bred with a female *fortis* "and produced 4 chicks in 1 brood."[9] This is a graphic example of different "species" interbreeding and that the alleged 13 new species of finch on the Galapagos Islands are, evolutionarily speaking, nothing of the sort.

In both undergraduate and graduate school, I was taught the synthetic theory — otherwise known as neo-Darwinism. This is defined as bringing together natural selection with Mendelian genetics and mutation theory. But neo-Darwinism (macroevolution) is not empirical science. It is not observable, repeatable, nor testable. Perhaps this is why the late L. Harrison Matthews said:

> The fact of evolution is the backbone of biology, and biology is thus in the peculiar position of being a science founded on an unproved theory — is it then a science or a faith? Belief in the theory of evolution is thus exactly parallel to belief in special creation — both are concepts which believers know to be true but neither, up to the present, has been capable of proof.[10]

It is significant to note that every one of the alleged scientific evidences presented by Darwinists in the infamous Scopes trial of 1925

---

7. *Grolier Multimedia Encyclopedia*, fossil section.
8. *Quarterly Review of Biology* (June 2003): p. 218.
9. Jonathan Weiner, *The Beak of the Finch* (New York: Knopf, 1994).
10. Charles Darwin, *The Origin of Species* (London: J.M. Dent & Sons, Ltd., 1971), introduction.

have failed the test of scientific scrutiny. Yet, Theodosius Dobzhansky, one of the co-authors of the synthetic theory (neo-Darwinism) loftily stated, "Nothing in biology makes sense except in the light of evolution." The biology student and the public are constantly exposed to variations on this tired refrain, but science is silent as to a mechanism. As a biology student, I was routinely taught the macroevolution party line, but was never told how it actually occurred. Editor Michael Allaby stated, "There is no agreement as to whether macroevolution results from the accumulation of small changes due to microevolution, or whether macroevolution is uncoupled from microevolution."[11] In college, I used the 1974 edition of *Integrated Principles of Zoology*.[12] Not a single fact for macroevolution was listed in those pages. Interestingly, the 1997 edition[13] has even less to say in regard to macroevolution, including:

> The origin of the ciliates [e.g., the *Paramecium*] is somewhat obscure (235).

> Unraveling the origin of the multicellular animals (metazoans) has presented many problems for zoologists (240).

> One of the most intriguing questions is the place of mesozoans in the evolutionary picture (242).

> The origin of the cnidarians and ctenophores [comb jellies] is obscure (275).

> Any ancestral or other related groups that would shed a clue to the [evolutionary] relationships of the Acanthocephala is probably long since extinct (317).

> The primitive ancestral mollusk [snails, clams, squids] was probably a more or less wormlike organism (346).

---

11. Michael Allaby, ed., *The Concise Oxford Dictionary of Zoology* (New York: Oxford University Press, 1992).
12. Cleveland P. Hickman Sr., Cleveland P. Hickman Jr., and Frances M. Hickman, *Integrated Principles of Zoology* (St. Louis, MO: C.V. Mosby, 1974).
13. Cleveland P. Hickman Jr., Larry S. Roberts, and Allan Larson, *Integrated Principles of Zoology* (Dubuque, IA: Wm. C. Brown Publishers, 1997).

No truly satisfactory explanation has yet been given for the origins of metamerism [segmentation] and the coelom [a fluid-filled cavity], although the subject has stimulated much speculation and debate over the years (365).

What can we infer about the common ancestor of the annelids [clam worms, earthworms]? This has been the subject of a long and continuing debate (365).

Controversy on [evolution] within the Chelicerata [arthropod] also exists (379).

The relationship of the crustaceans to other arthropods has long been a puzzle (399).

The [evolutionary] affinities of the Pentastomida are uncertain (439).

The [evolutionary] position of the lophophorates [invertebrates] has been the subject of much controversy and debate (447).

Despite the excellent fossil record, the origin and early evolution of the echinoderms [sea stars] are still obscure (450).

Despite the existence of an extensive fossil record, there have been numerous contesting hypotheses on echinoderm [evolution] (465).

Hemichordate [evolution] has long been puzzling (476).

Zoologists have debated the question of vertebrate origins. It has been very difficult to reconstruct lines of descent because the earliest protochordates were in all probability soft-bodied creatures that stood little chance of being preserved as fossils even under the most ideal conditions (485). (In other words, there is *no evidence* for their evolution.)

However, the exact [evolutionary] position of the chordates within the animal kingdom is unclear (480).

The evolutionary origin of insect wings has long been a puzzle (429).

The fishes are of ancient ancestry, having descended from an unknown free-swimming protochordate [a tunicate or lancelet] ancestor (499).

In graduate school in the mid 1980s, we used Ayala and Valentine's well-respected 1979 text titled *Evolving*. But once again, no facts to prove macroevolution were offered, other than the authors asserting on page 257 that people and butterflies had "a remote common ancestor"![14]

Secular biologists cannot name a single, unambiguous example of the formation of a new species by the accumulation of random genetic mistakes. Can they present a single example of a neo-Darwinian mechanism or process that can be observed and investigated at the genetic level? Can they give references of empirical research that proves duplicated genes can take on different functions? If evolutionists can answer these questions, why were they not listed in Jeffrey S. Levinton's second edition of *Genetics, Paleontology and Macroevolution*[15]? Indeed, in his review of Levinton's book, Peter Forey lamented, "Do not expect answers."[16] *Genetics, Paleontology & Macroevolution* is a substantial book at 617 pages and 1,600 references. Surely, there should be some positive empirical proof of macroevolution in this important tome — but there is none. Why shouldn't these candid observations and admissions by atheist scientists be exposed to public school students in America? For example, in Forey's quote above, no Scripture is cited, there's no reference to "intelligent design," and the quote is in context.

In my biological science education, I learned that minor biological change in this grand ecosystem called *earth* is everywhere. The Creator has designed His living creation to be genetically flexible. Populations commonly make slight behavior and physiological modifications in response to environmental pressures. But do such minor changes lead to

---

14. Francisco J. Ayala and James W. Valentine, *Evolving* (Menlo Park, CA: Benjamin/Cummings Pub. Co., 1979).

15. Jeffrey S. Levinton, *Genetics, Paleontology and Macroevolution* (Cambridge; New York: Cambridge University Press, 2001).

16. *Journal of Paleontology* 77 (1): p. 200.

large changes that cross the borders between the created kinds? If large genetic changes do occur, do they — in time — result in a completely different plant or animal? The answer, according to many decades of research, is *no*. Such radical change is the foundation of macroevolutionary theory, a purely theoretical extrapolation of the minor changes that we observe. Because we observe the fact of minor variation in nature is hardly cause to proclaim the validity of macroevolution.

> Quite suddenly the situation has changed. The mother lode has been tapped and facts in profusion have been poured into the hoppers of this theory machine. And from the other end has issued — nothing . . . the entire relationship between the theory and the facts needs to be reconsidered.[17]

A non-Darwinian conclusion regarding our origin is not uniquely religious. A host of non-Christian — even anti-Christian — scientists exist who have the same insights into, and criticisms of, the failed neo-Darwinian synthesis. Professor Lynn Margulis of the University of Massachusetts formulated the theory of endosymbiosis. A supporter of the Gaia hypothesis, at one of her many public talks she asked the molecular biologists in the audience to name a single, unambiguous example of the formation of a new species by the accumulation of mutations. Her challenge goes unmet.[18]

This is not surprising. Random mutations are destructive, or at best, are neutral because mutations are random relative to need and because organisms generally fit well into their environments, mutations normally are either neutral or harmful; only very rarely are they helpful — just as a random change made by poking a screwdriver into the guts of your computer will rarely improve its performance.[19]

Decades ago Dobzhansky stated:

> The most serious objection to the modern theory of evolution is that since mutations occur by "chance" and are undirected, it is difficult to see how mutation and selection can add

17. R.C. Lewontin, speaking in regard to population genetics, "The Paradox of Variation," M. Ridley, ed., *Evolution* (Oxford; New York: Oxford University Press, 2004), p. 67.
18. Michael Behe, *Darwin's Black Box* (New York: Simon & Schuster, 1996), p. 26.
19. Paul Erlich, *Human Natures* (Washington, DC: Island Press, 2000), p. 21.

up to the formation of such beautifully balanced organs as, for example, the human eye.[20]

A half-century later, Darwinists are no closer to answering this "most serious objection to the modern theory of evolution" because, domain shuffling aside, it remains a mystery how the undirected process of mutation, combined with natural selection, has resulted in the creation of thousands of new proteins with extraordinarily diverse and well-optimized functions. This problem is particularly acute for tightly integrated molecular systems that consist of many interacting parts, such as ligands, receptors, and the downstream regulatory factors with which they interact. In these systems it is not clear how a new function for any protein might be selected for unless the other members of the complex are already present, creating a molecular version of the ancient evolutionary riddle of the chicken and the egg.[21]

In the 1960s, secular scientists were excited about the emerging field of molecular biology. In 1966, they began to apply it to evolutionary theory (molecular systematics) using protein electrophoresis to estimate genetic variation. They hoped that biomolecules, such as mitochondrial DNA (mtDNA) and proteins, would finally give them the badly needed evidence for neo-Darwinism. But then scientific research crushed these hopes. For example, geneticist Peter Foster stated in the *Annals of Human Genetics* (January 2003), "More than half of the mtDNA sequencing studies ever published contain obvious errors." Comparing fossilized evidence (morphology) and biological molecular results does not result in support for macroevolution. Darwinists find it difficult — if not impossible — to decide which evolutionary tree to use when morphological and molecular trees disagree (which they often do). The late Colin Patterson and fellow authors conducted a detailed survey using molecular systematics (attempting to explain the diversity in the life sciences in an evolutionary context). Their conclusion was, as "morphologists with high hopes of molecular systematics, we end this survey with our hopes dampened. Congruence between molecular phylogenies is as elusive as it is between molecules and morphology."[22]

20. "The Genetic Basis of Evolution," *Scientific American*, 182 (1950): 32–41.
21. Thornton and DeSalle, "Genomics Meets Phylogenetics," *Annual Review of Genomics and Human Genetics* (2000), p. 64.
22. *Annual Review of Ecology & Systematics*, v. 24, p. 179.

Years later, *Nature* magazine[23] (v. 406) printed a sobering article by Trisha Gura, "Evolutionary Trees Constructed by Studying Biological Molecules Often Don't Resemble Those Drawn up from Morphology [fossils]. Can the Two Ever be Reconciled [?]" Evolutionist professor James Trefil said in regard to the origin of modern humans, "We have two bodies of evidence [fossils and molecules], each with seemingly impeccable credentials, that lead us to mutually contradictory conclusions." Trefil said a page later that he was "skeptical of arguments like those of the molecular biologists, based on long strings of theoretical assumptions."[24] In 2003, Peter Forey of London's Natural History Museum wrote molecular evidence is "fraught with difficulties of interpretation."[25] With these refreshing admissions, it is surprising that in the 2004 edition of the *Annual Review of Ecology, Evolution and Systematics,*[26] Kenneth Halanych noted in regard to the modern evolutionary synthesis, "The new view of animal phylogeny [is] based largely on molecular data"!

In the 21st century, neo-Darwinists continue to be plagued with basic questions regarding the false premise of macroevolution. Examples include: they have no coherent theory of variation (it's a paradox!), alleged environmental feedback mechanisms regarding mutations are unknown, and they cannot reconcile cladogram information.

". . . ARE CLEARLY SEEN . . ."

Atheist Francis Crick (d. 2004) stated in 1988, "Biologists must constantly keep in mind that what they see [in molecular biology] was not designed, but rather evolved."[27] Is there a better example of one who is "willingly ignorant"? Richard Morris echoes Crick's statement, saying, "It is almost as though the universe had been consciously designed in such a way that life would be inevitable."[28] English atheist Richard Dawkins states on page 1 of his book, "Biology is the study of

23. *Nature,* v. 406 (July 20, 2000): p. 230.
24. James Trefil, *101 Thing You Don't Know About Science* (New York: Mariner Books, 1996), p. 268–269.
25. *Journal of Paleontology* 77 (1) (2003): p. 199.
26. *Annual Review of Ecology, Evolution and Systematics* (Palo Alto, CA: Annual Reviews, 2003).
27. Francis Crick, *What Mad Pursuit* (New York: Basic Books, 1988) p. 138.
28. Richard Morris, *The Fate of the Universe* (New York: Playboy Press, 1982).

complicated things that give the appearance of having been designed for a purpose."[29]

Evolutionist and moralist Garrett Hardin (d. 2003) edited the *Scientific American* book, *39 Steps to Biology*. In this fascinating volume (which will never go out of date), he admitted that nature itself challenges evolutionary theory, asking his readers if creationist William Paley was right. He then said, "Think about it!"[30] The Human Genome Project has shown all of us just how much we do not know regarding our genetic makeup. Current DNA sequencing, linkage (or genetic) mapping, and physical mapping has revealed large areas of the human genome that have been missed. Theories and estimates regarding this fascinating field are being radically altered or thrown out monthly. It is presently estimated that we are composed of somewhere under 25,000 genes, but it was once thought the number was as high as 200,000! Regardless of total gene number, the Creator has designed this genetic network to interact in an unwavering manner and to resist change.

The apostle Paul is indeed correct. God's creation is so visible even atheists can see it — from the bewildering microscopic world to the physical construct of planet Earth. Creation scientist (and my mentor) Gary Parker described a conversation he had with a noncreationist, evolutionist friend of his who once told him:

> The best evidence for the [creation model] he knew was that *any land existed at all on the earth*. If our planet had spun down from a gas cloud, he said, the outer layers would consist of basaltic ocean crust (density 3.5 g/cm cubed), covered by a concentric layer of granite (3.0 g/cm cubed), the whole thing covered by more than two miles (3 km) of water (density 1.0 g/cm cubed)! He said it looked as if "someone with big hands" (the closest he could come to saying "God") took the granite and shoved it up into a pile to form the dry land. Then he added that the "guy with big hands" was also smart enough to thin the basalt under the granite piles to maintain the earth

---

29. Richard Dawkins, *The Blind Watchmaker* (England: Longman, 1986), p. 1.
30. Garrett Hardin, *39 Steps to Biology* (San Francisco, CA: W.H. Freeman, 1968), p. 105.

in gravitational balance (isostasy) so it wouldn't fracture as it rotated.[31]

This is hardly a simple solution. This gravitational balance of the earth involves a 35-km-thick continental crust composed of feldspar and quartz-rich rock. Mantle rock found beneath the continental crust is 20 percent more compact. Thus, the continental crust is buoyant, floating like icebergs on the dense mantle rock. The oceans only have a relatively thin (6 km) basaltic crust with an average depth of 3.7 km below sea level. And it turns out that the oceans, their relation to the continental crust, and both of their interactions with the moon (and vice versa!), are all critical for our survival.

Such observations, and many more like these, have not been overlooked by unbelievers. Two secular scientists from the University of Washington–Seattle give a graphic example in their book *Rare Earth: Why Complex Life Is Uncommon in the Universe*:

> If some god-like being could be given the opportunity to plan a sequence of events with the express goal of duplicating our "Garden of Eden," that power would face a formidable task. With the best intentions, but limited by natural laws and materials, it is unlikely that Earth could ever be truly replicated. Too many processes in its formation involved sheer luck.[32]

Through the decades, biblical creationists have maintained a grip on the historically accurate creation account amid waves of skepticism from within and without the Christian community. Sadly, many have caved in to the pressure to compromise with secular scientific conjecture. This has spawned corrupt philosophies, such as theistic evolution, progressive creation, and other "old-earth" views. While in college, I was told by other Christians that the earth *had* to be billions of years old (and that secular science had proven this). Intimidated, I remained silent for years on this volatile subject. In time, research findings in both the physical and life sciences helped geologists realize the doctrine of

---

31. Gary Parker, *Creation: Facts of Life* (Green Forest, AR: Master Books, 1980), p. 203.
32. Peter Ward and Donald Brownlee, *Rare Earth: Why Complex Life Is Uncommon in the Universe* (New York: Copernicus, 2000), p. 37.

strict uniformitarianism, which had been dogma since the early 1800s, simply could not be defended. This has led to a limited revival of catastrophism, which had been the view before the dark ages of Darwinism.

In the last half of the 20th century, many geologists again began to accept catastrophic explanations of local (and even continental) scale events. The 1980 explosion of Mount St. Helens, for example, validated the proposition that layered sediment sequences can form rapidly. Recently, creation geologist Steve Austin has documented evidence for rapid geological process in the Redwall limestone (the most prominent sedimentary rock formation) of the Grand Canyon. Nothing short of a massive kill event associated with a gigantic underwater landslide explains billions of creatures called nautiloids (as well as corals and brachiopods) buried in a thin layer over tens of thousands of square miles across northern Arizona, southern Utah, and into Nevada. One of the best books on the revival of catastrophism is by evolutionist Trevor Palmer of Nottingham Trent University, titled *Controversy: Catastrophism and Evolution*.[33]

In astronomy, evidence of galactic structures that are too early and too mature to fit the standard big-bang model is growing. Secular scientists will be forced to seek an explanation that encompasses these disturbing discoveries — as long as it's not creation. In biology, frustrating "explanations" of genetic mistakes (mutations) and natural selection rang increasingly hollow as researchers uncovered in ever more detail the mysteries of life. Something else had to be at work — enter the creation model (and recently intelligent design). Scientists with no theological axe to grind are now going where the biological evidence leads — an investigation of the exquisite inventions and designs in nature (and possibly their Designer).

ALL SCIENCE IS CREATION SCIENCE

To conclude, my reasons for becoming (and remaining) a biblical creationist are based on scriptural, scientific, and philosophical grounds. Scientists holding to a biblical worldview can both observe (and measure) rates of change in the natural world, and rather than being forced

---

33. Trevor Palmer, *Controversy: Catastrophism and Evolution* (New York: Kluwer Academic, 1999).

to interpret all natural phenomena within a Darwinism straitjacket, they are free to think God's thoughts after Him. Just as all truth is God's truth, all science is creation science, and all science is the search for truth — God's truth (John 14:6). Even though we have a finite mind clouded by sin — it is still created by God and able to discern substantial truth. Utilizing true science and true reason will always lead one to the true Creator (Rom. 1:20–23). Unintentional support for this is found in the writings of evolutionary naturalist Jeff Levinton:

> Either our laws are inadequate and we have not described the available evidence properly or no laws can be devised to predict uniquely what should have happened in the history of life. It is the field of macroevolution that should consider such issues. For better or worse, macroevolutionary biology is as much historical as is astronomy, perhaps with looser laws and more diverse objectives. If history is bunk, then macroevolutionary studies are . . . well, draw your own conclusions![34]

---

34. Levinton, *Genetics, Paleontology and Macroevolution*, p. 7.

Mocker Turned Apologist

**Chapter 32
Dr. Richard Lumsden
(1938–1997)**

By David F. Coppedge

Sure, Christians have done good science, but that was before Darwin. Right? Wrong! One staunch Darwinian who converted first to creation, then to Christ, is Richard Lumsden.

Dick Lumsden's faith did not come from the culture in which he lived, like someone from the 1500s. If anything, he was a product of the anti-creationist second half of the 20th century. Dr. Richard D. Lumsden was fully grounded in Darwinian philosophy and had no reason or desire to consider Christianity. Science was his faith: the facts, and only the facts. But at the apex of his professional career, he had enough integrity to check out the facts and made a difficult choice to go where the facts led him, against what he had been taught, and against what he himself taught. His life took a dramatic turnaround, from Darwinist to creationist, and from atheist to Christian.

Dr. Richard Lumsden was professor of parasitology and cell biology at Tulane University. He served as dean of the graduate school and published hundreds of scientific papers. He trained 30 PhDs. Thoroughly versed in biological sciences, both in knowledge and lab technique, including electron microscopy, he won the highest world award in the field of parasitology. All through his career, he believed Darwinian evolution was an established fact of science, and he took great glee in ridiculing Christian beliefs.

One day, he heard that Louisiana had passed a law requiring equal time for creation with evolution, and he was flabbergasted — *how stupid*, he thought, *and how evil!* He used the opportunity to launch into a tirade against creationism in class and to give his students his best eloquence in support of Darwinism. Little did he know he had a formidable opponent in class that day — no, not a silver-tongued orator to engage him in a battle of wits; that would have been too easy. This time it was a gentle, polite, young female student.

This student went up to him after class and cheerfully exclaimed, "Great lecture, Doc! Say, I wonder if I could make an appointment with you; I have some questions about what you said and just want to get my facts straight." Dr. Lumsden, flattered with this student's positive approach, agreed on a time they could meet in his office. On the appointed day, the student thanked him for his time and started in.

She did not argue with anything he had said about evolution in class, but just began asking a series of questions: "How did life arise? Isn't DNA too information-complex to form by natural law and chance? Why are there gaps in the fossil record between all major kinds of animals? What are the many missing links between apes and man?" She didn't act judgmental or provocative; she just wanted to know. Lumsden, unabashed, gave the standard evolutionary answers to her questions. But something about this interchange began making him very uneasy. He was prepared for a fight, not for a gentle, honest set of questions. As he listened to himself spouting the typical evolutionary responses, he thought to himself, *This does not make any sense. What I know about biology is contrary to what I'm saying.* When the time came to go, the student picked up her books, smiled, said, "Thanks, Doc!" and left. On the outside, Dr. Lumsden appeared confident, but on the inside, he was devastated. He knew that everything he had told his student was wrong.

Dr. Lumsden had the integrity to face his new doubts honestly. He undertook a personal research project to investigate the arguments for evolution and over time, found them wanting. Based on the scientific evidence alone, he eventually decided he must reject Darwinism, and he became a creationist. But as morning follows night, he had to face the next question, "*Who is the Creator?*" Shortly thereafter, by coincidence or not, his sister invited him to church. It was so out of character for this formerly crusty, self-confident evolutionist to go to church! Not much earlier, he would have had nothing to do with religion. But now, he was open to reconsider the identity of the Creator and whether the claims of the Bible were true. His atheistic philosophy had also left him helpless to deal with guilt and bad habits in his personal life. This time he was open. This time, he heard the good news that God had sent His Son to pay the penalty for our sins, and to offer men forgiveness and eternal life.

A tremendous struggle was going on in Dr. Lumsden's heart as he listened to the sermon. When the service ended, the pastor gave an invitation for sinners to come to the front and decide once and for all, publicly, to receive Christ. Dr. Lumsden describes the turmoil he was in: "With flesh protesting every inch of the way, I found myself walking forward, down to the altar. And there, found God! Truly, at that moment, I came to know Him, and received the Lord Jesus Christ as my Lord and Savior."[1] There's room at the Cross even for know-it-all science professors, if they are willing to humble themselves and bow before the Creator to whom the scientific evidence points.

Dr. Lumsden rejoiced in his newfound faith, but discovered there is a price to pay also. After his dynamic conversion to Christ and creationism, he was removed from the science faculty where he had served so well for so many years. The Institute for Creation Research invited him to direct their biology department, which he did from 1990 to 1996. Dr. Henry Morris said of him, "He had a very vibrant testimony of his conversion only a few years ago and of the role that one of his students played in confronting his evolutionism with persistent and penetrating questions. He became fully convinced of the bankruptcy of his beliefs and realized that the only reasonable alternative was that there must be a Creator."[2]

Lumsden was also appointed to the science faculty of The Master's College, and used his intimate knowledge of electron microscopy to help the campus set up an operational instrument for training students. There was a joy present in his life and manner that made his lectures sparkle. He loved to demonstrate design in the cell that he showed could not have arisen by Darwinian processes. In discussions with evolutionists, he knew "just where to get them" (he would say with a smile), having once been in their shoes. His students appreciated the depth and

1. From an undated taped lecture.
2. http://creationsafaris.com/wgcs_5.htm.

breadth of knowledge and the years of experience that he brought to the classroom and to the lab.

Richard Lumsden gave his personal testimony on Dr. D. James Kennedy's *Coral Ridge Hour*. In the feature, he re-enacted that day in his office when the student made him rethink his beliefs. In January 1996, he also spoke to the Bible-Science Association in Southern California, in a response to atheist Richard Dawkins's book *The Blind Watchmaker*. In his talk, called "Not So Blind a Watchmaker," he gave several detailed descriptions of organs that could not have formed by Darwinian natural selection. In the question-and-answer session, he shared his testimony of how God had saved him from his former life as a bragging evolutionist. Unfortunately, years of unhealthy habits as an unbeliever, including alcohol and tobacco abuse, took their toll on his body, and he died too soon, at age 59, in 1997. His students all miss him very much.

In September 2001, PBS aired an eight-hour series portraying evolution as fact and as the central theme of biology. It tried to portray the only opponents to Darwinism as being motivated by religion. Dr. Richard Lumsden, if he were still with us, might have called up the producers and asked, *Say, I wonder if I could make an appointment with you; I have some questions about what you said, and just want to get my facts straight.* It would have been an interesting interchange. Doc would have known just where to get them.

A Miracle of New Birth

Chapter 33
Nick Contor

I grew up with a very firm spiritual foundation: I was in church every Sunday and attended Christian schools from the sixth grade on. The church that we attended was very orthodox, and I learned a lot about the Bible and Christian doctrine there, but there was little emphasis on a relationship with God. While I was still in school, we started attending a new church, which was full of people who radiated God's love and were genuinely excited to know Jesus Christ. For the first time, I began to see Christianity as a *relationship* worth pursuing, rather than an academic program to be mastered.

I got plugged into the fellowship's youth group and attended high school in the institution that was started by the church. Although I was not always thrilled to be attending a small school (my graduating class was me and a friend), I now fully appreciate the advantage that such an education gave me. Not only were the academics superior to that of the local public school, but the spiritual atmosphere was also invaluable and gave my newfound faith fertile soil in which to grow.

Although I value my Christian education, the one area that I now feel could have been better taught was origins science. Darwinism was covered and argued against, but I'm not now sure how effectively the issues were presented. I still recall the material presented to refute Lamarckianism, but Darwinism was covered in less detail and was contradicted more in a theological and philosophical way rather than from a scientific view.

As a consequence, college overwhelmed me. I started off with a broad base of studies, but soon found myself drawn to the biology department. I began to focus my efforts in the science department and became a lab assistant, coming under the tutelage of a wonderful instructor named Robert Miller.

I admired him greatly, though he was a fully convinced evolutionist. This was a big influence on me. With nothing to counter the evolutionary doctrine I was receiving in my classes, I compromised my creationist beliefs. In retrospect, I don't believe that I was ever an outright evolutionist, but I soon became fond of phrases such as "The Bible is not a book on science." I also became a strong proponent of the gap theory, to which I was exposed in my youth.

I quit college after three semesters to get married. At the time, my motivations were not spiritual: I wanted to get married and I was goofing off academically, so I figured that work and marriage were a better way to go. In hindsight, though, I think that God was insulating me from the atheistic worldview promoted by my professors. I spent the next few years settling into married life, working various jobs, and not thinking much about creation/evolution issues.

Although my wife and I continued to attend church on a fairly regular basis, the compromise that began in college continued to the point where my relationship with God was almost nonexistent. But even though I was faithless, God was faithful, using a series of events to steer me back.

The first was the birth of my son in 1993. As he began to grow, I became more aware of how my life would very soon influence him, and I took a hard look at the example I would be setting for him to follow. The second factor was breaking my knee two days after my son's second birthday. I had begun working for a sign company when I fell 25 feet onto a basketball court, breaking my knee and cracking my skull in the process. While I was in the hospital, I began to blame God for my injuries. My wife gently reminded me that it was not God who had walked away from me. I recovered quickly, slowly learning to rely on God for strength and realizing that I still had a lot of growing to do.

I had been exposed to some of the secular world's arguments against the Bible, but didn't have much in the way of answers to those questions. As a consequence, my faith was still somewhat weak and I had many objections to overcome. But through God's grace, I now had the will to search for solutions. I began to study the Bible seriously again, this time as a way to really deepen my relationship with my Savior. A real eye-opener for me in this search was the writings of C.S. Lewis, particularly *Mere Christianity*. This was my first exposure to "natural" theology, and I was impressed by the use of a logical progression to defend the historical truth of Christianity.

My pastor recommended that I join a Bible study that was in the Book of Genesis at the time, and so I talked to the teacher of the class. He lent me the first few tapes of a Genesis study given by Chuck Missler, which he was using as source material for the class. I consider my exposure to Chuck's presentation of the Book of Genesis my baptism into creationism.

Chuck's style was engaging, thoughtful, intelligent, and above all, based upon Scripture. Although I didn't (and don't) agree with Chuck on all points, I respect the fact that he feels a need to base everything he said on a Scripture verse, not merely on his or any other man's opinion. I was impressed, for instance, that he rejected the documentary hypothesis solely on the basis of Christ's attribution of the Torah to Moses and felt no need to back that up with any scholarly treatise from an expert. It was certainly different from other Bible teachers I had heard.

I also praise God for leading me to such great ministries as Answers in Genesis and the Institute for Creation Research. Their books, magazines, and web pages have been a tremendous source of encouragement and education to me. Considering that I live in a rural area, I have been extremely blessed to have heard and talked with such creationist luminaries as Russ Humphries and John Baumgardner.

As a fully convinced creationist, I feel confident in my faith and bold enough to talk openly about my Lord, when once I was fearful of encountering the objections of skeptics. I used to feel guilty for needing the "crutch" of physical evidence to believe the words of Scripture, but I now believe that God does not mind us needing the assurance that His Word is verifiable and factual in all respects. I feel that God will always honor honestly asked questions and provide us with a firm platform of evidence from which to make any leap of faith that He requires of us.

SPECIAL FEATURE

FOUNDING FATHERS OF THE CREATION MOVEMENT

From Theistic Evolutionist to Creationist

**Chapter 34
Dr. Henry M. Morris
(1918–2006)**

Many people have asked me how a professor such as myself became interested in writing books about evolution and creation. During my college days, I was a theistic evolutionist and Sunday-morning Christian, but this began to change soon after graduating from Rice University. As a junior engineer with the International Boundary and Water Commission in El Paso, with my fiancée back home in Houston, I began once again to read the Bible and think seriously about my Christian responsibility.

I had largely ignored spiritual matters only a few years after my conversion (which had also come about mainly through reading the Bible) and baptism as an eight-year-old boy in Corpus Christi. After my wife, Mary Louise, and I were married, we joined a sound Bible-preaching church and began trying to build a solid Christian home. We accepted jobs as teachers of junior-age Sunday school classes and in 1942, I joined the Gideons. The latter fellowship especially encouraged me to believe in the saving power of the Word of God through personal witnessing for Christ.

It was also at about this time that Irwin Moon came to El Paso with his very impressive "Sermons from Science." Although his visual electrical displays impressed me, it was a sermon dealing with fossils as a result of the Flood, and its implications, that got me thinking. I had never heard of this idea before, and suddenly I realized that it was possible to not only defend the Bible against its scientific critics, but to also use it as a guide to aid in scientific discovery. As a result of his talk, I realized the need for answers in science and apologetics and began to read everything I could find that seemed relevant. To make as honest an evaluation of these key subjects as possible, I read many books promoting evolution, as well as books attacking the Bible. On the creationist side, I found Rimmer's books, Price's *New Geology*, and some others were all very helpful. However, it was a matter of concern to me that very few of these were written by practicing scientists with graduate degrees from recognized universities. Furthermore, practically all of even the creationist books seemed to uncritically accept the geologic-age system, and it seemed clear, even then, that the gap theory and day/age theory — not to mention the local flood theory — involved forced biblical exegesis that one would never use elsewhere in the Bible.

Finally, to try to settle this question in my mind, I resolved to embark on a verse-by-verse search through the entire Bible, listing and categorizing every passage connected to creation, the Flood, science, nature, and other relevant topics. By this time, my earlier doubts about the Bible had been settled: there was no doubt in my mind that it really was the Word of God, inspired and inerrant throughout. I no longer believed there was any validity to Darwinism, having become convinced of this as much by the evolutionist literature I had read as by the creationist books. The standards of evidence supporting evolution seemed trivial compared to the evidence on which engineers have to base their work and also compared to the evidences for the divine origin of the Bible (such as fulfilled prophecy, the resurrection of Christ, etc.).

But I still had problems with the age of the earth and the geological column. If this could be settled, it would have to be in Scripture because prehistoric events, by definition, are beyond the reach of the scientific method, a fact that many evolutionists find hard to comprehend. It seemed that God would not have left an important matter such as this, with such profound ramifications in so many areas of life and study, unsettled in His Word. The very fact that this problem is still the main bone of contention in the modern creation/evolution conflict points to its importance. Surely God had the answer in His Word!

And that, of course, is exactly what my verse-by-verse study confirmed! The Bible could hardly be more explicit on this point. Everything was created and made in the six days of the creation week, several thousand years ago. There may be some uncertainty in the precise date, and different Bible scholars (all following the same premises) have arrived at different dates, but there is no legitimate way the Bible can be made to yield anywhere near an age of millions of years ago for the date of creation. Neither the gap theory, nor the day/age theory, nor the allegorical theory, nor the revelation-day theory, nor any other theory that tries to accommodate the evolutionary ages can satisfy the straightforward teaching of the Bible on this vital subject. Neither, for that matter, will any of these theories accommodate the scientific data.

This conviction became the basic premise of my own creationist studies and has continued ever since, after once it was settled in my own mind that this was the firm teaching of Scripture. Furthermore, this has been the basis of the strength of the modern creationist movement, and uncertainty on this point has been the real reason why earlier creationist defenses (including that of Bryan) have fallen by the wayside.

As a result of Dr. Moon's talk, I embarked on an intensive study of the scientific evidence (which I am still pursuing today) that eventually resulted in my first book. Although it did include the evidence for flood geology and a very brief outline of evidences for a young earth, it also allowed the possibility of the "gap theory" as a means of accommodating a great age for the earth. I soon regretted this and rejected the gap theory (and all other such accommodating views) in my later books.

Why I Entered Teaching

Back in 1943, I was offered a teaching position at Rice University. I had graduated "with distinction" (the only type of special honor then available to Rice graduates with high scholastic records) in 1939 from there. I had also earned membership in the three honor societies — Sigma Xi (science), Phi Beta Kappa (humanities), and Tau Beta Pi (engineering). Consequently, even though I only had a BS degree and three years' experience in hydraulic engineering on the Rio Grande, the Rice faculty believed I was qualified to teach undergraduates and appointed me as a full-time instructor in civil engineering. Good engineering teachers were in short supply then, and universities then did not place nearly as much emphasis on PhD degrees (especially in engineering) as they do now. I even had an invitation to teach at Stanford, which I declined.

At the time of my appointment at Rice, I was already approved for an ensign's commission in the Navy Seabees. Unknown to me, however,

Rice had arranged with the navy to release me so that I could teach, since most of the male students at this time were in the Navy V-12 and ROTC programs, and navy officials believed I would be more useful to the war effort as a professor. In retrospect, I now believe that this was the Lord's will: I had never entertained the remotest idea of being a teacher, but this call to Rice was the beginning of my lifelong career in education.

After arriving at Rice, I quickly felt the burden of reaching the students there for Christ. They were all destined for active duty in the war immediately on graduation, and I had been actively involved in witnessing to the servicemen in the El Paso Gideons. Many Rice students (including my own brother, who took a night course in surveying that I taught) were later killed in the war.

The most widely known creationist when I was researching the issue was probably Dr. Harry Rimmer (1890–1952), a Presbyterian pastor and self-made scientist.

A Voice in the Wilderness

Harry Rimmer was a very prolific writer, and his books were more popular and widely read than even those of George McCready Price. His two best-known creationist works were *Modern Science and the Genesis Record* (1940) and *The Theory of Evolution and the Facts of Science* (1941). At a time when I was still wrestling with the advantages of theistic evolution, the latter book helped to convince me that Darwinism was false. Even though the book had obvious scientific weaknesses and (as with all Rimmer's books) was unnecessarily laced with sarcasm aimed at evolutionists and others with whom he disagreed, the book did have enough solid, factual evidence and logic to settle the question for me. Although at the time not as well known as Bryan of the Scopes trial (Bryan apparently did not ask his help or advice), his books and lectures made him world famous during the thirties and forties. He was undoubtedly the most influential creationist before the 1959 Darwin centennial.

Rimmer's formal education was very heterogeneous (a year each at Hahneman College of Homeopathic Medicine, San Francisco Bible College, Whittier College, and the Bible Institute of Los Angeles [now Biola University]); he was eventually awarded two honorary doctorates, a DSc by Wheaton College and an L1D by John Brown University.

Like Price, he was a voracious reader. He also built his own laboratory and became very knowledgeable in the sciences pertaining to origins. A great public speaker, using a variety of appealing illustrations and much humor, his audiences were often in the thousands. Even his scientific books and lectures always had as their goal winning people to Christ.

Soon after coming back to teach at Rice Institute (now Rice University) in the fall of 1942, I first encountered Rimmer's books. At that time, the subject of biblical Christianity was new and exciting to me. To have an effective witness among the students (who, during World War II, were mostly science and engineering students, sent there for special training by the U.S. Navy), I really needed this kind of information.

I also thought it would be wonderful if the Rice students and faculty could also hear him speak. Accordingly, I got up enough nerve to ask the university president, Dr. Edgar O. Lovett, to set up a meeting on campus. I assured Dr. Lovett that Rimmer was an authority in Christian apologetics and it would be an honor to Rice for him to speak on our campus. Before coming to Rice, however, Dr. Lovett had been professor of astronomy at Princeton, and was at least nominally familiar with the great apologists on the Princeton faculty (Machen, Allis, Wilson, et al.), so he was justifiably skeptical and reached over to check Rimmer's biography in *Who's Who in America*. Rimmer was in the book, but his qualifications did not impress Dr. Lovett, and he declined my request. In the process, he grilled me rather intensively on matters such as creation, miracles, and the like. He was especially concerned about the Bible's astronomical miracles (e.g., the long day of Joshua). I have often wondered what he thought of this presumptuous young instructor (me) and the naive answers I gave to his tough questions. He was quite a gracious gentleman, however.

Although Dr. Rimmer was not allowed to speak to the whole campus, I was able to have him address our Rice Christian Fellowship group. About 60 students were present, a much smaller audience than that to which he was normally accustomed. I was happy with the turnout, because it had been an uphill battle to get our group started in the first place. Dr. Rimmer brought an excellent message but was unable to stay after the meeting. I had been eagerly looking forward to getting to know him personally, to secure his guidance for what I hoped might become a future testimony in the university world like his own.

Although I was disappointed, I did enjoy this one brief contact with the man widely recognized by conservative Christians as "the greatest Christian apologist of his generation." It was an unforgettable week for me. I had already read most of his books by then, and it was delightful to hear him speak so effectively on topics that had recently become a great concern of mine.

Many years later, after the Institute for Creation Research was started, Dr. Rimmer's wife (Mignon Brandon Rimmer) sent me a copy of the biography she had recently written (*Fire Inside*, 1968) about her husband. Dr. Rimmer had died of cancer in 1952, at the relatively young age of 62, but reading her account of his life was a great blessing to me — few men have lived such a full and rewarding life as he.

The one serious weakness in Rimmer's work (as with so many other creationists of the time) was that he compromised the vital issue of the age of the earth and flood geology. That was one question I *did* manage to ask him when he spoke to our Rice Christian Fellowship.

He still believed in an old earth and that the Noahic flood was only regional. He was also a proponent of the gap theory, with its pre-Adamic ruin corollary. He did believe in the six literal days of creation, even participating in (and as usual, winning) two friendly debates on that topic with his good friend, Dr. W.B. Riley (who advocated the day/age theory). He and many others — past and present — have been blind to the overwhelming biblical and scientific problems associated with great ages. Even Price allowed for the great age of the earth's core, as well as of the stars, while still insisting on a literal six-day creation, with all the fossils formed after the Fall and Curse. There seems to me to be overwhelming scientific evidence — and absolutely conclusive biblical evidence — that the entire universe was made in the six literal days of creation week.

At the time of Dr. Rimmer's visit to Rice, I was already working on my first book manuscript. To witness effectively to students on the campus, I felt a need for a small book on Christian evidences — one that would include the scientific evidences for creation and the Flood, as well as the general evidences for the Bible. I had devoured many Christian books and liked to write (I once had ambitions to be a journalist), so decided to write one myself. The book had one immediate purpose — to win students to Christ — so I didn't then realize I was contracting an "occupational disease" that would stay with me throughout my life! Even at age 90, I still write.

My First Book

Since the primary purpose of my first book was evangelistic, I titled it *That You Might Believe* from John 20:31. It was not easy to get published: I was an unknown author with only a BS degree. Since I knew Pat Zondervan personally through the Gideons, I offered it first to Zondervan. After a long delay, they turned it down. (Pat told me, many years later, that they had often regretted that decision.) I then offered it to Stacey Woods, head of the Inter-Varsity Christian Fellowship (IVCF), since I also knew him personally. The Rice Christian Fellowship was one of the first IVCF chapters in the United States (1945). We had seen many conversions among the students — at least 50 during my last year there, out of a student body of 1,200, including many of the student leaders. This was all the more amazing since Rice had a highly liberal and intellectual reputation. All of this, of course, had been accomplished without any compromise on strict creationism or full biblical inerrancy, perspicuity, and authority.

Stacey liked the book (as well as the fruitful results that had been demonstrated among the students with a no-compromise approach), but IVCF was not yet into book publishing in this country, so he got Clyde Dennis, founder and president of the Good News tract publishing, to publish it. Good News was in the process of setting up a book publishing division, and my book was one of the first that they published. However, they would only publish it if I would agree to underwrite the first 500 copies. I was unable to do this then, but a good Gideon friend, W.S. Mosher, president of the Mosher Steel Company, agreed to lend me the money, so the contract was signed.

I had been working on the manuscript since early 1943 and teaching the materials in it during that time, so many students were looking forward to reading the book. *That You Might Believe* was published in 1946. The war was over, and I would be leaving at the end of that school year to start graduate school. Mr. Mosher would not accept repayment, telling me to give away the 500 copies. I offered copies to all the students in my engineering classes, and to anyone else who would come to my office and request one. (I had been making a similar offer of Gideon

Testaments for several years, so students were not too surprised.) I also gave copies to many — probably most — of the Rice faculty. I had witnessed to many of these men, without much response, and had not found even one Bible-believing Christian on the faculty, let alone a creationist. The same was true with almost all secular faculties at the time (the number of Bible-believing Christian faculty members located either by Inter-Varsity or the Baptist Student Unions around the country was almost nil).

The response to my book offer was tremendous. A constant stream of students came to request copies, and a number of conversions followed, both before and after I left Rice. Even several faculty members wrote letters of appreciation, telling me how the book had helped them. Mr. Mosher was very pleased. Throughout all these years, I have continued to receive many letters telling how my first book has changed lives.

Only 156 pages long, by an unknown, uncredentialed author, published as a first venture by a small religious company, the book was not very promising. Amateurish in many ways, it went against the all-but-universal opinion of the scientific and educational establishments then. So far as I know, it was the first book (at least since the Scopes trial, if not since Darwin) published by a member of a science faculty of a secular university that advocated flood geology and a recent creation, as well as absolute biblical authority and inerrancy.

With all its faults, it received good reviews in various Christian periodicals and filled a need that had existed for years. One result was that a promising young Princeton University student named John Whitcomb read it in February 1947. He had accepted Christ as a freshman, and now was one of the student leaders of the Princeton Evangelical Fellowship. Dr. Richard Seume had been pastor of my church in Houston and had reviewed the manuscript before it was published. He had moved to a church in Paterson, New Jersey, about the same time I moved to Minneapolis, and he had arranged to give copies to the Christian students there, including John Whitcomb. John and I would eventually meet six years later, at Grace Seminary in Indiana and then, soon afterward, we would collaborate in writing *The Genesis Flood*.

Eventually, the publishers suggested that I expand and update the book. I worked on the revisions while I was working on my doctoral dissertation at the University of Minnesota. It was published just after I completed my thesis and moved to Louisiana as professor and head of the Civil Engineering Department at Southwestern Louisiana Institute (now the University of Southwestern Louisiana). By this time, Moody Press had bought the book. Ken Taylor (director of Moody Press at the time) persuaded me to change the name to *The Bible and Modern Science*. It was published in 1951.

One of the most competent creationists I knew was Arthur I. Brown. Dr. Brown was for many years a practicing physician in Vancouver, BC, until he felt the Lord calling him into a full-time ministry. He was a wonderful teacher of the Word, and I had the privilege of hearing him speak several times. However, his series of well-documented anti-evolution booklets and books had the greatest impact. After I met him and we began to correspond, it turned out that he believed the gap theory, although this subject did not come up in his books. He was not a geologist, so he did not understand the basis of the geological-age system. He died in a tragic automobile accident in November 1947.

When I first met him in Minneapolis, I had an unforgettable interview with him at his downtown hotel. He had already been using (and widely recommending) my book *That You Might Believe*, so he seemed quite willing to talk with me. I had just come to the university to do my PhD, knowing that I would need a PhD to stay in academia. However, Dr. Brown had been preaching the imminent return of Christ: The atomic bomb had just been released, and it looked like the end was near. Consequently, I wondered if I should acquire further secular education when the Lord might well return momentarily. Wouldn't it be better to devote the few remaining months or years to winning people to Christ? I expected Dr. Brown to advise me to leave engineering, as he had medicine.

Instead, he fervently advised me to stay with my graduate studies! My testimony and influence would be greatly increased and more productive in the long run, and we had no way of knowing when the Lord would return. The greatest need of the Christian world today, he assured me, was not more preachers, missionaries, or lay witnesses, but dedicated, Bible-believing scientists who were willing to undertake the hard training and study needed to bring science, with all its tremendous influence over the minds of men and women everywhere, back to God. This was excellent advice, and I followed it. Over the years, many promising young Christian students have come to me with essentially the same question, and I have given them all the same answer.

In time, the creation movement grew in size and influence so that now almost half of all Americans believe that God created humans about 6,000 years ago. I found that persons especially in the Seventh-Day Adventist, Lutheran, Catholic, Baptist, Presbyterian, Brethren, and various other denominations, particularly the conservative evangelicals, all tended to work together in support of creation in the creation/evolution controversies. I am very humbled by the fact that I played a role in this very important work.

Persuaded by the Evidence to Always Be a Creationist

Chapter 35
Dr. Duane T. Gish

I am one of the few creation scientists today who always was a creationist (and was convinced by the evidence to remain a creationist). I became a Christian when I was about ten, and I accepted the biblical account of creation in Genesis, believing that God did exactly what He said He did. I have never discovered a single passage in the Bible that could be interpreted as support for the notion that God used some sort of evolutionary process to create the universe and living organisms on the earth. God did not command onions to evolve into roses or apes to evolve into humans, but each kind to reproduce after its own kind. In Genesis we read that God used very special processes to create Adam and Eve.

Coming from a poor family in the midst of the Great Depression of the 1930s, my ambition, limited by finances, was to be a high school chemistry teacher. The Second World War changed all of that. After graduating from Dodge City High School in Kansas, I attended Dodge City Junior College for a year and then joined the Kansas National Guard. Called into active duty on December 30, 1940, by President Roosevelt, I was with the 35th Infantry Division in Camp Robinson, Arkansas, when the war began. After serving in the army for five years, including two years in the Pacific, I was eligible for G.I. Bill benefits. I married and graduated with a BS degree in organic chemistry from UCLA. I then earned a PhD from the University of California at Berkeley, majoring in biochemistry. During these seven years, in addition to studying biochemistry, I studied physics, math, microbiology, and physiology. Yet, as far as I can recall, I never heard the word *evolution* mentioned once. No time was wasted listening to just-so stories about how this or that could have evolved: our time was completely devoted to learning good, empirically based science. Had I majored in biology, I'm sure the situation would have been different.

After I received my doctorate, I spent three years in research at Cornell University Medical School as a member of a team of chemists working on the synthesis of arginina vasopressin, a posterior pituitary hormone. I then returned to Berkeley, where I served for four years on the research staff of the virus laboratory, during which time I was part of a team that worked out the amino acid sequence of the protein coat of tobacco mosaic virus. While there I was given a booklet that changed my life. This booklet, authored by a Canadian physician who chose to remain anonymous to protect his career, was titled *Evolution: Science, Falsely So-Called*. It was an excellent summary of the scientific evidence from various fields of science that described the weaknesses of evolutionary theory and provided solid evidence for creation. This material greatly excited my interest in creation versus evolution. When I mentioned the contents of this booklet to my Sunday school teacher, it happened that the next Sunday he had planned to begin a series of lessons on the Book of Genesis, and invited me to speak to his class. I related to the class much of what I had learned from the booklet. Our pastor was in the class that day and arranged for me to speak to the faculty at Western Baptist Bible College, which was located near Berkeley at that time. My lecture was not only attended by the faculty, but also by several pastors who served as part-time faculty. From several of these pastors I received invitations to lecture in their church services, Sunday schools, men's groups, etc. Thus, my career in lecturing on the scientific evidence for creation had begun.

As a biochemist, I was particularly interested in theories on the origin of life. I read a book by Russian chemist A.I. Oparin, one of the first major theoreticians in this field, and journal articles relating speculations on this subject. I also was aware of the great importance of the fossil record and the field of thermodynamics as related to the question of origins, so I also began to read books and articles on these subjects.

In 1960, I left the virus laboratory to accept a position in the research division of Upjohn, a large pharmaceutical firm in Kalamazoo, Michigan. At that time, I had also received an offer as associate professor in chemistry at the University of Hawaii. I am sure that my decision to pass up an opportunity to live in the beautiful city of Honolulu to live in Kalamazoo (which was coated with snow and ice when I visited) was the Lord's will. If I had gone to Hawaii, I would have been isolated from the mainstream of creation scientists and never would have joined with them in efforts to document and articulate the tremendous scientific evidence for creation. In my first year in Kalamazoo, a writer for a Christian publication, distributed to about 500,000 Sunday school students, published an article in *Power* magazine about me. This brought invitations to speak from pastors and others not only in Michigan, but also from neighboring states, such as Illinois and Indiana.

While at Berkeley, I had become a member of the American Scientific Affiliation, an organization of Christian men and women of science. I published articles in their journal, was elected as a fellow, and attended national meetings, where I lectured. I assumed that all members were creationists but soon learned that some were theistic evolutionists, and the majority of the members of the governing board were evolutionists. At one meeting I actually debated a particles-to-people theistic evolutionist on the subject of the origin of life.

I once attended a joint meeting of the American Scientific Affiliation and the Evangelical Theological Society in Goshen, Indiana. At this meeting, a book by a theistic evolutionist was reviewed. During the discussion that followed, I gave remarks from the viewpoint of a creation scientist. After the meeting, Dr. William Tinkle, who had earned a PhD in genetics, introduced himself to me. He told me about a group of scientists who were planning to form a creation science organization, and arranged for me to join the group. Ten of us met in 1963 in Midland, Michigan, the home of Dow Chemical Company, to found the Creation Research Society (CRS). According to the constitution that we adopted, members had to sign a statement that they were Christians who accepted the biblical accounts of the creation and the Flood. We wanted to make sure that CRS would never be taken over by theistic evolutionists as had happened in the American Scientific Affiliation.

One other important rule that was adopted was that only those who had obtained master's or doctoral degrees in scientific fields would be eligible to hold office in the society and to vote for members of the executive board (others who signed the statement of faith could be members only). The society has published a quarterly journal since its inception and now has about 600 voting members and a research center in Chino Valley, Arizona.

My service on the executive board of the Creation Research Society was indirectly responsible for another important change in my life. Another founding member who served on the executive board of the society (and who served as president for five years) was Dr. Henry Morris. Dr. Morris and Dr. John Whitcomb were co-authors of the 1961 seminal creation book, *The Genesis Flood* which was a major factor in invigorating the creation science movement. At that time, the only creation science organization, known then as the Evolution Protest Movement, was located in England (now a vigorous organization with headquarters in Portsmouth, England, known as the Creation Science Movement, and whose commitment and goals are the same as those of the CRS). I had the opportunity to be with Dr. Morris at each of the annual meetings of the CRS executive board. Thus I became aware that he resigned his position in 1971 as chairman of the civil engineering department of the Virginia Polytechnic Institute and University (where he was over 27 professors) to join with Dr. Tim LaHaye and others to found Christian Heritage College and a joint research institute, known then as the Creation Science Research Center. The purpose of the center was to conduct research in all scientific fields relative to the question of origins.

I soon felt led by the Lord to leave my position at Upjohn and join Dr. Morris. I wrote to Dr. Morris concerning my willingness to do so, and several months later I received a letter from Dr. Morris relating that the executive board had extended an invitation to me. In the fall of 1971, I joined the staff of the research center with a professorship and teaching position at the college. In the spring of 1972, Dr. Morris and I left the Creation Science Research Center (they wished to pursue political means to get creation into schools and we did not) while we continued with the goal of developing scientific evidence to establish creation as a viable alternative to evolution. Our new organization was named the Institute for Creation Research (ICR) and presently has 11 full-time scientists on its staff, 9 of whom have doctoral degrees in science from major universities (the other two have master's degrees).

My first lecture on a major university campus was in 1972 at the University of California at Davis. A campus daily newspaper reporter had heard me lecture in nearby Sacramento several months earlier. The day of the lecture, she published a full-page article in a newspaper with the bold headline "Have You Been Brainwashed?" The author related some of what she had heard in my lecture and challenged faculty members and students to come and hear the evidence I would present. This fact is probably why the auditorium was packed to overflowing (people were sitting in the aisles, along the walls, and in the doorways). The professor who had invited me to lecture had to sit on the floor in the front of the auditorium! I had no idea how these students would react to the evidence I was to present.

My evidence for creation was based on the fossil record, thermodynamics, the probability of an evolutionary origin of life, and the evidence for purpose and design, using a series of slides. My lecture was followed by prolonged applause. G. Ledyard Stebbins, one of the world's leading evolutionists and a visiting professor at the university, was in the audience. Immediately after the applause ended, he jumped to his feet to offer a rebuttal. We then had several exchanges defending our positions. Later, a young professor, a paleontologist, declared that evolutionists had changed their theory. Now, he said, instead of predicting transitional forms in the fossil record, they were predicting lots of gaps. I enjoyed pointing out to the audience that, after looking for nearly 120 years, the failure to find the transitional forms Darwin predicted has forced evolutionists to predict the evidence that creationists had always maintained was evidence for creation, namely gaps!

The account of this impromptu debate in the ICR monthly publication *Acts & Facts* served as an inspiration for creationists to organize formal debates between evolutionists and creationists. The first formal debate was between Dr. Henry Morris and a geology professor at the Kansas City campus of the University of Missouri. There was no doubt that Dr. Morris was the clear victor. Dr. Morris and I formed a team to debate evolutionists on university campuses. Dr. Morris was a very capable debater and I enjoyed being on a team with him, but after some time he grew weary of debating (which can be very tiring), so I continued to debate alone.

Altogether I probably have had nearly 300 debates, the majority of which took place on university campuses. They have proven to be popular, drawing large audiences, some with several thousand in attendance. Many other creation scientists also participated in debates with evolutionists. Although I have never claimed to win a debate (it would be vain to do so), evolutionists have suggested that creationists have won almost every debate. They have offered a number of excuses why. They always have an equal opportunity, however, to present the scientific evidence for evolution and to offer rebuttals. If they have convincing evidence for evolution, and their creationist opponents are hardly more than people misled by their religious beliefs, the evolutionists should be able to win over the creationists. Creationists win the debates for one reason: they have overwhelming evidence on their side.

In the Bible we read, "Because what may be known of God is manifest in them, for God has shown it to them. For since the creation of the world His invisible attributes are clearly seen, being understood by the things that are made, even His eternal power and Godhead, so that they are without excuse" (Rom. 1:19–20; NKJV). Thus, all that creation scientists are doing is describing the things that God has made, and this evidence is so obvious (and sufficient) that no one has an excuse for not recognizing and acknowledging the origin of all things as the handiwork of God.

Creation scientists are often asked to describe the strongest evidence they have for creation. In my lectures and debates, I present the scientific evidence from the fossil record, the laws of thermodynamics, the origin of life as related to laws of probability, and the evidence for purpose and design that is pervasive in the universe and living organisms. I begin by pointing out that evolution is no more scientific than creation, and since they are both theories about history, neither can qualify as a scientific theory. I describe the fact that increasing numbers of evolutionists are abandoning the neo-Darwinian theory of evolution, the theory taught as fact in most schools and universities and defended by every evolutionist I have ever debated. I always quote Soren Lovtrup, a well-known Swedish biologist and evolutionist, who published a book titled *Darwinism: The Refutation of a Myth*. In one of his closing comments he states, "I believe that one day the Darwinian myth will be ranked the greatest deceit in the history of science."[1] Lovtrup has not given up his faith in evolution but is convinced that Darwin's mechanism is wrong. Darwin's suggested mechanism was responsible for the acceptance of evolution by the majority of scientists.

Dr. Ruse is a very widely known philosopher of science who has published many books (several of which I own) and many articles. He was one of the main witnesses for the evolutionists in the 1981 challenge in federal court in Little Rock, Arkansas, to the constitutionality of the

---

1. Soren Lovtrup, *Darwinism: The Refutation of a Myth* (New York: Croom Helm in association with Methuen, 1987).

creation/evolution equal-time law enacted by the Arkansas legislature. The federal judge, who declared the law unconstitutional, relied heavily on Ruse's testimony that evolution was science and creation was religion. Ruse has now publicly acknowledged that evolution is a religion. In an article published May 13, 2000, in *The National Post*, a Canadian newspaper, Ruse related the fact that he was a major witness in the Arkansas trial. He described an encounter, during the trial, with me (I was among those witnessing the proceedings of the trial), and related that I claimed evolution was just as religious as creation. He said that at that time he dismissed the idea, but the more he thought about it, the more he thought that there was some truth to my claim. He said that he had devoted a significant amount of time during the past 20 years researching the relationship of evolution to religion and acknowledged that his conclusion now was, "Evolution is promoted by its practitioners as more than mere science. Evolution is promulgated as an ideology, a secular religion: a full-fledged alternative to Christianity, with meaning and morality. *Evolution is a religion*" (emphasis added). This was the philosopher of science who was quoted innumerable times by evolutionists that evolution was science and creation was religion. Evolutionists have never won a single battle in court (or before school boards) by demonstrating that *the scientific evidence* shows evolution is superior to creation as an explanation for origins. They simply maintain that evolution is science and creation is religion: end of discussion. This acknowledgment by Professor Ruse demolishes such claims.

The fossil record is the history of life inscribed in the rocks. It is the only history of life except that found in the Bible, and it's critically important in the question of creation versus evolution. Evolutionists Glenister and Witzke state, "The fossil record affords an opportunity to choose between evolutionary and creationist models for the origin of the Earth and its life forms."[2] Futuyma expressed a similar belief when he said:

> Creation and evolution, between them, exhaust the possible explanations for the origin of living things. Organisms either appeared on the Earth fully developed or they did not. If they did not they must have developed from preexisting species by some

---

2. B.F. Glenister and B.J. Witzke, *Did the Devil Make Darwin Do It?* D.B. Wilson, ed. (Ames, IA: Iowa State University Press, 1983), p. 58.

process of modification. If they did appear in fully formed state, they must have been created by some omnipotent intelligence.[3]

If evolution is true, then millions of species have evolved during hundreds of millions of years as each species developed from some preceding form and in turn gave rise to a succeeding form. Furthermore, evolutionary doctrine holds that evolution proceeds by survival of the fittest, and the fittest are defined as those species that can reproduce in the largest numbers. Thus, the population of each intermediate species would be considerably large and would exist from tens of thousands to millions of years. As a result, enormous numbers of the transitional forms generated by evolution would have lived and died during that vast stretch of time. If evolution is true, our natural history museums should contain millions of undoubted transitional forms. The evidence for evolution should be obvious, even for an untrained eye.

Conversely, if creation were true, then we would expect to find a very different fossil record. We would expect to observe that each basic kind of plant and animal, each basic morphological design, would appear fully formed with no series of transitional forms revealing an origin from some other basic type. Cats were always cats, dogs were always dogs, monkeys were always monkeys, and humans were always humans. We would expect to see variation within each kind: many varieties of finches, as Darwin noted in the Galapagos Islands. Nevertheless, as creation scientists point out, finches are not only still birds but are also still finches and interbreed with one another. To believe that finches, canaries, ducks, eagles, hummingbirds, etc., evolved from a common ancestor that evolved from a reptile requires a great leap of faith not documented by the fossil record.

From the very beginning, the fossil record contradicts evolution, but provides the evidence predicted by creationism. The fossils of a vast array of complex invertebrates abruptly appear fully formed in the so-called Cambrian rocks. Evolutionists believed a few years ago that these Cambrian rocks began to form about 600 million years ago. Now geologists claim that these rocks began to form no more than 520–530 million years ago, and that the duration of the Cambrian was only about 5–10 million years rather than their earlier estimate of 80 million years.

3. D.J. Futuyma, *Science on Trial* (New York: Pantheon Books, 1983), p. 197.

These fossils include those of clams, snails, trilobites, brachiopods, jellyfish, sponges, worms, etc. Multibillions of fossils from these creatures are found in Cambrian rocks on every continent of the world. These animals supposedly evolved from microscopic single-celled creatures. Evolutionists also believe Precambrian rocks were laid down during hundreds of millions of years preceding and leading up to the Cambrian period. If evolution is true, these Precambrian rocks should contain many billions of fossils of the evolutionary ancestors of the complex invertebrates. Where are these fossils of transitional forms linking these complex invertebrates to common ancestors? Many of the Precambrian rocks are undisturbed and perfectly suitable for fossil preservation. If the fossils were there, they would be found. There are now many reports in the scientific literature of the discovery of fossils of microscopic, soft-bodied, single-celled organisms, such as bacteria and algae, in Precambrian rocks. If fossils of such creatures can be found, it is obvious that there would be no difficulty in finding fossils of the evolutionary ancestors and transitional forms leading up to the complex invertebrates whose fossils are in Cambrian rocks. No one, however, has yet found fossilized ancestors or transitional forms linking, say, sponges with jellyfish, brachiopods with clams, snails with trilobites, or any other possible linkages for a single one of the Cambrian invertebrates.

Douglas Futuyma, ardent anti-creationist, in his book on evolutionary biology, states, "It is considered likely that all the animal phyla became distinct before or during the Cambrian, for they all appear fully formed, without intermediates connecting one form to another."[4] Thus, Futuyma confesses that *all* animal phyla (a phylum is the broadest category or taxon of plants and animals; for example, all vertebrates: fish, amphibians, reptiles, birds, and mammals, including man, are placed in the phylum Chordata), or at least all the invertebrate phyla, have appeared in the fossil record with absolutely no evidence that they arose from preceding forms. All attempts to appeal to geological, climatic, atmospheric, and chemical explanations for this sudden and dramatic appearance of complex invertebrates have failed.

The origin of vertebrates in the fossil record is equally sudden and dramatic. Evolutionists believe that fish were the first vertebrates. We

---

4. Douglas Futuyma, *Evolutionary Biology*, 2nd ed. (Sunderland, MA: Sinauer Associates, Inc., 1986), p. 325.

have many billions of fossils of complex invertebrates, and countless billions of fossils of the various major kinds of fish entombed in the rocks all around the world. If evolution is true, we should be able to find the fossils of many billions of each stage of evolution of some invertebrates into fish and many billions of transitional forms linking various basic kinds of fish to one another. None have been found. This can be easily documented by a study of the fossil record. Evolutionist Arthur Strahler has published an anti-creationist book, in which he critiques two of my earlier books on the fossil record. The latest edition, *Evolution: The Fossils Still Say No!* was published subsequent to his book. In his discussion of the origin of fishes, Strahler says the "origin of the vertebrates is obscure: there is no fossil record preceding the occurrence of fishes in the late Ordovician."[5] Concerning ancestors and transitional forms for fishes, Strahler says:

> Mainstream paleontologists have found no fossil record of transitional chordates leading up to the appearance of the first class of fishes, the Agnatha, or of transitional forms between the primitive, jawless agnaths and the jaw-bearing class Placodermi, or of transition from the placoderms (which were poorly structured for swimming) to the class Chondrichthyes, or from those cartilaginous-skeleton sharklike fishes to the class Osteicthyes, or bony fishes. Neither, says Gish, is there any record of transitional forms leading to the rise of the lungfishes and the crossopterygians from the lobe-finned bony fishes, an evolutionary step that is supposed to have led to the rise of amphibians and ultimately to the conquest of the lands by air-breathing vertebrates.

> In a series of quotations from Romer (1966),[6] Gish finds all the confessions he needs from the evolutionists that each of these classes appears suddenly and with no trace of ancestors. The absence of the transitional fossils in the gaps between each group of fishes and its ancestor is repeated in standard treatises on vertebrate evolution. Even Chris McGowan's 1984 anti-creationist work, purporting to show "why the creationists are wrong," makes no mention of Gish's four pages of text

---

5. A.N. Strahler, *Science and Earth History — The Evolution/Creation Controversy* (Buffalo, NY: Prometheus Books, 1987), p. 316.
6. I used Alfred S. Romer's 1966 treatise.

on the origin of the fish classes. Knowing that McGowan is an authority on vertebrate paleontology, keen on faulting the creationists at every opportunity, I must assume that I haven't missed anything important in this area. This is one count in the creationists' charge that can only evoke in unison from the paleontologists a plea of *nolo contendere.*[7]

Nolo contendere is, of course, a type of guilty plea by a defendant who must admit that he has no defense. The fact is, the fossil record has not produced any ancestors or transitional forms for the major fish classes. Such hypothetical ancestors and the required transitional forms must, based on the known record, be merely the products of speculation. How then can it be argued that the explanation offered by the evolution model to explain such evidence is more scientific than that of the creation model? In fact, the evidence *required* by evolution theory cannot be found anywhere. Conversely, the evidence is precisely what would be expected if creation is true.

Endless arguments are generated by the question, "Is *Archaeopteryx* a transitional form between reptiles and birds or not?" and by the question, "Is one of the australopithecines transitional between apes and humans or is it not?" Even evolutionists argue among themselves on these questions. In the case of the origin of the Cambrian, complex invertebrates and the origin of fishes, the evidence is crystal clear: not a shred of evidence exists to support the notion that these creatures evolved. Conversely, the abrupt appearance, fully formed, of all of these creatures is exactly the evidence demanded by creation. The entire fossil record also provides powerful support for creation: each basic type of plant and animal is set apart with no series of transitional forms linking it to another basic type.

Some years ago, the late Luther Sunderland read the book *Evolution* by Colin Patterson, a senior paleontologist at the British Museum of Natural History. Luther wrote to Patterson and after a few good words about the book, Luther asked Dr. Patterson why he had not included actual examples of transitional forms in his book. In a letter dated April 10, 1979, Patterson thanked him for his letter and then agreed that he had not included descriptions of transitional forms in his book because

---

7. Strahler, *Science and Earth History — The Evolution/Creation Controversy*, p. 408.

if he had known of any, either among the living or the fossils, he would have included them. This evolutionary paleontologist, sitting among one of the greatest collections of fossils in the world, admitted that he wasn't aware of a single clear fossil transitional form!

One modern popular notion about the origin of the universe is the so-called big-bang theory, or variations of it, including the inflation theory. According to this theory, billions of years ago, all the energy and matter in the universe was crammed into a cosmic egg or perhaps a primeval atom. Nobody knows where it came from or how it got there.

Someone suggested perhaps a cosmic chicken laid the cosmic egg, which suddenly exploded (or expanded) at an unbelievable speed. Out of this hypothetical primordial explosion and chaos essentially only two elements were created: hydrogen (75 percent) and helium (25 percent). These simple gases expanded until almost a perfect vacuum existed at a very low temperature. From these simple gases, it is believed, everything in the universe has evolved: stars, galaxies, our solar system, all living things, including man (constructed from 50 trillion cells of about 200 different kinds, and a brain with 12 billion brain cells and 120 trillion connections).

Thus, according to evolutionists, the universe began in a state of chaos and disorder and the simple hydrogen and helium gases, which transformed itself into the incredibly complex universe, including all living organisms around today. If this is true, matter must have some intrinsic ability to transform itself from disorder to order, from simple to complex. Scientists should have observed this fact and incorporated it into a natural law. On the other hand, if creation were true, it would not be expected that matter would have this natural ability. If anything natural has happened since creation to change the original created state, it could only cause matter to deteriorate, to go from order to disorder. Thus, these two theories postulate diametrically opposed observations. What do we observe in the real world?

We observe a natural tendency for all observed natural systems to go from order to disorder, toward increasing randomness. This is true throughout the entire known universe, both at the micro and macro levels. This tendency is so invariant that it has never been observed to fail. It is a natural law: the second law of thermodynamics. On the other hand, according to the general theory of evolution, there is a general tendency of natural systems to go from disorder to order, toward an ever higher and higher level of complexity. This tendency supposedly operates in every corner of the universe, both at the micro and macro levels. As a consequence, it is believed that particles have evolved into people.

The famous science writer, biochemist, and atheist evolutionist, Isaac Asimov, described the second law of thermodynamics as follows:

> Another way of stating the second law then is: "The universe is constantly getting more disorderly!" Viewed that way, we can see the second law all about us. We have to work hard to straighten a room, but left to itself it becomes a mess again very quickly and very easily. Even if we never enter it, it becomes dusty and musty. How difficult to maintain houses, and machinery, and our own bodies in perfect working order: how easy to let them deteriorate. In fact, all we have to do is nothing, and everything deteriorates, collapses, breaks down, wears out, all by itself: and that is what the second law is all about.[8]

Evolutionists believe the universe is an isolated system. No one outside did any work on it and no matter or energy was brought in from the outside. Everything that took place within it, and which is now taking place, occurred, and is occurring, by a process of *self-transformation*. The second law states that the total order, organization, and complexity of an isolated system can *never* increase, but can only run down and deteriorate with time. And just as Asimov stated, the universe is obeying this law. The universe is dying, and if there is no God, or God would not intervene, the universe eventually will be dead: no order and no life anywhere. Yet evolutionists believe the universe is an isolated system that began in a state of chaos and disorder and the simplicity of hydrogen gas and transformed itself into the exceedingly complex universe existing today in clear violation of the second law. If the universe could not have created itself naturally, the only alternative is that it had to be created by an outside, thus supernatural, agency.

Although the big-bang theory, including various variations of it, is widely accepted by evolutionary astronomers, a significant number of evolutionists totally reject it, based upon scientific evidence. These scientists seek other ideas on how the universe evolved. An article by Eric

---

8. Isaac Asimov, *Smithsonian Institute Journal* (June 1970): p. 6.

Lerner, titled "Bucking the Big Bang," (published in *New Scientist* and signed by 33 other scientists from ten other countries) notes that exponents of the big bang must invent many imaginary entities, or fudge factors, including dark matter and dark energy, in order to eliminate some of the contradictions of their theory with scientific evidence. Lerner states, "The big bang theory can boast of no quantitative predictions that have subsequently been validated by observation."[9] Another article, titled "Once again, Dark Matter Eludes a Supersensitive Trap," reported that "the first results from the most sensitive dark-matter detector ever built had failed to reveal the invisible particles that theorists believe make up most of the mass in the universe."[10] Earlier, evolutionary astronomers believed that the universe is expanding at a rate that is slowing down. Based on new data related to type 1A supernovas, these astronomers now assert that the rate of expansion is *increasing*. They now claim there must be an enormous amount of energy in the universe that nobody has ever seen and that cannot be detected. Furthermore, this energy has a strange property: instead of possessing ordinary gravity, as does matter and the usual sort of energy, this energy possesses anti-gravity that *accelerates* the rate of expansion. Ordinarily, in science, when empirical data contradicts a theory, the theory is abandoned. This is not the case with evolutionary theory: tooth fairies are invented as often as necessary to evade data that falsifies the theory. After all, what other theory do they have?

More than 50 physical constants govern the operation of the universe, including Boltzman's constant, Planck's constant, gravitational constant, the pion rest mass, neutron rest mass, electron rest mass, unit charge, mass-energy relation, the gravitational, weak interaction, electromagnetic, and strong interaction fine constants. Each of these physical constants must be precisely what they are or the universe (and life) could not exist. They cannot be a minute fraction less or more. If one calculates the probability that just one of these constants happened to be exactly correct, being produced by a hypothetical big bang, the probability is essentially nil: But two? Three? Fifty? To anyone willing to admit the obvious, the universe was created for the existence of humankind. As someone once suggested: For geologists, the equations are an approximation of reality;

---

9. Eric Lerner, *New Scientist* (May 22, 2004): p. 20.
10. *Science* 304:950 (May 14, 2004).

for physicists, reality is an approximation of the equations; for cosmologists, reality is irrelevant. In reality, the scientific evidence reveals that beyond a reasonable doubt, the universe could not have created itself naturally. "The heavens declare the glory of God; and the firmament [the heavens] showeth his handiwork" (Ps 19:1; ASV).

Fifty years ago, evolutionists were confident that within just a few years, origin-of-life chemists would solve most of the problems related to the evolutionary origin of life. Today, however, it can be said that practically not one problem has been solved, and evolutionists are becoming more and more discouraged with such efforts. What has come out of origin-of-life chemistry is the revelation of a series of impassible barriers to a naturalistic, evolutionary origin of life. These include:

- The absolute necessity for the exclusion of a significant quantity of molecular oxygen from the hypothetical primitive atmosphere. If oxygen were present, all organic molecules would be oxidized to simple gases, such as nitrogen, carbon dioxide, and water. Thus, an evolutionary origin of life would be impossible. A reducing atmosphere would be required, one containing, for example, ammonia, methane, and hydrogen. Geological research has established that the universe never had such an atmosphere, and good evidence exists that the earth has always had an atmosphere similar to the present atmosphere. Certainly the earth never had an atmosphere required for an evolutionary origin of life.

- The hypothetical primitive earth could never have had a protective ozone layer. Most of the energy coming from the sun is deadly destructive ultraviolet light. Life on earth is only possible because the ozone surrounding the earth filters out and absorbs almost all of the ultraviolet light, permitting the visible light to reach the earth. Since, however, according to evolutionary theories of the origin of life, the primitive earth could not have possessed oxygen, then it could not have had ozone. Ozone is triatomic oxygen, produced by the action of radiation from the sun on the diatomic, or molecular, oxygen we breathe. Life could never have evolved in the absence of ozone.

• All sources of raw energy available on the hypothetical primitive earth are destructive, not constructive. These include mostly ultraviolet light, along with lightning, radioactive decay, and heat. With these sources of energy, the rates of destruction of organic molecules vastly exceed their rates of formation. Utilizing the incredibly complex systems within a living cell or the special reagents, conditions, and manipulations of an organic chemist, it is possible to convert simple chemicals into complex molecules, but utilizing the raw energy sources available on the hypothetical primitive earth could never produce significant quantities of even relatively simple molecules. The widely heralded experiment by Stanley Miller, utilizing methane, ammonia, hydrogen, and water exposed to electrical discharge (simulating lightning), still appears in high school and university texts today even though this experiment has been thoroughly discredited. As Dr. Gary Parker said, Miller's starting materials were wrong, his experimental conditions were wrong, and his products were wrong. Otherwise, it was a brilliant experiment![11]

• No method exists for producing, under primitive earth conditions, the large complex macromolecules, such as proteins, DNA, and RNA, needed for life. The amino acids that are the subunits of proteins, and the phosphoric acid, sugars, pyrimidines, and purines that combine to form DNA and RNA, do not spontaneously chemically combine with one another, but require the input of very controlled kinds of energy. Proteins, DNA, and RNA spontaneously degrade into their subunits, releasing energy. That the subunits of these large, complex molecules would combine with

---

11. From an undated interview.

one another under plausible primitive earth conditions is nonsense. That only takes place in living cells or in a chemistry laboratory.

- The formation of a single biologically active protein, or a DNA (or RNA) molecule, requires the precise positioning of hundreds of subunits, just as the 176 letters of this sentence had to be arranged in precise order. The average protein contains 400 amino acids (of 20 different kinds). The amino acids in a protein of only 100 amino acids can be arranged in 10^{130} (the number 10 followed by 130 zeros) different ways. That number is so large that it is nearly incomprehensible — 10^{130} electrons would be sufficient to fill every cubic inch of the universe. Another way to visualize the enormity of that number is to realize that only 17 amino acids can be arranged in more than 355 trillion different ways. The probability that a single molecule of a biologically active protein would form by chance is essentially nil. The origin of life in a primitive ocean containing millions of cubic miles of water would require billions of tons each of hundreds of different kinds of proteins, DNA, and RNA molecules — an impossibility. Sir Fred Hoyle calculated the probability of an evolutionary origin of life, assuming a minimum number of enzymes required for a living cell, that every star in the universe had a planet like the earth, and that the universe is 20 billion years old. He was astounded by his results: an evolutionary origin of life anywhere in the universe in 20 billion years is essentially nil. He declared that the probability of an evolutionary origin of life is equal to the probability that a tornado sweeping through a junkyard would assemble a Boeing 747. Wherever life exists in the universe, Sir Fred declared, it had to be created; therefore there must be a God. When he began this research on this problem he was an atheist.

- There are many other impossible barriers to an evolutionary origin of life, but I will mention only one more. No isolated organic molecule has any significance whatsoever. There is no information in a DNA molecule unless there is a system to decode it. There must be a system to transcribe the information in DNA into messenger RNA. There is then no information in the mRNA unless there is a system to translate the information in the mRNA into a protein, which requires transfer RNA, ribosomes, numerous enzymes, a flow of energy, etc. The protein has no significance whatsoever unless it is designed to interact with other molecules. Even if it were possible for an isolated protein, DNA, or RNA molecules to form in a primitive ocean, the molecules would have not have survival value and would rapidly degrade. That life comes only from preexisting life is a law of biology that has always been true. Life on the earth did not arise, and could not have arisen, from nonlife. Without a doubt, God created life on this earth.

One of the most persuasive evidences for creation is the evidence for purpose and design seen throughout the physical universe and in living organisms. Even the atheist evolutionary biologist Richard Dawkins stated, "Biology is the study of complicated things that give the appearance of having been designed for a purpose." Dawkins, all appearances to the contrary (he said), preferred to believe that "Natural selection, the blind, unconscious, automatic process which Darwin discovered," and which has no purpose in mind, was what created these complicated things.[12] Of course, Darwin discovered no such thing. The idea of natural selection is only that, an idea. It is an idea that evolutionists such as Pierre Grasse, Soren Lovtrup, Richard Goldschmidt, Lynn Margulis, Gareth Nelson, Norman Platnick, and other leading scientists have denied had anything important to do with evolution. Creation scientists have for many years stressed the

---

12. Richard Dawkins, *The Blind Watchmaker* (England: Longman, 1986), p. 1.

importance of intelligent design as evidence for creation. There are innumerable examples from biology. Even a microscopic bacterium reveals evidence of purpose and design in every detail of its structure and function.

One of my favorite examples is the metamorphosis of the monarch butterfly. It is said that 87 percent of insects go through a process of metamorphosis. Every step in the life cycle of the butterfly reveals design, from the egg to the caterpillar to the chrysalis and finally, to the butterfly. The monarch butterfly lives exclusively off of milkweed. The caterpillar has legs for crawling and mouthparts for eating leaves, and that is all it does during the caterpillar stage. After going through several molts, the caterpillar begins a miraculous process: it attaches itself by its tail end to a hard surface, such as a stem, using sticky, silklike material. Next, it goes through one last molt, shedding its legs and eyes. From that stage to the origin of the chrysalis requires less than three minutes.

Evolution is a blind process that has no goal or purpose other than to survive and reproduce. All changes that occur in the hypothetical evolutionary process take place by random genetic errors, almost all of which, evolutionists admit, are negative. I have never seen any convincing evidence for a single, clear information-gaining favorable mutation for the plant or animal itself in the natural environment. Very rarely does a mutation give the individual an advantage in the struggle for existence versus other individuals. After thousands of generations, and tens or hundred of thousands of years, the good mutant would completely replace the original, bringing about a slight change. Hundreds or thousands of these slight changes eventually, we are told, results in a new species or higher life form.

The question is, how would evolution with no goal or purpose "know" that a chrysalis is needed? How could a caterpillar be slowly changed into a chrysalis in even thousands of years, let alone the few minutes required? How could a multitude of transitional forms exist between a caterpillar and a chrysalis? The chrysalis is an engineering marvel inside of which is a little heart beating. Evolution also has another impossible task: it must program the chrysalis jellylike interior via random genetic errors to transform it into a butterfly, a creature that has no resemblance to either the chrysalis or the caterpillar. The butterfly is a marvelous creature with wings for flying and a strawlike proboscis for sucking nectar. Evolution would have no way of "knowing" what a but-terfly even looks like, let alone "knowing" how to create one. I have often challenged my evolutionary opponents to describe how metamorphosis could have evolved. Not one, even a biologist whose lifetime of research was devoted to butterflies, has been able to respond to the challenge. In the book, *The Insects*, Peter Farb,[13] in his chapter titled "The Marvel of Metamorphosis," refers to metamorphosis as a "miraculous change of form" that there "is no evidence how such a remarkable plan of life ever came about."

The process of metamorphosis is one of thousands of examples in biology that cannot be explained by any naturalistic evolutionary process and can only be explained as the product of an agent whose intelligence is unfathomably greater than human intelligence. Dr. Michael Behe of Lehigh University, in his book, *Darwin's Black Box*,[14] describes many irreducibly complex biological processes. These processes, such as the biochemistry of vision, the biochemistry of our immune system, the bio-chemistry of blood clotting, and others all involve a suite of molecules that are so complex its origin cannot be explained by Darwinism. Yet the loss of only one of the needed molecules results in total loss of function. The system is irreducibly complex. The origin of such systems demand creation by the master engineer of the universe, our Creator God. There is much more scientific evidence that informs us that the best scientific statement we can make about our origin is still "In the beginning God created the heaven and the earth." These are only some of the reasons why I was "persuaded by the evidence" to remain a creationist.

13. Peter Farb, *The Insects* (New York: Time, Inc., 1962), p. 56.
14. Michael Behe, *Darwin's Black Box* (New York: Simon & Schuster, 1996).

I Preached Evolution: A Biology Professor's Story

Chapter 36
Dr. Gary E. Parker

I wasn't just teaching evolution, I was *preaching* it. "It was millions of years of struggle and death that brought mankind and all the other animals and plants into being," I told my college students. I praised Darwin for being the first to understand how evolution worked: "From the war of nature, from famine and death, the production of higher animals [and man] directly follows."

It was not God who made mankind in His image, I confidently asserted, but the other way around. When humans reached a certain stage in evolution, they made God in their image, a reflection of their emerging thoughts about morality and eternity. "God," in essence, was just another product of evolution.

Some Christian students told me that I could believe in evolution and the Bible at the same time, that evolution was just the means God used to create the world. My response usually went something like this: "Who would want to believe in a God who used millions of years of struggle and death to create things? Who'd want to pray to a God who made countless mistakes and buried His mistakes in the ground to become fossils? Besides that," I used to say to Christians, "don't you believe that God is love, and that He sent His Son Jesus to remove suffering and to conquer death? If God were using millions of years of struggle and death to create the life existing today, then Jesus would be opposing God's plan for evolution!" I was actually harder on students who tried to put the Bible and evolution together than I was on those who stood for what the Bible clearly says.

But I tried not to be nasty about it. I liked being considered a nice guy, and I really did think the Christian faith was a nice religion and that it would be nice to go to heaven and to have good triumph over evil. I let students freely express their religious beliefs, but would not let them use their personal faith to challenge what I considered the rock-hard science of evolution. I thought it was part of my duty as a science teacher to deliver my students from silly old superstitions, like taking the Bible literally and trying to refute evolution with "creation science."

If that's what I once believed and taught, what happened? The change began when Dr. Charles Signorino, a chemistry professor at the college where I was teaching biology, invited my wife and me to his home for Bible study. The last thing I wanted to do was to study a dusty, old, outmoded pre-scientific book like the Bible. But for social reasons (and the free coffee and donuts), we began attending, and I started studying the Bible, primarily to criticize it more effectively.

The Bible's opening chapters described a perfect creation, completed in six ordinary days, where there was no suffering or death, animals ate only plants, and people were designed to live forever. In light of my knowledge of radiometric dating, sequences of fossils thousands of feet thick, the food chain, and human physiology, the Bible's description of the Edenic creation seemed more than absurdly ridiculous.

The corruption of creation by human sin recorded in the third chapter of Genesis at least introduced the key elements in the evolutionary process, struggle and death, and chance was given its due elsewhere. But the Christians in the Bible study seemed bent on using evolutionary processes (time, chance, struggle, and death) to explain the origin of disease, disease organisms, and birth defects, not the origin of species. It was strange (and a little irritating) to hear people blaming the decline on time, chance, struggle, and death, instead of crediting these processes for upward evolution.

It was disconcerting to find intelligent scientists who believed in a perfect six-day creation ruined by struggle and death brought on by sin. But I was more astounded to learn that they also believed thousands of feet of fossil-bearing strata found all over the world were largely laid down during the one year of Noah's flood! At first, only the free coffee and donuts (and very friendly people) kept me coming back to the Bible study. At the time, the concept of a yearlong worldwide flood seemed ludicrous to me, but I also began to wonder about a God who could create a perfect world and then wipe it out because some woman ate a "forbidden fruit." I didn't appreciate at first, of course, that her sin (and our sin and my sin) involved a total rejection of God's love and God's gifts, setting our self-serving opinions above His absolute truth and love.

I finally learned that, even though we turned away from God, He did not turn away from us. He sent His willing Son, Jesus Christ, to die for our sin and to rise again so that all who believe receive eternal life, rich and abundant, in a restored relationship with their Creator Lord. The flow of biblical history can be summarized in "4 Cs": God's perfect *Creation*, ruined by man's sin (*Corruption*), destroyed by Noah's flood (*Catastrophe*), restored to new life in *Christ*.

When I first understood the gospel message, I thought, *Wow! I can see why someone would want to be a Christian. According to the Bible,* **life wins**: *new life in Christ. According to evolution, it's millions of years of struggle and death until finally* **death wins***, and all that's left of the universe is chaotic, random, thermal motion.*

But then I thought, *Yeah. The Bible has a happy ending: just like all those other fairy tales.* Even when I understood the happy hope of the Bible versus evolution, I couldn't accept it. The facts of science (falsely so-called, I found out) had convinced me that evolution was a fact. And the "fact of evolution" meant that God was just a figment of the evolved human imagination. No matter how beautiful the story, there was no Creator God out there who could keep those wonderful promises of a "new heaven and new earth" (2 Pet. 3:13) filled with righteousness, harmony, and happiness. It was pleasant to think about a place where the wolf and lamb would lie down together and there would be no more hurt or destruction (Isa. 11:6–9). However, my commitment to the "science" of evolution meant I could never consider such a place any more than a myth.

Make no mistake about it — creation/evolution is a salvation issue. I do *not* mean you have to have a detailed knowledge of creation science to be a Christian; I simply mean that belief in evolution can be for many, as it was for me, a powerful stumbling block to accepting (or even considering) the claims of Christ. Paul warned Timothy to avoid the oppositions of science falsely so-called, which some have erred concerning the faith (1 Tim. 6:20–21; KJV). Evolution is really "humanism dressed up in a lab coat," a man-centered worldview that uses scientific jargon to put man's opinions far above God's Word (as Eve did in the Garden). As such, evolution qualifies as "science falsely so-called," and just as Paul warned, it has been very effective in causing many to "err concerning the faith."

My extensive knowledge of, and zeal for, evolution certainly prevented me from even considering God might be real and the Bible true. So what happened? Well, Dr. Signorino, the colleague who invited me to the Bible study, was not only a superb Bible teacher, he was also a scientist respected internationally for his work in chemistry. He challenged me to look again at the science I thought I knew so well. Confident that science would support evolution and refute "4C" biblical literalism, I gladly accepted the challenge.

The battle began. For three years, we argued creation/evolution. For three years, I used all the evolutionary arguments I knew so well. For three years, I lost every scientific argument. In dismay, I watched the myth of evolution evaporate under the light of scientific scrutiny, while the scientific case for Creation-Corruption-Catastrophe-Christ just got better and better. It's no wonder that the ACLU (actually the anti-Christian lawyers union) fights by any means to censor any scientific challenge to evolution!

A turning point in my personal battle with creation/evolution came when Professor Allen Davis, a biologist newly hired at the college where I was teaching then, introduced me to the famous (or infamous) book *The Genesis Flood*, by Drs. John C. Whitcomb (theologian) and Henry M. Morris (scientist). At first, I reacted very negatively to the book, writing nasty notes in the margins and asking Allen how he, as a scientist, could respect such drivel. But as I read deeper into the book, I got answers to my evolutionary questions. Then I got scientific evidence and concepts that pointed away from belief in evolution and toward acceptance of the biblical record as earth's real history!

About that time, I got a copy in the mail of the first book I ever wrote, a programmed science instruction book called *DNA: The Key to Life*. Up until that time I thought people who wrote books, especially textbooks in science, knew what they were talking about. I had a nearly straight *A* average and earned numerous academic awards, and my book had been reviewed by experts on DNA, but I knew all the uncertainties that went into it. (Indeed, when I published the second edition five years later, I put the first edition aside and started fresh; so much additional knowledge about DNA had been gained.) It finally dawned on me: if experts in science can write books that have to be continually corrected, revised, and updated, perhaps God could write a Book in which He said what He meant and meant what He said: eternal and unchanging truth, an absolutely sure foundation for understanding life useful to all people at all times in all places!

Looking now at the Bible as the truly true "History Book of the Universe," I was lifted out of the prison of time, space, and culture, and enabled to see past the shallow and ever-changing words of human experts to the deep and never-changing Word of the Lord God, Maker of heaven and earth! I experienced who Jesus is and what Jesus meant when He said, "You shall know the truth, and the truth shall make you free" (John 8:32; NKJV).

My IQ didn't go up 100 points the day I became a Christian (and some friends thought it dropped by that much!), but I could now look at familiar facts in unfamiliar ways — ways that made more sense scientifically and helped me to solve some of the origins problems that had puzzled me as an evolutionist. As I looked at biology with the blinders of evolution finally removed, the biblical theme of Creation-Corruption-Catastrophe-Christ was reflected everywhere!

Take DNA, for example. Without realizing its significance, I had long known that DNA really contains only the genetic alphabet, not the genetic code. Evenly spaced along the length of a DNA chain are various combinations of four bases, the genetic "letters" called A, T, G, and C. In groups of three (triplet codons), these letters make up code names for amino acids, the building blocks of protein molecules. DNA is the molecule of heredity; proteins are the molecules of structure and function. All living systems (bacteria, plants, animals, and people) depend on this genetic coding relationship, using a reproducible series of bases in DNA, taken three at a time, to line up the series of amino acids giving each protein its unique structure and function.

But DNA has no means for determining which three of its evenly spaced "base letters" go together. The task of correctly grouping base letters into triplet code names for amino acids is carried out by ribosomes, which are huge cellular "machines" consisting of at least 50 different specific proteins and several huge RNA molecules! Then it takes a set of at least 20 highly specific multi-site protein enzymes (activating enzymes or "translases") to pair each amino acid with its correct genetic code name! In short, it takes a highly coordinated set of specific proteins to turn DNA bases into a genetic code and to use that code to produce the highly coordinated set of specific proteins for life and for the genetic code.

Darwin believed that each feature of every living system was produced one step at a time by changes that slowly and gradually improved reproductive potential; he boldly asserted that even one feature that could not be produced by this step-by-step process would completely disprove his theory. Based on ignorance and astonishing misconceptions about cellular complexity, belief in chemical evolution may have been possible in Darwin's time (the late 1800s), but astounding advances in molecular biology have completely disproved every attempt to evolve life from nonlife. It takes scores of interacting and interdependent parts ("irreducible complexity") to use even one DNA sequence as a code for producing even one protein among the thousands in a "simple" cell.

Besides refuting evolution, discoveries in molecular and cellular biology provide strong scientific evidence for creation. That surprises some people. Even some Christians believe creation is only something you believe or don't believe, and that you can't find evidence for creation. Actually, nothing is easier or more natural than finding and recognizing evidence for creation. All of us can tell the difference between a pebble shaped by time and chance and an arrowhead molded with plan and purpose; all analysts would agree an airplane is put together by creative design and organization, not by chemical properties of aluminum doing what comes naturally; and even evolutionists working on the Search for Extra-Terrestrial Intelligence (SETI) are convinced there is a difference between signals produced by natural process and those sent with intelligent design. What does it take to distinguish patterns produced by time and chance (evolution) from those produced by plan and purpose (creation)? All you need are the ordinary tools of science, logic, and observation.

Imagine you have just finished reading a fantastic novel. Closing the covers you exclaim, "Wow! Great book! I wonder where I can get a bottle of that ink?" You would never say that, of course. The credit for writing the story goes to the author, not to the ink and paper. The ink and paper were merely the means the author used to communicate his information. No laws of physics and chemistry were violated in the writing of the book; properties of the ink and paper were used (and harmful properties, like blotching, were avoided), but the ink and paper did not produce the coded sequence of letters nor their meaning to the reader. Likewise with the genetic code — the properties of DNA and protein are utilized (and numerous harmful interactions avoided), but DNA and protein did not write the genetic manuscript. Credit for writing the genome, or "book of life," for each kind goes to the Author of life, the Lord Jesus Christ.

As clearly as the genetic code provides scientific evidence for creation, however, it also demonstrates the corruption of creation that followed human sin. Mutations, random changes in the genetic code that occur in our fallen world, have produced defects, disease organisms, and more than 5,000 genetic diseases in the human population alone! Evolutionists have called mutations the "raw material for evolutionary progress," but scientists refer to accumulating mutations as "genetic burden" or "genetic load" inexorably dragging down the genetic quality of each species. Furthermore, mutations do not make new genes from scratch; they merely alter genes that already exist. Therefore, mutations point back both to creation (the prior existence of genes) and to corruption (defects, disease, and decline) following man's sin. Following Christ's example of bringing healing to the sick, scientists properly applying genetic techniques are now overcoming some of these ills.

What about Darwinian natural selection? Natural selection, yes; evolution, no. Selection is based on variability within species sorted out in the struggle for survival. As noted by Edward Blyth, two dozen years before Darwin published his *Origin of Species* book in 1859, variability was introduced at creation so living things could "multiply and fill the earth," and the struggle for survival was introduced when man's sin corrupted God's creation. Working together, variability and struggle help to explain how and where living things survived as they multiplied and filled the earth after the Fall and Flood. Scientists have observed (or inferred) many examples that show how varieties of a created kind survive in different areas as they spread over the earth: peppered moths in England, finches on the Galapagos Islands, antibiotic-resistant bacteria. All these are examples of variation within kind; none are examples of one kind of organism changing into something different. None of them even hint at the addition of new genetic information and complexity required to make evolution even a legitimate scientific hypothesis. Evolutionary selection failed completely as a science; unfortunately, what Darwin called "the war of nature" succeeded only too well as an alternate religion, atheistic humanism dressed up in scientific jargon devoid of scientific content.

When I finally realized how strongly science pointed away from evolution and toward biblical creation, I decided I needed to discuss this evidence with my biology students. To my surprise, three members of the college's Bible department challenged me to a debate! When chemist Charles Signorino and biologist Allen Davis joined my side, the stage was set for the Great Debate: the Bible department defending evolution and the science department defending creation!

After the Great Debate, no one asked me further about biology. But some said that if I only knew more about fossils, I would give up this "creationist nonsense" and accept the "fact of evolution." Then the Lord did something fabulous for me: a fellowship from the National Science Foundation for 15 months of full-time doctoral study. With fear and trembling, I added a doctoral minor in geology, emphasizing paleontology and origins, to check out the fossil evidence firsthand.

I had excellent professors, including some Christians, but all assumed evolution without question. However, what they taught me about fossils made it hard to believe in evolution and easy to accept the biblical record of a perfect creation, ruined by man, destroyed by the Flood, restored to new life in Christ: Creation, Corruption, Catastrophe, Christ!

The professor introduced the course in fossil plants by saying that Darwin called the origin of flowering plants "an abominable mystery." Then he added that the many fossil discoveries since then failed to change that statement. What we would find, he said, is that our modern plant groups go way back in the fossil sequence. Sure enough, the "first" fossils of each of the major plant groups were just as complete and complex as those today — well designed to multiply after their kind. In fact, fossils show a far greater variety of plants existed in the past than at present: *creation*, followed by *corruption*, the exact opposite of evolution. Shredded remains of plants spread out deep and wide in cross-continent layers of coal testify to worldwide flooding (*catastrophe*). Remnants of once-great groups, called living fossils, have been saved, including the "dinosaur pine" in Australia and the ginkgo tree in Asia.

The courses in invertebrate paleontology included mostly geology majors, and I thought I might have to work extra hard to catch up. My experience was exactly the opposite. Unlike most geologists, I already knew the long Latin and Greek names for major animal groups and parts because they were the same names, features, and criteria for classification used for modern groups. Once again, the fossil lessons were clear: complex, varied beginnings for each of the major groups (*creation*); death, disease, and decline (*corruption*); rapid, deep burial on a worldwide scale (*catastrophe*); and preservation and repopulation (*Christ*).

The "first" (deepest buried) animal fossils are trilobites, incredibly complex creatures in the most complex of all invertebrate groups (the arthropods). The professor said we should never let anyone call the trilobite a simple animal! Trilobites are found with representatives of all the other major groups of animals in the "first" or "simplest" group of once-living things to leave an abundance of fossil remains, the Cambrian geologic system. Evolutionists, who had hoped the first group of fossils would be simple, few, and quite different from modern forms call this unexpected, sudden appearance of complex, varied, and familiar forms the "Cambrian explosion." It seems these first fossils were not the first evolved but the first of the created kinds buried in Noah's flood! No wonder Darwin called the fossil evidence the most obvious and serious objection to his theory.

The biological and geological evidences that helped convert me from evolution are detailed in the book *Creation: Facts of Life*. But for me, like most Christians, the most difficult decision to make about origins concerned the amount of time involved in the earth's history. The study of fossil deposits worldwide (including for me over 40 week-long study hikes and two raft trips through the Grand Canyon) provided abundant evidence that it was a lot of water, not a lot of time, that covered the earth in a blanket of sedimentary rock layers. The evidence for a globe-covering catastrophe like Noah's flood is so convincing scientifically that even reluctant evolutionists are now calling themselves "neo-catastrophists." While the world watched, the eruptions of Mount St. Helens in 1980 and 1982 did in minutes, hours, and days what evolutionists had taught would take millions of years.

But what can we say about carbon-14, uranium-lead, and other methods of radiometric dating? Could a Christian committed to the serious study of both God's Word and God's world still accept and defend a six-day creation a few thousand years ago? Again with fear and trembling, I signed up for geophysics primarily because it included an extensive unit on radioactive decay dating.

After explaining why rubidium-strontium isochrons were one of the best dating methods, the professor assigned us the problem of dating a rock using two sets of data. Neither my classmates nor I could get the dates for that one rock to agree. After making us sweat for a while, the professor explained that he wanted to show us the method doesn't always work! Indeed, Rb-Sr isochron ages show lava flows at the bottom of the Grand Canyon are younger than ones at the top, suggesting, if taken literally, that the canyon formed upside-down! At one of my creation/evolution debates, my opponent acknowledged that creationists could make a very good case for creation from DNA and genetics, and he freely admitted that the fossil links to support evolution were still missing. But then he claimed he could prove the earth was billions of years old using rubidium-strontium and spent the rest of his hour explaining the assumptions that go into that method! An international team of prestigious scientists organized by ICR (Institute for Creation Research) just completed a ten-year research project titled *Radioisotopes and the Age of the Earth* (RATE), showing that radiometric evidence really supports an age for the earth of thousands, not billions, of years.

At the end of my geophysics unit on radiometric dating, the professor was going over the long list of assumptions required to convert any measurement of radioisotope amounts into some estimate of age. Midway through the list of unwarranted assumptions and inconsistent results, the professor paused to joke that if a Bible-believing Christian ever became aware of these problems, he would make havoc out of the radiometric dating system! Then he admonished us to "keep the faith."

"Keep the faith." At bottom, that is all there is to radioactive decay dating: a faith the facts have failed. At bottom, that's all there is to evolution: a faith the facts have failed. Evolution was only able to get a toe-hold on science because of 19th-century ignorance of molecular biology, cellular ultra structure, ecology, and systematics. Discoveries in these fields completely crushed evolution as a science, but it persists only too well as a secular religion protected from contrary evidence by the anti-American censorship lawyers united.

The Bible is based on faith, too, of course — faith that God is telling us the truth in the Bible about our world and ourselves. What's the difference between faith in evolution and faith in creation? Evolution is a faith the facts have failed; creation is a faith that fits the facts! All the so-called facts I once used to "prove" evolution to my students have now been disproved. Because nothing better has come along, many modern textbooks continue to use "proofs" for evolution that are 50–150 years old (making it easy for creationists in debates). In the meantime, the scientific case for 4C biblical creation has gotten better and better. I was once somewhat shy about discussing plate tectonics, carbon-14, or starlight and time in a debate or university talk, but now if evolutionists don't bring up these topics, I will! Because scientific knowledge is always incomplete, there will always seem to be some conflicts between science and the Bible. Just hang in there; science will catch up and show the Bible has been right all along!

I must always remember, however, that the surest foundation for the Christian faith is God's Word written (the Bible) and God's Word living (Jesus Christ). Whether creationist, evolutionist, or undecided, people are finite and our knowledge is always limited. We must live by faith; we can do no other. But it can be a faith with eyes wide open, and a heart that understands the other person.

At one point, I had let evolution pervert science away from a search for truth about nature to a close-minded search for naturalistic explanations about life. As a Christian, I was finally free to pursue science as a search for truth, even if that search led me to Jesus Christ, who is "the way, the truth, and the life" (John 14:6; NKJV). I recommend it highly!

A Geologist's Story: How and Why I Became a Creationist

Chapter 37
Dr. Andrew A. Snelling

Reared in a Christian home from birth, I attended a Bible-believing church where God's Word was faithfully preached. As a young child, I remember going to church every Sunday where we lived in Sydney, Australia. I especially remember the joy of learning God's Word and the fellowship with Christian friends. Our elderly pastor was a godly man who preached from the Scriptures in a systematic and thorough manner, proclaiming truth without compromise. A shepherd who loved and cared for his flock, he regularly visited our homes to listen, exhort, and pray. There was also much fun and laughter at social events, picnics, and family celebrations. It was no wonder that we were a close-knit group of Christians.

As soon as I was old enough to sit still, I participated in church services. I also attended Sunday school classes at the appropriate level for my age. Lessons were always thoroughly Bible-based, and I was encouraged to study the Bible for myself and even entered annual Scripture learning and knowledge competitions. Because my brother is two and a half years older than me, I often tagged along on Bible studies and other activities designed for older children (and was forced to keep up with them in learning and studying Scripture). Older godly adults in our church knew the Scriptures thoroughly and taught these Bible studies in depth, encouraging discussion and personal expression of what was being taught. Even at school we attended weekly Scripture classes that were, and still are, provided for in Australian public (state) schools. I remember when, in third grade, in the weekly Scripture class (run along the lines of church affiliation) I was successfully competing with children from other grades up to sixth grade in Scripture quizzes and memorization (much to the consternation of my older brother in the same class)!

Although I grew up with a solid biblical foundation, had head knowledge of the Scriptures, lived in a Christian home, and attended a Bible-believing church, this did not make me a Christian. Outwardly, I did and said everything that would be regarded as the hallmark of a Christian, but inwardly my heart had not yielded to God.

Not long before my ninth birthday, I went with my brother to a six-day holiday camp organized by our denomination at a campsite where there were lots of fun outdoor activities. We were housed in rooms by age, with an appropriate camp leader assigned. There were Bible lessons and outdoor adventures in the surrounding bushland and nearby river. The climax of the week was a Friday night concert at which each room had to contribute a story, the funnier the better. Although there was much laughter, the evening closed on a serious note when the senior camp leader spoke on how one became a Christian by recognizing our failure before God, and then asking His forgiveness on the basis of Jesus Christ taking our deserved punishment on the cross, yielding our hearts to Him, and inviting His Spirit to take charge of our lives and make us completely new as a child of God.

I remember the emotions as the words sunk in beyond my mind, where I was familiar with them, to my very heart, so that my deepest emotions were touched. I knew I needed to make that transaction with God. So at bedtime I spoke with my room leader, who counseled me in the steps that I should take. That night I knelt by my bed and prayed, asking for God's forgiveness, and inviting Him to take charge of my life and make me a born-again child of God. I remember the peace that flooded my inner being, and the joy I had of knowing as I went home to my parents (and my church) that I had been changed from within, and was now truly a Christian, not just outwardly, but also inwardly.

A year later, just before my tenth birthday, we went on a family holiday to Tasmania, Australia's southernmost and island state. We drove our car onto the boat for the overnight voyage across the 200-mile stretch of water that separates Tasmania from mainland Australia. We then drove around to take in the magnificent scenery and historic sites. On the west coast we visited Queenstown, where large copper-gold mines had been operating for decades. In those days before present environmental laws, unchecked sulfur fumes from the smelters (where the sulfide ores were roasted) killed off the vegetation on the surrounding hills and stained them with red, orange, and yellow ochres, making the Queenstown area appear to be another world. Through a friend of the family, we had contact with one of the mine workers. He organized a personal tour of some of the opencast pits from which the copper-gold ore was mined. I was even free to pick up and keep rock and ore samples. All of this fascinated me so much that I went home with a new interest in rocks and minerals. Back at school I remember giving a talk on our family holiday, specifically describing the rocks and minerals that I had collected, and which I had there for show. My rock and mineral collecting continued, and I began reading and learning about geology. My parents encouraged this newfound passion, as did my teachers, and as my knowledge grew, my passion was fed by the fact that soon I seemed to know more about the subject than my teachers! I was thoroughly hooked, and my rock and mineral collection steadily grew through the remainder of my primary school years.

High School Years

When I started in junior high school in 1965, I was convinced that I was heading for a career as a geologist. In the school library was a geology textbook that was more than 1,000 pages long, *Principles of Physical Geology* by Sir Arthur Holmes. As an avid reader, I used to sit in the school library during lunch hours reading that textbook (much to the consternation of the librarian who felt that, while my reading habit was good, I still needed the regular physical activities in the school yard). He therefore sought to restrict my access to that geology textbook. However, at the end of that first year of high school, I used my academic achievement prize money to purchase my own copy of that geology textbook! Five years later, it was one of the textbooks used for my first-year geology studies at university, by which time I already knew its contents from cover to cover!

For my two years in senior high school, I wanted to make geology one of my major subjects to prepare me for geology at university and a geology career. However, the public (state) high school I attended did not have a geology class. Sensing my disappointment, the science master and the deputy headmaster suggested that if I could recruit enough students interested in enrolling in a geology course, they would organize one. They did this to placate me, not expecting the outcome; I not only convinced enough of my fellow students to enroll in geology, but geology was also the second largest class for a science major in the senior high school for the next two years! Moreover, the teacher who was assigned to the course for the first year got so excited about geology, and the weekend geology excursions, that at the end of the year he resigned as a teacher and took a job as a geologist.

A Conflict Resolved

As my head was being filled with all this newfound knowledge, and the millions of years geologists claimed was responsible for the accumulation of the earth's rock strata and the shaping of the earth's surface, a deep internal mental struggle developed. I knew full well the Book of Genesis clearly taught God supernaturally created the earth in six literal days, and that, subsequently, a global catastrophic flood destroyed all life from the earth's surface in the days of Noah, who was kept safe with his family and many animals on an ark he built under God's direction. So how was I to reconcile the millions of years explanation for the earth's rock strata, and the countless fossils in them, with this clear teaching from the Scriptures that, as a devout Christian, I saw as the final authority, God's written communication to mankind? Because I was preparing for a career as a geologist, these were not questions that I could simply shelve and ignore.

I turned to my mentors at church and consulted the relevant footnotes in the *Scofield Reference Bible*, both of which taught that there was a time gap between Genesis chapter 1, verse 1 and verse 2, between a primeval creation that was destroyed at the fall of Satan and God's subsequent six literal days of "re-creation." It was into this gap, I was told, that the millions of years claimed by geologists could be fitted, the fossils in the rock strata representing life forms in the primeval creation that were destroyed by "Lucifer's flood." I was initially somewhat happy to live with this gap theory, both because it had been held by many well-respected Bible-believing Christian leaders for more than a century, and because it seemed to be faithful to both the Scriptures and the evidence of geology. However, I was not totally convinced and remained uncomfortable because it didn't seem to make sense to me why God would have to re-create many of the animals and plants destroyed during the gap. This seemed to imply that God was unable to otherwise look after His original creation. And besides, there didn't seem to have been much geologic work done at all by Noah's flood, for which there were three chapters of detailed description in the Bible, compared with the lack of description of "Lucifer's flood" that had occurred (unmentioned and unnamed) between two Bible verses!

During my high school years, my parents became more and more aware of the struggle I was having reconciling what the Scriptures clearly said with the claimed countless millions of years for earth history that I was learning about in my geology books. With their encouragement, I began reading all the relevant books available in the local Christian bookshops then, but there was no clear consensus among the authors. Some even advocated another view, that the days in Genesis were not literal, but rather were vast geological periods of time. Even my geology teacher in my final senior year at high school, who was a Christian, advocated the theistic evolutionary position, which made me feel even more uncomfortable trying to reconcile the millions of years with Genesis. In my final year in high school, my mother sought the advice of an elderly owner of a Christian bookshop in downtown Sydney. He recommended a book that they had only recently stocked from the United States, a book that was then being widely read and acclaimed — the 1961 volume by Drs. John C. Whitcomb and Henry M. Morris titled *The Genesis Flood: The Biblical Record and Its Scientific Implications*. My mother bought a copy of this book for me, which I devoured.

What relief and satisfaction it brought! I immediately resonated with the authors' high view of Scripture, as they cogently and logically argued the basic arguments for why Noah's flood had to be a global, catastrophic event, and then skillfully and decisively responded to all the counterarguments made by prominent Christian writers. I could see immediately that these authors were also faithful to the scientific evidence, which pointed to catastrophic geologic processes having been responsible for the accumulation of the megascopic fossil-bearing rock strata and for shaping the earth's surface. Furthermore, they ably answered all potential objections, and more than adequately dealt with what detractors would claim to be problems for a biblically based construction of geology. All my internal turmoil was gone, and I was ecstatically convinced! I was persuaded by the evidence of catastrophic geological processes that had deposited the many vast rock layers of the geologic record and the enormous numbers of exquisitely preserved fossils in them. And the clear evidence of the problems with the radiometric methods for dating the rocks meant that they could not be used to bolster the claimed millions of years as an objection to the authority of God's inerrant Word, which had to be true in all matters of science and history.

UNDERGRADUATE UNIVERSITY YEARS AND A CALLING

Armed with this reaffirmed confidence in the reliability of God's Word, and convinced the framework for earth history provided by the straightforward reading of the Scriptures made perfect sense of the real-world geologic data, in 1971 I started at the University of New South Wales in Sydney to do four years of study for a geology degree. During those four years, I found nothing factual in my geological studies that conflicted with the literal six-day creation, young universe, and recent, global, catastrophic flood framework for earth history. Recognizing minerals based on their properties and naming them, and the description and classification of rocks, simply involved repeatedly observing and testing minerals and rocks in the laboratory and in the field and did not in any way require assumptions about millions of years. Describing coal, oil, and mineral deposits and the methods for finding them likewise did not require a belief in millions of years. And even though the rocks and coal, oil and mineral deposits were described as requiring millions of years to form, the evidence in question could still be alternately viewed as consistent with the scriptural framework of earth history. Not that there weren't lots of apparent problems and conflicts, but such was my confidence in God's Word that I instinctively knew that such apparent conflicts could (and would) be resolved by future research.

I began to regularly visit bookshops, looking for every available published book about creation, evolution, geology, and Noah's flood. These books were avidly read and digested. I soon sensed that there didn't seem to be many who were working to resolve the apparent conflicts between the uniformitarian interpretation of the geologic data and the scriptural young universe-recent global flood viewpoint.

Furthermore, as I began to enthusiastically speak to other Christians about my absolute confidence that the earth's history could be explained by a straightforward reading of the Scriptures, I usually found either disinterest or bemusement about the relevance of the topic to the gospel message. Sometimes there was even pleasantly spoken opposition on both scriptural and scientific grounds, but usually with the subliminal inference that, once my enthusiasm wore off in the face of the supposedly overwhelming geologic evidence in favor of the millions of years, then I would "come back into the fold."

However, instead, I increasingly sensed that it was no coincidence that I was studying geology and was deeply immersed in learning about, and arguing for, compatibility of the geologic data with the scriptural framework of earth history. Furthermore, even though I knew that there were those who had written on this subject, I perceived there was a definite need for such apologists to defend the literal veracity of the Scriptures. Thus, by the time I had completed my four-year degree in geology, I was convinced that God was calling me into a full-time Bible/science ministry that would involve research, writing, and speaking on geology, creation, and the Flood.

PhD Studies

But how could I do this when, at that time, I knew of no organization that could, or would, support me? At graduation, what would be my next step? Through the kindness of one of my professors speaking to his contacts, I had benefited from the invaluable experiences of working during my summer vacations with a mining company in several remote locations around Australia, studying ore deposits in operating mines and helping search for new ones. Although this mining company had offered me employment as a geologist, my application for a government scholarship to study for a PhD in geology had been successful. I spoke with valued friends, including our pastor, and my high school geology teacher (who was a Christian) about my growing passion to be involved in creation/Flood research and Bible/science ministry. The overwhelming advice I received was to accept the government scholarship to do a PhD. I was told, even if people don't agree with you, once you have a PhD you have earned the right to be heard!

So I accepted the scholarship, and in 1975, I enrolled to study for a PhD at the University of Sydney. My research topic was soon selected — the mineralogy and geochemistry of the (then recently discovered) Koongarra uranium deposit in the Northern Territory of Australia, focusing on the make-up of the ore itself and the hydrothermal alteration surrounding the ore that had been produced during its formation. My research involved extensive analytical work on the minerals making up the ore and the surrounding host rocks, using the electron microprobe recently installed in the university. Rock and ore sections had to be made and studied under the optical microscope to decipher what the textures of the interlocking minerals might reveal about the order in which the various minerals crystallized and formed as the ore deposit accumulated. It was an absorbing study that involved a number of field visits to the site to study (and sample) the thin cylindrical rock columns (or cores) retrieved from drilling through the ground surface into the ore deposit.

MEETING OTHER CREATIONISTS

In late July 1975, during my first year on the University of Sydney campus, the Bible Union of Australia advertised a lunchtime meeting with biochemist Dr. Duane Gish, then associate director of the Institute for Creation Research in San Diego, California, who would speak on the topic "Creation and the Origin of Life." I was absolutely enthralled at his defense of biblical creation using scientific evidence. At last, I had found someone engaged in full-time creation research, writing, and speaking with an organization established for that purpose. After the lecture and subsequent question time, I went with a small group of students who had gathered around the speaker on the lawn near the lecture theater to listen to the continuing discussions and meet him personally. I shared with him my background and my burden, and he was delighted to hear of my passion. He mentioned that there was another young geologist, Steve Austin, also studying for his PhD, and he would pass on my interest to his co-worker, Dr. Henry M. Morris. A few weeks later I wrote to Dr. Morris. His gracious response (which I still have) included a catalog of books sold by ICR, and an application for membership in the Creation Research Society. Now, I was able to obtain copies of the latest creationist books from ICR.

Over the next few years, as I continued my PhD studies, I started speaking on the subject of geology, creation, and the Flood to the young adults and others at our church, and put together notes on those studies. This came to the attention of the interim pastor, who at that time was also the editor of a bimonthly Australian Christian magazine. He soon asked me to write a short article on the topic "Is the Earth Millions of Years Old?" The article I produced was published in early 1978. Within days of that article appearing, I was contacted by a medical doctor (Dr. Philip West) living and working in the northern suburbs of Sydney, who himself had begun speaking and writing about creation, the young earth, and the Flood. He was in the process of preparing to speak at a seminar organized at a seminary, and asked me to join him. The seminar proved very successful, and we sold some of the books he had imported.

About the same time, the same interim pastor became aware of a medical doctor in Adelaide who had started publishing a little magazine called *Ex Nihilo*. Several high school science teachers and others in Brisbane were also conducting seminars and selling creationist books, calling themselves the Creation Science Educational Media Services. I signed up for the first issue of Dr. Carl Wieland's *Ex Nihilo* magazine, and started communicating with Ken Ham and his associates.

From the Mining Industry to Full-Time Creation Scientist

After more than four years at the University of Sydney, all the data for my research project had been collected and the task of writing my thesis was well under way. But as my scholarship was coming to an end, I needed to look for work. I applied at a major international mining company for a job as a mineral exploration geologist. I was hired, and in May 1979, my wife of three years, Kym, and I moved to Darwin, from where I also completed and submitted my PhD thesis. For the next two years I worked on mineral exploration surveys and projects throughout northern and central Australia, and then was recruited by another mining company as chief geologist for the development of the Koongarra uranium project, not far to the east of Darwin.

Throughout this time, I kept in contact with Ken Ham and others at what had now become the Creation Science Foundation (CSF) based in Brisbane. I had several discussions with them about the future possibility of joining their growing full-time staff. I traveled to Perth to join them for a week of a ministry program there, and on several occasions assisted Dr. Carl Wieland with weekend seminars near Sydney. The time now came for a major decision — continue in the mining industry, take a government research scientist position in Sydney, or follow the call God had laid on my heart years before. A fleece was laid, doors closed, and an invitation was received to join the full-time ministry staff at CSF. Following the Lord's leading, Kym and I decided that I would quit the mining industry, and we moved with our two young sons from Darwin to Brisbane at the end of 1983 to begin full-time ministry with the CSF.

Now, at last, I had the time and opportunity to devote myself full-time to creation/Flood research, writing, publishing, and speaking. During my first year at CSF (1984) I established and edited the *Ex Nihilo Technical Journal*, which became the *Creation Ex Nihilo Technical Journal* (now simply the *TJ*). Over the next 15 years, I traveled widely around Australia, to the United States, Britain, New Zealand, South Africa, South Korea, Hong Kong, China, and Indonesia, to speak on the scientific evidence for creation, a young earth, and a recent global flood, as well as the relevance of these issues to the good news that Jesus Christ our Creator came to earth to die for our eternal salvation. After all, if there had been death over countless millions of years before Adam, and the Fall was not a literal event, then why would we even need Jesus to be our Savior? Field research was conducted, and articles written and published, including in the *Ex Nihilo* magazine, which became *Creation Ex Nihilo*, and now simply *Creation*.

In 1990, I was graciously invited by ICR to assist them in their Grand Canyon tour, and from then on I have participated in every subsequent Grand Canyon tour, apart from one, hiking and rafting, as well as being involved in research and sample collection authorized by the National Parks Service. My research eventually led to attendance and presentation of papers at the International Conferences on Creationism in Pittsburgh, commencing with the third conference in 1994. Then in July of 1997, I was invited by ICR to contribute to the establishment of what became the RATE (Radioisotopes and the Age of The Earth) research project, which has enabled me to aggressively pursue my passion for research, especially on the vexed radiometric dating of rock issue.

After almost 15 years at what had now become Answers in Genesis, in late 1998 I joined the staff of the Institute for Creation Research.

The Evidence That Persuades

The evidence that persuaded me has not changed through all these years and continues to persuade me that the scriptural account of earth history alone explains the world in which we live. This evidence persuaded me years ago, but there is now even more evidence that is stronger and more powerful, leaving those who reject the evidence (and the Scriptures) without excuse. From the standpoint of a geologist, most of the fossilized creatures in the strata record bear all the same attributes and qualities as their modern counterparts, and they too show all the evidence of having been designed as integrated working "machines" that functioned perfectly while they lived in their respective biological communities. The fossil creatures appear suddenly in the strata record, fully formed and fully functioning, without any hint of an evolutionary ancestor, or of how their uniquely designed features could have evolved by time, natural law, and chance.

Furthermore, the formation and exquisite preservation of so many remarkably complete fossils, many with delicate structures and soft tissues meticulously fossilized, required special conditions and virtually instantaneous burial. Such beautifully preserved fossils are not isolated specimens but are found by the countless thousands over vast areas in what are known as "fossil graveyards." This required a scale and magnitude of catastrophic deposition to bury so many organisms over such vast areas of the earth's surface, so nothing less than a catastrophic global flood could have accumulated (and preserved) the fossil record. Indeed, the most extensive fossil graveyards, such as the chalk and coal beds, stretch right across continents and have a global distribution.

However, geologic strata also bear testimony to the catastrophic geologic processes operating on a global scale that were responsible for depositing them. Six recognizable successive strata sequences can be traced across North America, each representing a major cycle of ocean waters advancing across the North American continent, and then retreating. Some of the strata in these sequences, such as the sandstone at the base of the first of these six sequences, can be traced from southern

California and Texas northward to Canada and across to Maine. Even strata composed of sand, pebbles, and boulders cover tens of thousands of square miles, having been deposited by massive sheets of rapidly flowing water, totally unlike anything we observe or experience today. And in conventional thinking, the whole strata sequences that were supposed to have been deposited over hundreds of millions of years instead contain internal evidence of the massive quantities of rapidly flowing water that had to have been deposited within days. Yet there is no evidence of the supposed millions of years of nondeposition and/or erosion between these strata. Rather, these complete strata sequences, supposedly representing hundreds of millions of years, were folded without fracturing, implying that these whole sequences were still pliable after just having been deposited. This combined evidence alone eliminates more than 500 million years in the conventional time scale for the earth's history.

Nevertheless, the fallacies in the radioactive methods for dating rocks pointed out in 1961 by Drs. Whitcomb and Morris remain the same: the initial conditions under which the rocks formed need to be known, there would have to have been no changes in the rocks since they formed apart from radioactive decay, and the rates of radioactive decay have to have remained constant during the earth's entire history. Strictly speaking, none of these assumptions are provable, but they are needed to make these methods work. Evidence of this is the perplexing discovery that recent and historic lavas on ocean islands and from active continental volcanoes often yield radioactive dates of between one and two billion years. Equally revealing is where dating the same rocks by the different radioactive methods has yielded totally different ages by hundreds of millions of years. Yet coal beds that are supposed to be hundreds of millions of years old have consistently yielded radiocarbon ages of only thousands of years, which supports numerous other evidences of the earth's youthfulness.

These are some of the many evidences that persuaded me in my youth to become an avid biblical creationist and Flood geologist. It is my prayer that the Lord will use these evidences, and the many more that my fellow creationists are today researching and presenting, to convince and convict countless more people around the globe, for His kingdom and His glory.

Fulfilled Journey — The Influence of a Triple-PhD Creationist

Chapter 38
Dr. A.E. Wilder-Smith
(1915–1995)

BIOGRAPHY BY DAVID F. COPPEDGE

The Intelligent Design movement is much in the news today, but did you know much of the scientific reasoning behind it came from a European organic chemist? William Dembski, author of several key books in the ID movement, credits Dr. A.E. Wilder-Smith for the inspiration to make the study of origins his life's work. Dean Kenyon, the evolutionary origin-of-life researcher turned creationist, called Dr. Wilder-Smith one of the two or three most important scientists in his life. Much of the literature coming out of the modern intelligent design movement contains echoes of powerful arguments made by A.E. Wilder-Smith decades ago.

In his books and tapes, Arthur Edward Wilder-Smith stressed the importance of *information* in biology, stressing that the materialist's formula for life — energy plus matter plus time — was deficient because it left out the information factor. He convincingly argued that the information transfer from DNA transcription to protein synthesis had to follow a *language convention*. In other words, it presupposed an agreement between parties needing to communicate with one another. For example, he explained how SOS is a meaningless sequence of letters unless there has been a convention (a "coming together" agreement in advance) that it is a signal for distress. Similarly, the DNA triplet codon for alanine, GCC, looks and smells nothing like alanine by itself. Unless both the translation mechanism (the ribosome) and the DNA code both have a convention that GCC means alanine, the system will not work. This, he explained, was prima facie evidence of intelligent design.

He also argued effectively against Thomas Huxley's old monkey-typewriter analogy, the claim that a million monkeys typing on a million typewriters would eventually produce Psalm 23 by chance, given enough time. This often-told story has undermined the faith of many over the years. Wilder-Smith appears to have been the first to point out a fatal flaw that undermines the whole argument. By showing that since the chemical reactions that would have led to life in a primordial soup are reversible, that fact rendered the analogy useless. In the monkeys' case, if the letters often fell off the page as soon as they were typed, no meaningful sequence would ever be produced. Huxley, therefore, had cheated by claiming that the letters typed would remain intact and never be lost. The fact is, the laws of chemistry do not permit the needed level of stability in chemical evolution scenarios. Using the results of scientific research, Wilder-Smith argued that creation was scientific and naturalistic evolution was unscientific.

As a highly qualified organic chemist, A.E. Wilder-Smith was uniquely positioned to critique so-called "chemical evolution." This kindly gentleman was merciless in his cogent scientific responses on Miller, Oparin, Fox, and other evolutionists who claimed to be making progress explaining life's origin by chance and necessity. His effectiveness stemmed not from vituperative ability or rhetoric, but rather because of his intimate acquaintance with the facts of chemistry. No knowledgeable chemist could deny Dr. Wilder-Smith's calm, rational application of scientific principles. His skill at dismantling the philosophical and scientific assumptions underlying his opponents' errors was original and effective. Dr. Wilder-Smith was one of the first scientists to emphasize the necessity for one-handed molecules to hold genetic information, and to apply the laws of thermodynamics and equilibrium to discussions about the origin of life.

A.E. Wilder-Smith was one of few scientists in the world to have three earned doctorates. He obtained his first PhD in physical organic chemistry at Reading University, England, in 1941. A research scientist during the war, he subsequently became a fellow of the University of London, and then director of research for a Swiss pharmaceutical company. After becoming a full professor at the University of Geneva, he earned a second doctorate in pharmacology, and later, a third doctorate in pharmacological sciences at ETH, a senior university in Zurich, Switzerland. In addition, he was a fellow of the Royal Society of Chemistry and a NATO three-star general!

Dr. Wilder-Smith's expertise in chemotherapy, pharmacology, organic chemistry, and biochemistry were enhanced by his communication skills. He was a gifted teacher, a popular public speaker, and a courageous debater. He did not shy away from entering the lions' dens of the evolutionary establishment. At a time when communism was strong and evolutionary science reigned with unchallenged bravado, he was like a Daniel aided by divine power to shut his opponents' mouths.

Once, in a manner reminiscent of Paul turning the Pharisees and Sadducees against each other (see Acts 23), he got the better of a hostile audience composed of Finnish and Russian students by adroitly turning their hostility to his advantage by using a word that meant one thing in Finnish and another in Russian. The Finns, who disliked the Russians (Russia had concurred Finland several times in the past), were incensed to hear Dr. Wilder-Smith claiming this word had the Russian meaning, but the Russians agreed with him. As they were shouting at one another, some English students in the audience jumped in and argued that the word was a meaningless syllable. Thus, the professor got his point across: without a language convention, a sequence of letters carries no information.

Dr. Wilder-Smith confronted Communists with scientific arguments that undermined their political philosophy. God only knows how much his work contributed to the eventual demise of communism, but it clearly affected numerous individual Communists. Dr. Alma von Stockhausen, a philosophy professor in Germany, said, "It is to Professor Wilder-Smith that I owe the scientific falsification of evolutionary theory, which had become the scientific concretion of Hegelian dialectics as the alternative to metaphysics and theology." Continuing, he noted, "Dr. Wilder-Smith was the first and only person to have the courage to refute evolutionary theory as a whole on a principal level."[1]

A.E. Wilder-Smith was also partly responsible for making Richard Dawkins reluctant to share a platform with a creationist. In 1986,

1. http://www.wildersmith.org/testimonials.htm.

Wilder-Smith and Edgar Andrews debated the two leading Darwinian lions in Britain, Richard Dawkins and John Maynard Smith, at their home den, Oxford. Yet even there, 150 out of 348 in the staunchly pro-evolution audience voted that the creation side had won the debate. The vote count became a contentious issue. On the tape, it sounds like 150 aye votes (that creation is more valid than evolution), but published reports gave the count as 115. Some accused the AAAS of publishing a lie, fudging the vote count down to 15 by replacing the first digit 1 with the letter i. When they were confronted, the AAAS did not correct this error, allowing incorrect information to stand. The evolutionists apparently were embarrassed that the creationists made such a strong showing.

Contrary to the ground rules of the debate, Dawkins and Maynard Smith repeatedly attacked religion, while the creationists stuck to scientific arguments. Dawkins himself had to be reprimanded by the moderator for attacking Wilder-Smith about his religious views. During the debate, Dawkins implored the audience not to give any votes to the creationists lest it be a "blot on the escutcheon of ancient University of Oxford" (an odd remark, considering Oxford was founded by Christians). Of note is the fact that Dawkins has refused to debate creationists ever since.

Following the debate, there were accusations of a cover-up by the university and the press. Normally, Oxford Union debates are news given prominent publicity in the press, radio, and television. This one, however, which should have rivaled the historic 1860 Huxley-Wilberforce encounter in importance (and was even titled the "Huxley Memorial Lecture"), was silently dropped from the radar screen. The Oxford Student Union inexplicably lost some of the details from its records. Dr. Wilder-Smith felt the record had been expunged. In his memoirs, he commented, "No records of my having held the lecture as part of the Oxford Union Debate could be found in any library. No part of the official media breathed a word about it. So total is the current censorship on any effective criticism of neo-Darwinian science and on any genuine alternative."[2]

2. http://www.amazon.com/Fulfilled-Journey-Arthur-Ernest/dp/0936728752/ref=sr_1_1?ie=UTF8&s=books&qid=1214809096&sr=8-1. His memoirs are published in a book titled, *Fulfilled Journey: The Wilder-Smith Memoirs*, A.E. Wilder-Smith and Beate Wilder-Smith (Costa Mesa, CA: The Word for Today, 1999).

A sought-after public speaker, Dr. A.E. Wilder-Smith shared his insights with tens of thousands of students and others throughout America and Europe. His rapport with audiences and unhurried manner made them feel at ease, even when hearing him talking about abstruse scientific concepts. He would occasionally glance into their faces to see if they "understood his point" and if not, would ask if a term or concept needed to be explained in more detail before he went on. With charming simplicity, he could be found discussing comfortably anything from black holes to one-handed molecules, to Shannon information theory, time dilation, DNA transcription, AIDS, criminal psychology, history, natural theology, natural selection, and why God allows suffering.

A devoted husband and father of five children, a devout born-again Christian, and an unquestionably capable scientist, he left no chinks in his armor. To the consternation of his scientific colleagues, here was a young-earth creationist they could not pigeonhole as an ignoramus. He could not only hold his own among the best, but he could also silence his opponents on scientific ground, making them retreat to personal attacks. Wilder-Smith authored more than 70 scientific publications and more than 30 books. Some of these have been published in 17 languages and are still in print. Many of today's leading creationists consider him a major influence in their own intellectual development and call him a pioneer in anti-evolution arguments.

Dr. A.E. Wilder-Smith narrated an award-winning creation film series called *Origins: How the World Came to Be*. Still available from ChristianAnswers.net, this series keeps his wit and wisdom alive. These films are a good way to become acquainted with the man and his message. In one episode, he holds up a living plant and a dead stick to the energy of the sun and asks the viewer what is the difference. If energy is all that is necessary to produce life, why does one grow and the other decay? Clearly, the energy must be directed through programmed instructions and conversion mechanisms to harness the energy for growth. Such pithy illustrations using familiar objects are a good teacher's art. In another taped lecture (*The Seven Main Postulates of Evolution*), he held up a sardine can. "Could new life evolve from this can?" he asked. "After all, it has all the ingredients necessary for life, because the sardines in it were once alive. It's an open system, too," he explained.

"We can heat it or cool it any way we wish." Everyone knew that nothing would ever happen.

If life could originate from the can, he pointed out, the food processing industry would be in turmoil, because no one would be able to predict what new life forms could emerge in our food. He drove the point home by asking what would happen if *E. coli* bacteria were inserted into the can: an explosion of life would result. Thus, he cleverly taught that matter and energy are insufficient to produce life under the best of conditions. An essential ingredient is information in the form of the genetic instructions and a processing apparatus to utilize the matter and energy to carry out the program.

To know A.E. Wilder-Smith from his legacy of literature and lectures is to love him, not only as a great scientist and thinker, but also as a winsome Christian man of integrity. He had the look of a kindly grandfather. His disarming personal appearance belied the sharp intellect inside. His soft-spoken and unhurried speech, seasoned with wry humor, had a way of getting right to the heart of important issues and conveying difficult concepts in terms accessible to everyone. A masterful teacher, he won the "Golden Apple" award three years in a row at the University of Illinois Medical Center for the best course of lectures. The last award was inscribed, "He made us not only better scientists, but better men."

Following his death in 1995, his wife Beate organized his memoirs into a biography, *Fulfilled Journey*, published by Calvary Chapel in Costa Mesa, California, his adopted American church. Pastor Chuck Smith provided the foreword, comparing him to the apostle Paul who had "fought the good fight, finished the course, and kept the faith." Dr. Dean Kenyon wrote on the book jacket that "Dr. A.E. Wilder-Smith . . . powerfully influenced my intellectual development," calling him a "courageous, supportive, and gracious man" who was instrumental in turning him from evolution to creation. He said, "The discussions I had with him were outstanding and had a great impact on my views and thoughts on origins." Dr. Duane Gish wrote of his "vast store of knowledge and unique and brilliant abilities to communicate," eulogizing him as a man who "has proclaimed the truth of God's creation and His sustaining grace through both the spoken and written word with tremendous effectiveness."[3]

3. http://www.wildersmith.org/testimonials.htm

Despite his busy life, A.E. Wilder-Smith loved classical music and enjoyed hiking in the Swiss Alps. The music of Haydn's *Creation* reminded him of God's creativity described in Genesis. Of his outdoor experiences, he said, "In God's beautiful nature, with the colorfully blossoming mountain meadows in front of you and the gigantic snow-capped ten thousand footers behind them, the murmuring brooks beside you and the ringing of the cow-bells around you, hearts automatically begin to admire God's creation and wisdom and cannot but praise the intelligence behind such manifold beauty."[4]

---

4. A.E. Wilder-Smith and Beate Wilder-Smith, *Fulfilled Journey: The Wilder-Smith Memoirs* (Costa Mesa, CA: The Word for Today, 1999).

Crusade against Evolution

**Chapter 39
Dr. Mortimer Adler
(1902–2001)**

SPECIAL BIOGRAPHY
BY JERRY BERGMAN, PhD

D r. Mortimer Adler (December 28, 1902–June 28, 2001) was considered one of the greatest thinkers of all time, and according to a 1987 *Time* magazine article was the "last great Aristotelian." Adler wrote (or co-authored) more than 45 books (all of them very successful) and more than 200 articles. He was also chairman of the board of editors of *Encyclopedia Britannica* for many years. His 54-volume *Great Books of the Western World* has sold more than a quarter of a million copies since 1952.[1]

Dr. Adler did his undergraduate work at Columbia University, where he finished a four-year program in only three years, yet still was ranked highest in his class and was first on the Phi Beta Kappa list.[2] He completed his PhD in psychology at Columbia and then served as a professor at the University of Chicago for 12 years, becoming a full professor before he became involved with Britannica. His work is of such stature that a national center based on his educational concepts was established in Chapel Hill, North Carolina.

Dr. Adler was an active and outspoken opponent of Darwinism for almost a half-century.[3] In 1985, *Time* magazine noted that Adler "dismasts Darwin" because, among many other reasons, Darwinism categorizes

1. Ezra Bowen, "The Last Great Aristotelian," *Time*, 129(18) (May 4, 1987): 84–85.
2. Anna Rothe and Evelyn Lohr, eds., *Current Biography* (New York: H.W. Wilson Co., 1952).
3. Martin Gardner, *Fads and Fallacies in the Name of Science* (New York: Dover, 1957).

humans "as simply an animal with higher sensory perceptions."[4] Martin Gardner even concludes that Adler "has for some time been carrying on a one-man crusade against evolution." In his book *What Man Has Made of Man*,[5] Adler branded evolution "a 'popular myth,' insisting it is not an established fact."[6]

Adler used the word "myth" to refer to his own conclusion that Darwinist belief *"vastly exceeds the scientific evidence.* . . . This myth is the story of evolution which is told to school children and which they can almost visualize as if it were a moving picture" (emphasis mine).[7] Specifically, Adler concluded that the theory of evolution "is not a theory in the sense of a systematic organization of scientific facts and laws, in the sense in which Newton's *Principia* is a theory" but is only a theory:

> . . . in the sense in which there is an attempt to explain certain facts, which have been scientifically established in the biological sciences, by making *hypotheses* which are not propositions to be proved, but are merely imaginative guesses about unobservable processes or events. This is the sense of hypothesis in which Newton said no scientist should make them (emphasis in original).[8]

Adler's lifelong interest in Darwinism eventually resulted in his writing two books on the topic. While still just a young man, Adler had read a collection of articles by different authors in a book titled *Evolution and Modern Thought*, which he said caused him to be "puzzled" by the "conflicting points of view" expressed by the different authors.

> Try as I might, I simply could not figure out how evolution was supposed to work. I spent hours writing notes to myself and making diagrams in an effort to put down the steps by which a new species came into being.[9]

---

4. Ezra Bowen, "A Philosopher for Everyman," *Time* (May 6, 1985): p. 68.
5. Mortimer Adler, *What Man Has Made of Man* (New York: Ungar, 1937).
6. Gardner, *Fads and Fallacies in the Name of Science*, p. 135.
7. Ibid., p. 135–136.
8. Ibid., p. 115.
9. Mortimer Adler, *Philosopher at Large; An Intellectual Autobiography 1902–1976* (New York: Collier-Macmillan, 1977), p. 13.

He adds that this puzzlement remained with him for years, and only when he read Darwin's *Origin of Species* for the third time did he believe that he finally understood Darwinism. However, when he finally understood evolution, he found much with which he disagreed. Gardner concluded that one of the things to which Adler objected was the view that life lies "on a continuum in which one species fades into another by imperceptible changes. The evidence indicates, he argues, that 'species' differ not in degree but in kind, with a radical 'discontinuity' separating them."[10]

Adler devoted an entire book to the "radical discontinuity" between humans and animals. In this book, titled *The Difference of Man and the Difference It Makes,* he argues that the difference is critical. In his autobiography, Adler stresses that the theme of this entire book is that humans and animals differ not just in *degree* (quantity), but in *kind* (quality) as well. He later added that "since *The Difference of Man and the Difference It Makes* was published [in 1967], scientific investigations have turned up additional evidence relevant to [my conclusion] . . . that man, with the powers of syntactical speech and conceptual thought, differs in kind from all nonlinguistic animals remains as clear and certain as before."[11] This view is reflected in many of Adler's writings.[12] Adler adds that evolution as a theory is actually "wild speculation" and that:

> Darwin himself is partly responsible for much of this speculation. *The Origin of Species* is full of guesses which are clearly unsupported by the evidence. (To the extent that *The Origin of Species* contains scientifically established facts, these facts are not organized into any coherent system.) Furthermore, these guesses, which constitute the theory of evolution, are not in the field of scientific knowledge anyway. They are historical. This conjectural history, begun by Darwin, was even more fancifully elaborated by the 19th century evolutionary "philosophers."[13]

He adds that work of the "post-Darwinian 'scientific cosmologies': Spencer, Haeckel . . . [and] the post-Darwinian 'evolutionary

10. Gardner, *Fads and Fallacies in the Name of Science*, p. 136.
11. Adler, *Philosopher at Large: An Intellectual Autobiography 1902–1976*, p. 300.
12. I.B. Holley Jr., Review of "Intellect: Mind over Matter" by Mortimer Adler, *American Scientist*, 80(2) (1992): 202–203.
13. Mortimer Adler, *The Difference of Man and The Difference It Makes* (New York: Holt, Rinehart and Winston, 1967), p. 115–116.

philosophies': e.g., Bergson" consists of wild speculations. Adler's intensive study concluded that biological:

> ... "evolution" is not a scientific fact, but at best a probable history, a history for which the evidence is insufficient and conflicting ... [and that the] relevant facts are facts in embryology, genetics, palaeontology, comparative anatomy. These facts establish only one historical probability: that types of animals which once existed no longer exist, and that types of animals now existing at one time did not exist. They do not establish the elaborate story in which is the myth of evolution; nor do they establish any of the etiological guesses about the way in which species originated or became extinct, such as natural selection, adaptation to environment, struggle for existence, transmission of acquired characteristics, etc.[14]

He concludes by stating:

> If the grand myth of evolution, as a history of the development of the forms of life, and the grand theory of evolution, as an explanation of how it all happened, are not scientific knowledge, how much less are they philosophical knowledge. (This type of speculation, peculiar to the 19th century, did much to bring discredit upon the name of philosophy, which it so wrongly arrogated to itself.) For the most part, the wild speculations of Spencer, Haeckel, Schopenhauer and Bergson are now generally discredited both by scientists and philosophers.[15]

As do all creationists, Adler recognized that microevolution (variation within the Genesis kinds) is valid, and writes in detail about this problem in his book *Problems for Thomists*[16] (A Thomist — a follower of St. Thomas Aquinas — champions the view that there exists a "self-existent Prime Mover" an uncaused First Cause [i.e., a Creator-God]). In this book, Adler examines in great detail the question of how many "species" exist so he can answer the question:

---

14. Ibid., p. 116–117.
15. Ibid., p. 117.
16. Mortimer Adler, *Problems for Thomists: The Problem of Species* (New York: Sheed and Ward, 1940).

How many creative acts of God are required to explain the evolutionary jumps? . . . Adler's . . . view, which he considers "almost completely demonstrated," is. . . . Within a species, changes have occurred, but each species itself is a fixed type — immutable in its essence, and coming into being only by an act of God. Adler suspects that each species was created in several different types, underived from each other — for example, the separate creation of flowering and non-flowering plants.[17]

Adler was an active anti-evolutionist for many years before he died in 2001. Gardner concludes that one of many examples of what he calls Adler's "blasts" against evolution was in a lecture:

At the University of Chicago, in 1951. Men and apes, he declared, are as different "as a square and a triangle. There can be no intermediate — no three and one-half-sided figure." Most of Adler's arguments were straight out of the arsenal of Bible Belt evangelism. . . . If a scientist would only produce an ape that could speak "in simple declarative sentences," Adler said, he would admit a close bond between man and monkey. . . . Only two explanations will fit all the facts, Adler concluded his speech. Either man "emerged" from the brute by a sudden evolutionary leap, or he was created directly by God.[18]

He once said, "Scientists . . . are theologically naive. But that doesn't seem to stop them from talking about beginnings and endings. The beginning wasn't a Big Bang and the end won't be a final freeze. But don't try telling a scientist that."[19]

Mortimer Adler was one of millions of Americans (including more than 40,000 active scientists) who do not accept Darwinism.[20] Fortunately, in contrast to many, Dr. Adler was willing to speak out about his doubts in his lectures, articles, and books. As a result, he articulated some major concerns that have not been addressed by evolutionists even

17. Gardner, *Fads and Fallacies in the Name of Science*, p. 136.
18. Ibid., p. 137.
19. Terry C. Muck, "Truth's Intrepid Ambassador," *Christianity Today*, 34(17):32-34 (Nov. 19, 1990): p. 33.
20. Jerry Bergman, "The Attitude of Various Populations Towards Teaching Creation and Evolution in Public Schools," *Technical Journal* 13(2) (1999): 118–123.

today. And as expected, Dr. Adler endured his share of attacks by Darwinists, especially those in the atheistic community[21] who have called him everything from "an ignorant creationist" to an "anti-progressive."[22] Born of Jewish parents, he "fell away from religious observance" as a young man to the point of becoming a "religious scoffer."[23] Only in 1984 when he was 82 did he become a Christian,[24] and from that time he was active in writing and speaking about his faith. The reason he became a Christian is because he believed, "Christianity is the only logical, consistent faith in the world."[25]

Until he died, Dr. Adler was deeply concerned about the question of God's existence and trying to establish His existence "beyond reasonable doubt."[26] His confidence in God's existence was based on the cosmological argument (the conclusion that the existence of a creation proves the Creator), and the fact that evolutionism cannot account for the creation of either life or the cosmos.[27] Furthermore, he believed that belief in Christianity was very important in developing a system of ethics and morality.[28]

ADDITIONAL REFERENCE MATERIAL USED

Mortimer Adler and V.J. McGill, *Biology, Psychology, and Medicine* (Chicago, IL: Encyclopedia Britannica, 1963), "Darwin: The Origin of Species," p. 183–216 and "Darwin: The Descent of Man," p. 217–251.

21. See Gordon Stein, review of "The Angels and Us," by Mortimer J. Adler, *The American Rationalist*, 27(1) (1982): 14; and Muck, "Truth's Intrepid Ambassador."
22. Diane Ravitch, Ronald E. Gwiazda, Floretta Dukes McKenzie, Mary Francis Berry, Martin Carnoy, Steven M. Cahn, and Mortimer J. Adler, "Symposium: The Paideia Proposal," *Harvard Educational Review*, 53(4) (November 1983): 377–411.
23. Mortimer Adler, *How to Think about God: A Guide for the 20th-Century Pagan* (New York: Macmillan, 1980), p. 19.
24. Mortimer Adler, "A Philosopher's Religious Faith," p. 203–221 in *Philosophers Who Believe: The Spiritual Journeys of 11 Leading Thinkers*, Kelly James Clark, ed. (Downers Grove, IL: InterVarsity Press, 1993), p. 210.
25. Muck, "Truth's Intrepid Ambassador," p. 33.
26. Adler, *How to Think about God: A Guide for the 20th-Century Pagan*, p. 19; Mortimer Adler, *Truth in Religion; The Plurality of Religions and the Unity of Truth* (New York; Toronto: Collier-Macmillan, 1990), p. 107.
27. Adler, *How to Think about God: A Guide for the 20th-Century Pagan*, p. 136–137.
28. Mortimer Adler, *The Time of Our Lives: The Ethics of Common Sense* (New York: Holt, Rinehart and Winston, 1970).